PENGUIN BOOKS

THE DEATH OF GENTLEMANLY CAPITALISM

For over twenty years, Philip Augar was one of the City's top brokers. After steering NatWest's equities business into a leading position, he built a securities business for Schroders and was a member of the team that negotiated the sale of Schroders investment bank to Citigroup. He has a doctorate in History, is a Visiting Fellow at Cranfield School of Management and can be contacted through his website, *www.philipaugar.com*.

PHILIP AUGAR

THE DEATH OF GENTLEMANLY CAPITALISM

The Rise and Fall of
London's Investment Banks

PENGUIN BOOKS

PENGUIN BOOKS

Published by the Penguin Group
Penguin Books Ltd, 80 Strand, London WC2R 0RL, England
Penguin Putnam Inc., 375 Hudson Street, New York, New York 10014, USA
Penguin Books Australia Ltd, 250 Camberwell Road, Camberwell, Victoria 3124, Australia
Penguin Books Canada Ltd, 10 Alcorn Avenue, Toronto, Ontario, Canada M4V 3B2
Penguin Books India (P) Ltd, 11 Community Centre, Panchsheel Park, New Delhi – 110 017, India
Penguin Books (NZ) Ltd, Cnr Rosedale and Airborne Roads, Albany, Auckland, New Zealand
Penguin Books (South Africa) (Pty) Ltd, 24 Sturdee Avenue, Rosebank 2196, South Africa

Penguin Books Ltd, Registered Offices: 80 Strand, London WC2R 0RL, England

www.penguin.com

First published as a Penguin hardback 2000
Published with a new foreword in paperback in Penguin Books 2001

4

Copyright © Philip Augar, 2000, 2001
All rights reserved

The moral right of the author has been asserted

Printed in England by Clays Ltd, St Ives plc

To Denise, William and Rachel

Contents

CONTENTS

PART THREE
BANG, CRASH, WALLOP, 1986–9

PART FOUR
THE GRAND OLD DUKE OF YORK, 1990–94

PART FIVE
THE END GAME? 1995–2000

PART SIX
THE CITY UNPLUGGED

List of Tables

Acknowledgements

The views contained in this book are entirely my own and are not necessarily shared by the people who have agreed to be interviewed for this project. None the less, many colleagues and competitors have been generous with their time. Some have asked not to be named but I am as grateful to them as to the following contributors: Nicholas Angell, Bernard Asher, David Atkinson, Catherine Black, Keith Brown, Cazenove & Co., John Chiene, David Clementi, Howard Coates, Tony Cole, Scott Dobbie, Kevin Feeny, Tim Ferguson, Mike Geering, Sir Edward George, James Hanbury, Bill Harrison, John Holmes, Philip Kay, Philip Leeder, John Littlewood, Donald Macpherson, Michael Marks, Sir Peter Middleton, Rudolf Mueller, Jim O'Donnell, Geoffrey Osmint, Joy Palmer, Quintin Price, Ruth Sack, Richard Sadleir, Hector Sants, Ken Taylor, Martin Taylor, Sir David Walker, Derek Wanless, Nick Whitney, Fiona Worthington and Richard Wyatt.

I am particularly grateful to George Pearson, Professor Richard Taffler and Patrick Wellington who read and commented on draft MSS and to Susan Pollock and Daniel Hind at Penguin Books. Alison Buckley, Deana Plummer and Nancy Smith also made major contributions.

Preface

In the summer of 1978 I was finishing a thesis and collecting rejection letters. A handful of universities had jobs for newly qualified historians but not for me. Eventually I made the shortlist at a small teacher training college in Liverpool but the conversation between candidates as we were shown round made it quite clear that the other five had more experience and better qualifications. I left still without a job but with the certainty that I had to look outside the academic world to pay my debts and earn a living.

A friend in a similar mess told me that 'they do research in the city' and that I should try there. It took me a while to learn where the City was: not the centre of Cambridge, as I first thought, but a part of London where the great bankers and brokers worked. I found a list of firms who were hiring graduates, chose two with nice sounding names and wrote to them.

Quite soon they both replied. A miracle! Two interviews on successive days and one with an invitation to lunch. The first was at 2.30 p.m. and I arrived disorientated by the maze of narrow streets, the speed at which people rushed around and the rudeness of passers-by too busy to stop to give directions. I need not have worried. I sat on a comfortable sofa reading horsey, country magazines for half an hour. Just before 3.00, a chap ambled in, clearly having enjoyed a good lunch, and asked me a few introductory questions: school (grammar), university (Cambridge), contacts in the City (none), sports played (lots). I was on the alert: this was just to wrong-foot me and there would be a tough question on the economy any minute. But no, the next comment was, 'Well you seem like a decent type, we'll offer you a job.' The time was 3.20 p.m.; I had been with him less than half an hour, and I left elated at my performance, one that had been so brilliant that I had landed a job within minutes.

On the train home doubts set in: he seemed drunk; would he remember the offer in the morning? Even if he did remember, did I really want to work for people who took decisions on the hoof, were late for meetings, drank heavily at lunch, kept no records, and thought their guests would enjoy reading about hunting, fishing and shooting?

The next day I was back in the City to meet the second firm. There was a bit more structure to this interview: relevant questions were asked, the different functions in the firm were explained to me and I met someone called the administrative partner who talked about serious sounding things like pensions and season ticket loans. They took me to lunch (quite the best restaurant I'd ever been in) and effortlessly balanced a serious discussion with equally serious eating and drinking. My own contribution was handicapped by unfamiliarity with smart restaurants, the subjects under discussion and the tool I'd been given to eat my lobster with but, surprisingly, I was offered a job. It still seemed impossibly easy after the depressing trek through the lower reaches of academe and I did not really believe that either firm had the basis for making a decision about me. But the second firm, Fielding Newson Smith, seemed marginally more thorough and I started work there in September 1978 as a trainee investment analyst for a salary of £100 per week.

I spent most of the next twenty years in the City in an apparently successful career. I became a well-known investment analyst, writing reports on shares and recommending them to investors. I won several public awards for outstanding work and eventually became head of research at one of London's leading broking firms. I became managing director of the whole firm, responsible for a worldwide staff of 2000. I was then head-hunted and ended up in the inner sanctum of one of London's leading merchant banks. My annual earnings often exceeded £1 million and sometimes £2 million. A newspaper once described my reputation in the City as 'awesome'.

Yet throughout this I have carried a sense of unease. Could this fame and fortune be for real? How did we all earn so much when the firms we worked for generally lost money? How is it that greed, disloyalty and deception are tolerated and usually rewarded with even more money?

When every large investment bank in London was sold to a foreign owner within fifteen years, usually under distressed circumstances, did the managers of those firms really do a good job? If not, why did they keep getting paid so much? Why are the Americans so much more successful at this business than the Brits? Is it a matter of work ethic, experience, native talent or were there structural forces at work?

These questions have troubled me for years but I reached a crossroads in 1998 when I was offered one of the plum jobs in the industry. It was a position so grand that it would have been the crowning glory of a career in the City and the opportunity for even more money and power. The prospect filled me with dread. Another five years of jet lag, dinners with people I had little in common with, pampering to the burgeoning demands of staff whose desires knew no bounds. I turned the job down and worked out what I really wanted to do. A starting-point was to set down what has happened in the City over the last twenty years, particularly since 1983 when the reforms known as Big Bang were first contemplated. I wanted to review these extraordinary events in as detached a way as it is possible for a participant to do, firstly to check that what I thought had happened had really occurred and then to understand why.

Three themes run throughout the book: ownership, class and self-regulation. Ownership mattered. Partnerships and small companies performed better than megabanks. Big banks thought they needed big brokers and these proved impossible to manage. Results were poor and the institutional shareholders – especially British investors in British banks – created an environment where the investment banks and brokers had to be sold or closed. The final section explores whether it matters that the British investment banks of today are nearly all foreign-owned.

Class also came into it. The failure of a whole generation of managers in the 1980s was not solely to do with their background but they had emerged from the public schools and National Service with a respect for hierarchy, conservatism and with bags of self-confidence. The attitudes of the senior brokers of the 1980s were born out of their experiences in the 1950s and it showed in their inability to cope with a more complex, fast-moving world. This left the British firms gasping to keep up with the harder-working Americans.

Government and the regulators were conspicuous by their absence. I have often asked myself, why do the authorities allow this to happen? Who are the authorities? Do they know what is happening? Do they care? Are there no grown-ups watching us play? As I have worked through the sources I have begun to understand that London's softer regulatory regime compared with New York has ideological origins in the free market philosophy of Mrs Thatcher's heyday. The fashion for minimal Government interference was music to the ears of the City's fathers who were confident in their abilities to manage everything themselves. The absence of a tough regulatory regime has had important consequences for the City, not because it is a crooked place to do business – in fact, there still exists a strict moral dealing code which is far more stringent than the written rules, and broking in the City is largely free of corruption – but because the standards for training and financial reporting are so low that sloppy behaviour has been encouraged.

The early narrative of the book focuses on broking, a business that the merchant banks of the 1980s saw as the key to becoming successful investment banks in the 1990s. Gradually, broking and merchant banking became so entwined that the failure of one became inextricably linked with the other. The complication of assimilating and running brokers made the management task much harder and is at the heart of every failed investment bank. The book's conclusions relate to these wider investment banking issues.

There were 225 broking and jobbing firms that belonged to the London Stock Exchange in 1986. The top ten brokers and top three jobbers, which between them accounted for the majority of shares traded at the time, the banks that bought them before Big Bang and a few of the American firms that gradually took over in the City are followed in detail. I have limited the scope of the book to make it manageable to read and write. Those interested in the small- and medium-sized brokers will not find much mention and this has led to the exclusion of a few quite significant firms such as Laing & Cruickshank and Simon & Coates. The merchant banks have also been dealt with selectively, with little mention of smaller banks like Charterhouse, Hambros and Singer and Friedlander and less coverage of the major advisory banks, Rothschild and Lazards, than of those that followed an integrated advisory and capital markets strategy.

Firms are followed in detail until the moment when the strategy that was started in Big Bang was abandoned. For example, amongst the merchant banks, Hill Samuel disappears from the story after it was sold to TSB, as does Morgan Grenfell after the sale to Deutsche Bank and Warburg after the sale to Swiss Bank.

The story is about equities, not bonds, and institutional, not private, client broking, for these were the activities at the core of the new investment banks that emerged. Whilst Big Bang covered British Government securities as well as equities, corporate bonds were not affected. Many of the merchant and commercial banks were already experienced in issuing and trading corporate bonds and little changed as a result of Big Bang. The extra dimension came from equities and although banks did run into problems in their fixed-income areas, it was in equities that the worst problems arose. The two activities were quite separate and banks like NatWest and Barclays were able to continue in fixed-interest securities after they pulled out of equities and related corporate finance activities.

This was not a successful period for the industry and there are few individuals, companies or official institutions to emerge with credit. However, I can find very few cases where people behaved with malice. Staff, management and shareholders did their jobs according to the standards of the day, to the best of their abilities. My own performance was no better, but I hope no worse, than that of my peer group: a mixture of successes and failures. Soon after I started, my career was nearly ruined by stock market developments I had failed to anticipate. A colleague consoled me with some advice that has helped me to survive the occasional low periods that were inevitable in a long career in the City: 'If you can't take a joke, don't work in the Stock Market.' Those words gave me perspective and I hope that this book will do the same for anyone interested in a remarkable episode of modern business history.

Foreword to the Paperback Edition

In the year since I finished *The Death of Gentlemanly Capitalism*, my perspective on the City has altered. More time has passed since I was personally involved, memories have faded, relationships with individuals and institutions have changed. Events have moved on. Some of the outcomes that I predicted have already occurred, others have moved in unexpected directions making different conclusions now seem more likely. Reviewers, correspondents, visitors to my web site and people I have met while promoting the book have given me new ideas and I am grateful for all such comments.

Critics have made much of the inevitability of the US domination of the City, arguing that Wall St's profitability and the sheer size of the US economy meant that no British firm could survive. Wall St's power is indeed awesome but I remain unimpressed by the skill and commitment of us British competitors. Class, incompetence, the authorities' belief in 'free' competition, premature in a market where the Americans had a head start, and short-termism all contributed to the great British failure. We need look no further than Continental Europe to see how it could have been done better. There are no British investment banks in Europe's top ten but there, alongside the Americans, are Deutsche Bank, Credit Suisse, United Bank of Switzerland and Dresdner Bank. These European banks, comparable in size to the UK clearers who decided not to compete, have built credible investment banks, often with British components, and from a much less promising cultural and business background. Was the British failure really so inevitable?

My suggestion that foreign ownership of the investment banks might damage the City in the long term has been attacked by reference to both the past and the future. Looking back, the important role foreigners played in the City's history has been used to justify the present situation. But there is a difference between European families going to London, settling there and becoming Anglicized and companies that are headquartered across the Atlantic with no roots in or commitment to the UK. Whereas families such as the Schroders and Barings moved their bases to Britain, there is little prospect of Goldman or Morgan Stanley or Merrill doing so and nor should they. Looking forward, it has been argued that globalization makes the concept of corporate nationality obsolete but this is simplistic when the location of head office so often determines a firm's culture. Home is still where the head is in that social and commercial connections often cut across efficient resource allocation.

The issue of who owns the City will become pressing when the investment banks' clients on the Continent outweigh those in the UK, a time that is not far away. We shall then see whether London's charms, language and infrastructure are sufficient to keep the investment banks centred there. If by then monetary union has taken off without Britain or London has misplayed its hand in the global realignment of stock exchanges, the City's position as Europe's financial services capital will be tested. It seems too good to be true that there will be no adverse consequences arising from the failure of a whole class of financial institutions. We are about to find out.

Philip Augar
Cambridge, England,
February 2001

PART ONE

THE TWILIGHT WORLD OF GENTLEMANLY CAPITALISM

I

A Foreign Affair

A few years ago I had dinner with a future Governor of the Bank of England. He was already a powerful man and the conversation was as serious as befits someone in his position. We discussed the steady progress made by the American investment banks in London and the squeeze on the British firms. I was urged not to worry. My companion recalled the parallel with the Wimbledon Tennis Championships: held in Britain, staffed by locals, dominated by foreigners but still generating bags of prestige and money for the UK. The City would be the same: safe as Europe's financial capital and a strong environment in which Britain's investment bankers could work. I disagreed, preferring the example of manufacturing, where the failure of British firms has left the UK without control of strategic industries or employment. We had a good debate and went our separate ways, he to run the Bank of England, me to worry about the collapse of British broking.

Over the following years the British banks and brokers gradually fell into foreign hands, sometimes spectacularly, as when Barings went bust and Warburg's profits collapsed, sometimes with dignity, as when Smith New Court sold out. The bigger banks like Barclays and Nat-West soldiered on for a while before they too sold their equities businesses. The consequence is that investment banking today is a foreign affair. All of the City's top ten brokers and nine of the top ten corporate finance houses are American or Continental European.

This book is about what happened, why it happened and whether it matters. The twenty-year period is taken in five parts, the first of which, 'The Twilight World of Gentlemanly Capitalism', describes the City in the years immediately before the 1983 agreement between the Government and the Stock Exchange. This deal, by which the Stock

Exchange agreed to drop fixed commissions and open itself to competition to escape a Restrictive Practices case, ushered in the market reforms of 1986 known as Big Bang. The City's inability to cope with these changes is the central theme of the book. The run up to Big Bang in 1986 saw the brokers and banks get together in a series of hastily arranged marriages. The Crash of 1987 exposed cultural and managerial weaknesses and enormous losses were made in the following years. Some banks did a rapid about turn, others tried to learn from the lessons. The early nineties brought partial success until late 1994, when a combination of tricky markets, poor strategies and the pressure of globalization brought down the brokers and some of the banks that owned them.

The causes of the failure are analysed as the story unfolds. In the early years, managerial incompetence from a generation underprepared for the scale and complexity of the task they faced was the characteristic feature. The social and professional backgrounds of those involved contributed to this by putting hierarchies and conservatism above networks and flexibility. In the middle years, the benefits of tight ownership became evident as the partnerships, small companies and family-controlled businesses outperformed the institutionally held megabanks. Eventually many firms fell into traps laid in the earlier period when their overextended strategies carried them into the arms of the foreign competition. From the mid nineties, industry trends to scale and globalization posed major, often insurmountable challenges. These underlying themes are pulled together in the concluding section of the book, 'The City Unplugged', which also explains how many City practitioners were able to earn fabulous salaries and bonuses at a time when their firms were failing.

Does this matter? The book concludes by considering the current belief amongst many commentators that the lack of a domestically owned investment banking industry is of no consequence. This view is a matter of conviction for some, but generally it would be more credible if it had been the line taken all along. It is also the type of post-event rationalization at which the City excels. Analysts are much better at explaining eloquently and elegantly what has just occurred than they are at forecasting the future. Investment banks pitching for business present their credentials in the best possible light through careful selection of performance data. Head-hunters acting for invest-ment banks misrepresent their clients' failed strategies to candidates who gloss over too many career moves. Investment managers choose the best available time periods to conceal bad performance. The ability to distort the truth with plausible explanation is one of the City's most polished skills. In this case there is plenty of evidence that foreign ownership was not intended. There was widespread concern at the time of Big Bang that modernization, which nearly everyone recognized as essential if the City was to stay competitive, carried a risk that British firms might not survive. The authorities went to some trouble to assuage such fears. In December 1983 Alex Fletcher, the Minister at the Department of Trade and Industry responsible for Big Bang, gave an interview to the *Financial Times*:

Q: How important is it to have a British owned securities industry?
A: I think it is very important. If we want to maintain London as a prominent market, I think it is very important that the Stock Exchange and the majority of the institutions here should remain very firmly in British hands.[1]

The Bank of England was equally aware that the national interest could be as jeopardized by too much reform as by too little. Robin Leigh-Pemberton, then Governor of the Bank of England, stated in March 1984: 'We would not contemplate with equanimity a Stock Exchange in which British-owned member firms played a subordinate role.'[2]

The matter was grasped early on by the *Financial Times* which, after enduring the misfortune of being on strike at the time of the 1983 agreement between the Department of Trade and Industry and the Stock Exchange, covered Big Bang with increasing authority and incis-iveness. On 12 September 1983 it commented that, 'The authorities are anxious to see the emergence of strong British securities firms, capable of competing with the big Wall Street and Japanese houses. One school of thought is that some kind of ring fence should be placed on a temporary basis around the City to prevent foreign competition from over-running the UK securities industry.'[3]

Cabinet ministers, the Governor of the Bank of England and the most influential newspaper in the City all grasped the importance of there being an indigenous investment banking industry. Then, as now, they were reassured by the cooperative, non-threatening approach of the foreign firms: 'Mr Robert Conway, head of Goldman Sachs International, the UK offshoot of the giant US investment bank, has stressed that fears that the Americans will subsume British securities firms after the City's Big Bang are exaggerated.'[4]

It may not matter that boards of management in New York, Frankfurt and Zürich determine the resources committed to London by the leading investment banks, but the vulnerability of London's position is illustrated by the absence of any party with a vested interest in putting the opposite view. The investment banks themselves can be relied upon to keep mum. They have the right to run their business any way that they choose and will be the last to own up to the risks of a migration from London while they need the goodwill of British clients and authorities. The Bank of England and the other regulators will also play down the issue for they have allowed and unwittingly encouraged the domestic industry to fail and will not wish to admit that mistakes have been made. Senior figures in the City are in a similar position, having mismanaged their industry and being anxious not to draw attention to its fall.

The City of London is held up to be a great British success. Statistics are quoted showing that its share of such activities as foreign exchange and bond trade are increasing. All of the world's leading investment banks base their European operations in London. London's advantages – critical mass, language, skilled staff and a favourable fiscal and political environment for business – are trumpeted loudly and often. The City is widely believed not only to be currently unchallenged as Europe's financial services capital but also to be so far ahead of its rivals that it cannot be overtaken in any foreseeable time frame.

However, the absence of a single British-owned investment bank with meaningful global aspirations is a serious deficiency. It is currently unfashionable to talk of 'national companies', the globalization of staff, shareholders and clients being held to have superseded this old-fashioned notion. But ask any London employee of Merrill Lynch or Goldman, or UBS or Dresdner Bank the nationality of the company they work for and you do not have long to wait for an answer. As we have seen in manufacturing industry, head office determines the strategy, the culture and the commitment.

The position of New York is now so well established as the world's investment banking capital that it is unassailable and this is a consequence of the strength and size of the US economy rather than London's mistakes. But the failure of the City's investment banks means that London's position as the leading secondary centre is not as secure as it appears.

A hub-and-spoke structure radiating out of New York to a series of equally important secondary financial centres is now the most likely model, with London sitting alongside, not above, the other European capitals. Frankfurt and Paris can contemplate this with equanimity. They are currently behind London in the global pecking order and equal status would represent an improvement in their relative positions. With London riding high on the tide of prosperity created by the bull market of the 1990s this is hard to imagine. But in financial markets the story never stands still. Twenty years ago Tokyo was regarded as a serious threat to London and New York as the world's financial capital – now it is out on a limb. Ten years ago, it was inconceivable that all of London's investment banks would be sold to Americans and Europeans – now it has happened. Seven years ago Warburg was sweeping all before it and Goldman was laying off staff; within two years Warburg had been sold and Goldman was dominant. Five years ago the idea that London would find itself having to respond to a bid from the operator of a smaller European stock exchange would have been derided. The next few years are likely to bring equally dramatic changes. London's ability to benefit from them is weakened by the absence of a national investment banking champion. How did we get into this position?

2

Buy Side, Sell Side

'Buy Side, Sell Side' is an American term that describes the divide between customers (the buy side) and service providers (the sell side) in investment banking. Although this term was not widely used in Britain before Big Bang, it is a useful distinction. The buy side consists of those seeking help with Stock Market transactions: investors, companies and governments. The sell side consists of the providers of such services: brokers, merchant banks and, in Britain, before Big Bang when brokers were not allowed to take principal risk, jobbers.

BUY SIDE: INVESTORS

British institutions – companies that invest clients' money – accounted for two-thirds of turnover on the London Stock Exchange in 1983. Overseas institutions accounted for less than 10 per cent of turnover but this rose to around a quarter by the end of the 1980s as they increased their investments in Britain. Private individuals investing directly in equities through stockbrokers made up less than a third of turnover in the early 1980s and, despite the boost from Government privatisation, less than 20 per cent by the early 1990s.

Equity investing took off in the 1950s as an alternative to bonds in pension funds.[1] Initially companies managed their own pension funds but the growth of specialist departments at the merchant banks and insurance pension funds claiming to deliver better performance at lower cost led to the gradual closure of most of the independent pension fund investment departments. In this way the pension fund business came to be dominated by the asset management departments at the major merchant banks and insurance companies.[2] Pension funds accounted for about 40 per cent of the $500 billion of assets managed in the UK on the eve of Big Bang. The remainder was spread between insurance funds, mutual savings schemes (such as unit trusts and investment trusts) and charities.[3]

Institutional shareholdings were so large that teams of fund managers were built up to monitor them. The fund managers in turn required the support of teams of researchers. By 1983 fund management teams at the pension funds, insurance companies and in the asset management departments of the merchant banks included their own research departments and portfolio managers. This required the institutional brokers to develop their own organizations in a way that matched client needs. This is explained in a following section (see pp. 23–8).

BUY SIDE: ORIGINATORS OF EQUITY

Institutional and private investors bought and sold secondary equities – that is, shares already in issue – but the supply of shares was refreshed by primary issues from companies and the Government. Companies issued shares through rights issues if they were already listed on the Stock Exchange or through an initial public offering if they were not. Rights issues could be major events, such as BP's in 1981 and Barclays' in 1985 which raised over £500 million each, or more routine issues from smaller companies.[4]

The Government's traditional use of the Stock Market was for raising debt through issuing fixed interest securities known as gilts. After the election of the Conservatives in 1979 the Government found a second use for the Stock Market. Between 1981 and 1983 eight major privatisations were successfully completed, raising £1.4 billion and generating £25 million in fees and commissions for the professional advisers and substantial secondary market income for the brokers and jobbers.[5]

SELL SIDE

Merchant banks, brokers and jobbers were all involved in institutional equities in 1983. After Big Bang these three functions were to fuse into single entities called investment banks but in 1983 each occupied a distinct role in the hierarchy. The most prestigious organizations were the merchant banks, responsible for originating new equity into the system by arranging rights issues and flotations. In a rights issue a company seeking to raise capital offers new shares to its existing shareholders in proportion to their holdings. In a flotation, a company offers shares on a stock exchange for the first time. Distribution was via the brokers, who liaised between the Stock Exchange and corporate clients when new equity was being issued and advised the institutions on investment matters and handled their orders as agents. The brokers placed their clients' orders to buy and sell shares with jobbers, firms that traded in shares listed on the Stock Exchange as a principal, that is on their own account. Their role was to provide liquidity to the brokers and their clients.

The relationship between these three was determined by Stock Exchange rules and refined by custom: the merchant bank could deal with the corporate client and with brokers but not with jobbers or institutions; the broker could deal with jobbers, corporates and institutions; the jobber could deal with brokers but not with banks or institutions.

SELL SIDE: BROKERS

There were 214 broking firms in Britain on the eve of Big Bang. Some were full service businesses offering gilts and equities to institutional, corporate and individual clients, others were small partnerships specializing in private clients. Some of the firms had diversified from broking into related activities such as asset management and money broking. There was no clear market leader. Although some firms were very strong in certain lines of business – for example, Cazenove had the largest number of appointments as official 'corporate broker' to

Table 1. Stockbroking League Table Rankings, 1983[6]

Firm	Equities	Gilts	Research	Corporate broking	Overall rank
Hoare Govett	1	4	10	3	1
James Capel	3	9	1	^10	2
Scrimgeour Kemp Gee	2	9	2	10	3
Phillips & Drew	5	5	3	^10	4
Cazenove	4	^10	^10	1	5
de Zoete	6	7	7	5	6
Rowe & Pitman	6	^10	^10	2	7
Wood Mackenzie	6	^10	4	^10	8
Grieveson Grant	9	2	^10	4	9
Greenwell	^10	1	6	^10	10=

companies quoted on the Stock Market, James Capel led in research and Greenwell in gilts – no single firm had sufficient product differentiation to dominate.

In equities the market share of a firm like Fielding Newson Smith, ranking around fifteenth, was not much smaller than that of Greenwell in tenth place and only three percentage points behind that of the market leaders. The top three in gilts were different to the top three in equities and had a bigger grip on their market, accounting for 30 per cent compared to 16 per cent for equities. In research, four firms – Capel, Scrimgeour, Phillips & Drew and Wood Mackenzie – had established a franchise. The remainder had a few good analysts rather than in-depth research departments.

Hoare Govett, Cazenove and Rowe & Pitman scored more heavily in business terms than they did in research due to their strength in corporate broking. Institutions believed that they would get preferential treatment in attractive new issues if they maintained a good relationship with the brokers who were responsible for share allocation in over-subscribed issues and so firms with a strong corporate list were well favoured by the institutions.

In addition, a company's broker was more likely to receive price sensitive news before the rest of the market. Until inside dealing was made an offence in 1980 relationships with powerful corporate brokers were a source of price sensitive information for fund managers. There was suspicion in the City throughout the 1980s and 1990s that certain companies continued to use their corporate brokers to warn shareholders about forthcoming news in advance of a general announcement to the whole market.

SELL SIDE: JOBBERS

Every share traded on the London Stock Exchange had to pass through a jobber's book. Brokers were agents acting on behalf of the clients, jobbers were principals dealing only with the brokers. This separation of the agency and risk functions was known as single capacity and was at the heart of the dealing system before Big Bang. The advantage was held to be that the broker was known to be dealing in the clients' interests and not protecting his own book position. The jobber was simply there to provide liquidity and make a profit.

Table 2. Leading Jobbing Firms, 1983

Firm	Equity market share (per cent)
Akroyd & Smithers	30
Wedd Durlacher	30
Pinchin Denny	12
Smith Brothers	12
Bisgood Bishop	6
Charles Pulley	5

But the Wilson report on the City showed how difficult it had been for jobbers to make a profit and the consequent consolidation which was occurring in the jobbing industry. Whereas in 1959 there had been 104 jobbing firms in the London market, by 1980 there were only thirteen, of which five accounted for 90 per cent of turnover. The remainder, from Charles Pulley downwards, were specialized and not large enough or well enough capitalized to play a meaningful role in global markets. The jobbing market in gilts was dominated by Akroyd & Smithers and Wedd Durlacher, with an estimated 80 per cent of the market between them, a position which gave them a huge flow of business.

Akroyd and Wedd also dominated equities, followed by a group of three second-tier firms, Pinchin Denny, Smith Brothers and Bisgood Bishop, with Charles Pulley leading the long tail of smaller, more specialized jobbers. The fact that there were twenty brokers of size but only five large jobbers meant that there were not enough jobbing firms to go round when the Big Bang marriages occurred.

SELL SIDE: MERCHANT BANKS

The merchant banks were at the top of the hierarchy of firms in the City in 1983. Their traditional business was corporate finance, especially lending to finance overseas trade. By the 1980s this had developed into a broader range of financing services for companies operating in the UK and overseas. Advisory work, especially on mergers and acquisitions, was both high profile and profitable and sometimes created opportunities to help clients raise debt or equity capital. In addition to these core businesses different wholesale financial services were provided by the merchant banks, ranging from asset management, project finance, lending and leasing, commodities and bullion trading. Not every bank provided every service but corporate finance, underwriting and asset management were the core businesses of most major merchant banks.

The major merchant banks met together on the Accepting Houses Committee. The relative status of the banks changed with time, as each enjoyed its time in the sun. In 1983, Morgan Grenfell topped the *Financial Times* league table in rights issues and mergers and acquisitions and was third in flotations. It could claim at that stage to be the leading merchant bank, with Schroders, Kleinwort Benson, Warburg and Lazards not far behind.

Amongst the leading firms there were five quoted merchant banks – Morgan Grenfell (from 1986), Hill Samuel, Warburg, Schroders and Kleinwort – but the latter two had a significant family shareholding, as did the two unquoted companies (N. M. Rothschild and Robert Fleming). Lazards was a partnership and there were two subsidiaries

Table 3. Merchant Bank Rankings for 1983[7]

Flotations	1982	1983	Rights issues	1982	1983	Mergers and acquisitions/Takeovers	1982	1983
Schroders	1	1	Morgan Grenfell	2	1	Morgan Grenfell	2	1
Kleinwort Benson	5	2	Hill Samuel	5	2	S. G. Warburg	1	2
Morgan Grenfell	2	3	Kleinwort Benson	3	3	Hill Samuel	4	3
Lazards	6	4	N. M. Rothschild	–	4	Lazards	–	4
S. G. Warburg	3	5	Samuel Montagu	8	5	Kleinwort Benson	5	5
County NatWest	–	6	Schroders	1	6	Schroders	10	6
Samuel Montagu	8	7	County NatWest	4	7	Charterhouse	9	7
Robert Fleming	10	8	Robert Fleming	9	8	N. M. Rothschild	3	8
Charterhouse	–	9	S. G. Warburg	1	9	Samuel Montagu	7	9
N. M. Rothschild	–	10	Lazards	6	10	Barings	6	10

of larger companies (Samuel Montagu and County Bank). NatWest owned County and Midland had a 60 per cent share in Samuel Montagu, the US insurer Aetna Life holding the other 40 per cent in 1983. Barclays Merchant Bank was also a wholly owned subsidiary but did not get a single ranking position in the 1983 table.

SELL SIDE: OUTSIDERS

Although the highest positions in the league tables were occupied by British firms, there were 500 foreign banks and brokers in the City trying to break in by 1983. At this stage, with the Japanese market and economy still going strong, the Japanese were perceived to be as an equally formidable a threat as the Americans. However, the big four Japanese brokers, Nomura, Nikko, Daiwa and Yamaichi, were constrained by the UK authorities in retaliation for the difficulty British firms experienced in getting licences to operate in Tokyo and by the disinterest amongst Japanese investors in European securities. Most European banks were more interested in Eurobonds and their own domestic business than in international markets. Their London offices were mainly representative offices rather than aspirational investment banks. It was a similar story with the Americans. Goldman Sachs had maintained a small presence in London since 1969, but the whole office contained only 286 people in the early 1980s.[8] The other bulge bracket firms such as Merrill Lynch, Salomon Brothers and Morgan Stanley had also been in London for a long time without having made a real impact.[9] However, it was clear to some commentators that this situation would not last: 'Every major Wall Street investment house has been pitching hard at Britain's leading companies to obtain corporate work. Established ties between client and merchant banker are breaking down: no treasurer will stand blindly by the old guard if a newcomer can offer better terms.'[10]

THE SELL SIDE CONNECTED

Broking was the only activity before Big Bang that connected all other parts of the buy and sell sides. Jobbers could only deal with the buy side if they went through a broker; the buy side could only deal on the market if it went through a broker. The broker was the classic intermediary through which all business passed.

Equity broking was also a way into corporate clients. There was a value chain in such relationships which began with the corporate's treasurer, moved up to the finance director and peaked with the chairman and chief executive. The treasurer dealt with commodity services such as lending and foreign exchange and was usually serviced by the commercial banks. Next up was the finance director who might have a relationship with commercial bankers but would also have regular dealings with the merchant bankers and brokers. The highest level and the most prized relationship was with the chairman and chief executive. This was the preserve of merchant bankers discussing corporate finance matters such as mergers and acquisitions and equity funding, together with issues of group strategy and corporate governance.

However, brokers also had access to chief executives due to the peculiar nature of UK corporate underwritings. In the UK, a corporate's rights issue is underwritten by the merchant bank and distributed to sub-underwriting institutions by the corporate's appointed broker. The shareholders are then given the chance to subscribe for the new shares in proportion to their original holding at a fixed price within a set time period. The right of first refusal for existing shareholders is termed 'pre-emption right' and protects the existing shareholders' ownership from dilution. Any shares not taken up by or sold for the shareholders revert to the sub-underwriters; any shares not sub-underwritten are left with the issuing merchant bank. All shares left with the merchant bank are then placed in the market by the broker and, before Big Bang, were traded through the jobbers. A similar approach to underwriting is taken in flotations.[11] In rights issues and flotations, the broker's input on price, timing and demand is crucial to the tactics of the offering and gives them access to chief executives.[12]

The strategic importance of equity broking moved from the wings to centre stage with the Stock Exchange agreement of 1983 when it became clear that banks would be able to own brokers. This put into play the corporate broking relationships. For the merchant banks this created a situation that was both offensive, in that it was seen as a chance to win new business, and defensive, in that it was regarded as necessary to own in-house equity distribution in case all the independent brokers disappeared. For the commercial banks and the investment banks trying to break into the chief executive relationship there was now an opportunity to do so through the corporate broking route and the rush was on to buy institutional equity brokers.

3

Simple but not Easy

Broking and jobbing before Big Bang had three key characteristics: the firms were small; functions were clearly separated; the businesses were domestic. As a result the individual's role was simple (but not necessarily easy); the businesses were straightforward to run; relationships were everything; risk management skills were not widespread. It is essential to understand these characteristics of the old world when considering the changes that were to come in with Big Bang.

SIZE

The City was a small world. In 1983 the brokers and jobbers fitted neatly into the Square Mile, with many occupying the winding streets and narrow alleys around the Stock Exchange in Throgmorton Street. The overspill to Docklands was still a decade away, and Liverpool Street station's neighbour was still the crumbling Old Broad Street station, not the gleaming Broadgate development of the late eighties. The office blocks were post-war, stone-clad, six or seven storeys high, with a few brokers like Greenwell and Phillips & Drew in slightly higher concrete and glass structures left over from the sixties.

Most of the brokers and jobbers operated in only one location, although a few of the regionally based firms had London offices as well as their headquarters in provincial cities such as Glasgow, Edinburgh, Birmingham or Liverpool. The typical layout was a single head office with separate departments for institutional sales, private clients, fund management, gilts, research, and the back office, with a small box in the Stock Exchange close to the market floor for the dealers. The jobbers operated from pitches on the Stock Exchange floor with their main offices a few minutes' walk away.

The total number of people in stockbroking was around 10,000 and there were about a thousand in jobbing. The entire broking and jobbing community in London was smaller than some of the larger American firms of the day. The individual firms in London comprised a few hundred people at most and 300 was the median. The numbers of staff employed by the first firms to announce link ups with each other in 1983 and 1984 show the modest scale of the constituents. The combined operations of Scrimgeour Kemp Gee and Vickers da Costa were only 500 when Citicorp announced in September 1984 that it was to merge them. NatWest bought Fielding Newson Smith which employed around 200 at the time and Shearson Lehman Amex sought to break into London by buying L. Messel & Co., a firm numbering 270 staff. Even the leading jobbers employed only small numbers. At Smith Brothers, there was an average number of employees during 1982–3 of 165 plus twelve directors. Akroyd & Smithers was bigger but it contained only 435 employees in the year to September 1984, the last year before it linked up with Warburg. Pinchin Denny, which was to form Morgan Grenfell's jobbing arm, comprised 257 partners and staff.

A result of the modest scale and single-site location was that most people in a firm knew each other personally and quite a large proportion of the broking and jobbing community were able to recognize each other by name, face or reputation. At firms of up to about 250 employees, the senior partner would know everyone by name and sight and would have a working relationship with all the partners and senior executives. The salesmen and analysts would work as a closely knit team because they felt part of one family. The dealing staff who operated on the market floor and who belonged to a different set were somewhat remote from the salesmen and analysts but were still emphatically part of the same family. The personal relationships that were possible in such a small community were reinforced by the intimacy of a dealing system in which people dealt face-to-face rather than over the phone or via screens.

The fact that everyone knew and met each other had a major effect on the way the City operated. Close personal relationships discouraged bad behaviour in many forms. Within firms, it was harder to let down colleagues by shoddy work or disloyalty in the days of frequent personal contact than in the modern era of anonymous screen-based communication and sprawling global empires. In the market, those who did not play by the rules were ostracized. This was most evident on the Stock Exchange floor where there was a very strict code of behaviour, both formal and informal. The Stock Exchange rulebook set out clearly what was and what was not permitted and the system was operated in a meticulous manner. Disciplinary hearings did occur but the informal policing system was even more impressive. Word spread quickly when individuals or firms were consistently misbehaving and such parties very suddenly found it hard to get liquidity or to be shown business. Correct procedures were drummed into the most junior messengers, known as blue buttons, at a very early stage and it was a matter of honour not to let the side down. Even where deals were being struck on the most brazen inside tip, care was taken not to leave the jobber in a hopeless position and to complete the execution strictly by the rules. On the market floor, self-regulation was possible and it did work.

Size and ownership patterns tended to reinforce patterns of loyal behaviour. The sense of family was cultivated by the partnership structure. Paternalism was fostered by a few traditional rituals that continued right up to Big Bang. Christmas Eve morning in the City was marked by lorries outside many broking firms unloading turkeys, the traditional gift from the partners to the staff. This Dickensian touch brought the firm into every home on Christmas Day and guaranteed full attendance on Christmas Eve. The connection between firm and family was also made at births, marriages and deaths: a present from the partners at weddings and births, representation at funerals and informal financial after-care for the needy bereaved.

Redundancies and sackings were rare events and then only in the most dire economic circumstances or for high crimes and misdemeanours. Dundas Hamilton, the senior partner of the medium-sized broker Fielding Newson Smith at the time of Big Bang recalled, 'We never had a redundancy',[1] and the firm was not unusual in that.

Such loyalty to staff was generally reciprocated although this was beginning to break down by 1983. As late as the 1970s, it was rare for people to change firms in stockbroking and even then certain rules had to be obeyed. Haruko Fukuda moved from Vickers da Costa in 1974: 'It was not done in those days in the City to move from one firm to another and start speaking to clients from the previous firm. We had to generate new clients.'[2]

Old values were already crumbling by 1983. Head-hunters had been active in the City for some years and regular traffic was developing from the smaller firms to the industry leaders as the best people found their way to the leading houses. The earnings curve began slowly but, after a few years' experience and just before staff became prospective partners, mismatches developed between revenue-generating potential and rates of pay. Such candidates were ideal fodder for the head-hunters and there was increasing staff mobility between firms.

The redundancies and lay-offs that had been necessary in 1974–5 after the oil crisis may have broken the old trust between partners and staff and the new Government was also considered to have played a role in changing the mood: 'The City was changing. As new capital flooded in, an old honour code was breaking down. City firms had been partnerships that worked as a single unit. Brokers and merchant bankers would patiently wait their time to be partners and would then amass a decent wealth before retiring. Now the cult of the individual was growing, part of the ethos known as Thatcherism.'[3]

Whilst the general mood changed to one of entrepreneurialism, the change in the tax rate reinforced the new values and contributed to the breakdown of the old City:

When I started off most companies were paternalistic and there was tremendous loyalty from the people to the employer and the employer to the employee. Also because of the high taxation rate, it wasn't really worthwhile anybody moving from one company to another – if you got £10,000 per year more you got £1700 out of it and there wasn't much point destroying your life for £1700. So people stayed within their niches and this rather cosy situation built up. Then the tax rate came down to 60 per cent and people started becoming more mobile and when it came down to 40 per cent even more mobile. People became greedy. And the employers became less loyal to their employees because they were paying vast sums of money and if they didn't perform they were out.[4]

Considerable moral pressure was applied to staff who resigned. They were accused of letting down their colleagues, letting down the firm, and behaving in an ungentlemanly manner. If the resigner was turned round, then all was forgiven. If not, and he or she insisted on leaving, the culprit was made to feel ashamed and deemed to have let the side down. This took the form of quite subtle body language and a rather distant courtesy. In one part this was to discourage the others, and in another it was a way of expressing a genuine sense of betrayal.

Because the broking and jobbing firms were like large families, they could be managed in a minimalist way. Discipline, morale and momentum were self-generated by the peer group. Problems would be dealt with by mutual support and would be raised to the attention of the senior partners only in serious cases. There was no need for an infrastructure to deal with career development or training: the family helped its ailing members.

The brokers and jobbers were small in financial terms as well as in headcount. Taking a typical institutional broker with a staff of 270 and thirty partners, the profits available to the partners were between £5 and £10 million in the early 1980s, giving the average partner between £150,000 and £300,000 per annum, depending on the profitability of the firm. Junior partners earned less than £100,000, senior partners up to £500,000. Brokers' balance sheets were small. They were not allowed to take principal positions in securities so the only capital requirements were fixed assets and working capital. Not even the leading jobbers could be described as large companies. In the year ending 22 April 1983, and just before the agreement between the Government and the Stock Exchange, Smith Brothers reported record profits of £3.5 million. Market capitalization was less than £5 million and shareholders' funds totalled only £9.4 million. The sum of bull plus bear positions at the year end had been £88 million. The chairman was paid £105,000, eight directors earned between £95,000 and £100,000 but no employee earned over £65,000.

The small financial resources of the firms in the City meant that there was very little experience of running big enterprises and this is one reason why the old school appeared out of its depth when tasked with the challenge of Big Bang. There was a pool of more experienced management talent at the merchant banks which was bigger than the brokers and jobbers. The leading UK merchant bank in 1983, Morgan Grenfell, made post-tax profits of only £13.5 million for the year, that in itself a substantial increase over the £9.5 million made in 1982. United Kingdom employees totalled 842 in the average month in 1983, much bigger than the brokers and being of sufficient scale to require more organization and management than was typically found in broking and jobbing.

SIMPLE BUT NOT EASY

To a modern broker, the life of his predecessor before Big Bang would seem very simple. The business of selling to clients and researching companies was not dissimilar to the present day but the job ended there. The process of working with the in-house market makers and sales traders was unknown to salesmen before Big Bang and analysts hardly ever had to work with corporate finance. Their jobs were simpler and so was management of the firm.

The typical institutional equity broker in 1983 consisted of five departments: sales, research, dealing, corporate broking and back office. Each had a clearly defined role, not confused in 1983 as it was to be just three years later, by poorly understood technology, colleagues in other countries, or conflicting requirements from another part of the group.

The sales team consisted of up to thirty people whose job was to communicate the firm's investment ideas to institutional clients. This was done by telephone backed up by occasional meetings, often over lunch. The head of sales was usually a leader rather than a manager, leading by example, firing up the team when business was quiet and trying to generate the raw energy and self-feeding momentum that characterized a sales team that was working well. Each salesman was responsible for calling fund managers at the institutions with ideas and getting orders in return.

Formal marketing was a thing of the future although account targets and personal budgets were beginning to come in. The sales team followed a very broad marketing plan: there might be a year's target commission for each client but no direction was given on how to achieve it and it was just as likely that the formal target was left to each salesman's common sense. The clients rewarded the brokers for service with commission and the salesman's annual bonus and pay rise would depend on the total business he generated and on the firm's overall profitability.

Execution of the firm's business through jobbers involved the broking firm's agency dealers, who worked on the Stock Exchange floor. Although they came up to the office after market hours, the dealing department was always slightly remote from the rest of the firm. The dealers were closer in style and background to the jobbers they dealt with, although they were agency dealers and not risk managers. Orders successfully completed were processed by the firm's back office team of settlement clerks.

The crux of the dealers' job was to find the jobber who was most prepared to execute the firm's business on the best terms. The dealers would go round the market floor from pitch to pitch, asking 'What are xyz co?', being careful not to reveal whether they were buyers or sellers, before deciding to which jobber they would give their business. The skills they required were accuracy under pressure, a good nose for the market, the ability to forge good relationships with other market professionals, a quick mind and the ability to walk many miles per day around the Stock Exchange floor. The dealers were frequently under pressure from salesmen who demanded better prices. Clients often wanted to deal in more shares than the jobber would accommodate and the salesmen would ask the dealer to try for bigger size. Salesmen knew the jobbers themselves and often thought they could do better than the dealers; rows were frequent.

The relationship between the salesmen and the dealers was one of the few points of structural friction in the pre-Big Bang firm but it was the existence of these intermediaries that kept the broker's role simple. Because of the Stock Exchange rule requiring each member firm to operate in single capacity – that is, broking or jobbing but not both – the broking firms did not have to take principal risk. An order from a client was unequivocally good news for the broker. He got commission on the order and he did not have to worry about off-loading the risk it created. The broker's only requirement was to execute as speedily as possible at the best available price for the client.

It was this requirement that caused rows with the dealers because for some salesmen the price was never good enough and the size never large enough. But the rows were of a different type to those that ensued after Big Bang, when the risk positions that were created for the broker by client business could cause profit and loss account problems of some magnitude.

The salesmen got their ideas from the research department supplemented with personal knowledge. The salesmen's ability to sniff out their own stories, whether from their clients, an intelligent reading of the financial press or observation of the business world, or simply by noting the number of shoppers in the High Street on a Saturday afternoon, was and still is a priceless supplement to the output of research. But by 1983 the research department was the source of most of the firm's investment ideas. One factor in this was the insider dealing legislation of 1980 which made illegal some of the brokers' traditional research sources.

Originally the brokers' research departments were called 'the stats department' and the analysts' publications took the form of letters to clients. Even in 1983, brokers' circulars were still called letters by some veteran salesmen. In the early days, analysts were considered slightly eccentric boffins and there were residual signs of this in 1983. Graduates were finding their way into sales but the majority of the sales desk came direct from public school, the armed services or accountancy. The research department, on the other hand, was mainly staffed by graduates. The glossy publications which proliferated in the mid and late 1980s were very rare and the analysts' circulars still appeared amateurish in layout and content.

The research analysts worked in pairs in the bigger sectors, one senior and one junior, but the large teams of today were only just beginning to form in the early 1980s and in many firms each sector of the Stock Market was covered by an individual. The analysts were responsible for producing research reports on companies and whole sectors which were sent to clients. The sources were published information enriched by company contact. Company contact could take the form of a visit by a group of analysts to see an aspect of the company's operations and meet the management, or a one-on-one visit to meet the chief executive or finance director. The analyst would use these visits to form a relationship which would permit updating telephone calls.

Communications were on the verge of revolution in 1983 but personal mobile telephones were not yet in everyday use. This could cause enormous problems for analysts on group visits with an unseemly dash for the pay phone. Analysts would sneak out of presentations to get to the pay phone first in order to relay the news back to clients and colleagues in London. In 1980 the Distillers Company Limited took a party of thirty analysts to tour its distilleries on Islay and for the Chairman to update the analysts on current trading. The news was bad – demand for Scotch in America the next year would be down and so would profits. There was only one pay phone at the small hotel where the meeting took place and unseemly brawls broke out as the analysts jostled to be the first with the news.

The analysts communicated their views in print and verbally, giving the salesmen a daily briefing at the morning meeting and then spending the first part of the morning telephoning the relevant sector specialist at the clients. Written research was sent out to clients and backed up by telephone calls from generalist and specialist salesmen and by telephone calls and visits from the analyst himself.

Two developments which were to complicate the life of the analyst were underway in the early 1980s. Institutions were beginning to develop a system of giving points to broking firms for the quality of service that they received and these points would determine the level of business given to each broker. Individual members of the firm, especially the analysts, were allocated points, and the results were made known to the senior management. This 'panel voting' system was to transform the analysts' lives from idea generators to vote catchers.

The second development was the rise in importance of published surveys, ranking firms and their analysts. The magazine *Institutional Investor* had been running such polls of institutional fund managers for some years in the US and began to do the same in Britain in the early 1980s. The UK had its own well-established survey run in his spare time by a fund manager named Geoffrey Osmint; originally called the Continental Illinois survey after the bank which sponsored it, it became the Extel survey in 1985 under Extel's sponsorship. A good position in the Extel survey served as an advertisement to other firms and hence became a factor in analysts' pay. In corporate finance beauty contests a high Extel position helped to impress corporate clients.

But at this stage the requirements of corporate finance, the need to help the in-house market makers, and the demands for intensive marketing to service the institutions were not widely felt. Just before Big Bang the Extel survey asked the analysts how they spent their time. Seventy per cent of time was spent on fundamental research, including company visits, 22 per cent was spent on marketing and only 8 per cent on helping corporate finance. This was still a simple, one-dimensional world.

The jobbing firms were equally straightforward. The soul of the market depended on the existence of the exchange floor. The floor in use in 1983 had been in operation only since 1973, following modernization. It consisted of a large number of hexagonal booths around which the jobbers stood. Different sections of the market – gilts, gold mining shares, equities by sector – had their own areas. Each firm, whether jobber or broker, had its own small office at the side of the floor known as a box. This was the central point of communication between the salesmen giving orders from the main office to their dealers on the floor. Communication was by telephone from office to box and then by walkie-talkie from box to dealer on the floor. Having received the order from the box, the broker's dealer would walk out on to the floor and check the prices before giving his order to the most competitive jobber. No paper changed hands until the contract note was completed at the end of the day and the expression 'My Word is My Bond' was essential to the functioning of the floor.

London's jobbers quoted two prices in each share, the lower being the price at which they would buy, the higher being their selling price. The difference between the two, the spread, gave the jobbers the chance of making a 'turn' between buyers and sellers. The market makers' job was straightforward then. All resources were devoted to producing a positive trading account at the end of the day. In the days of single capacity, there were no salesmen to appease in pursuit of market share and no corporate financiers trying to impress clients with the volume of their shares traded. Sectors rarely moved for global reasons; the jobber's face-to-face clients were the key to supply and demand.

The internal workings of the jobbing firms were highly focused. They were divided into teams covering the various sectors and markets and the teams were hierarchical, with senior dealers grading down to blue button trainees. The term 'blue button' referred to the colour of the identification badges which were compulsory for anyone going onto the Stock Exchange floor. The aggregated risk positions of each team were monitored constantly to ensure that the firm's overall risk was in balance. This was much easier in the 1980s before foreign exchange and derivatives came along to complicate matters. Real time computer models, even spreadsheets, were years away. Notebooks, ledgers and the backs of envelopes were more common risk-management tools.

In the broking and jobbing firms, work was more straightforward under single capacity. Each function served no more than one internal and one external customer.[5] It was easier to focus and relationships were more straightforward. People were generally able to cope with what they had to do and therefore they tended to be happier. It was very unusual for management to have to reconcile conflicting demands and so people management was very rudimentary.

DOMESTIC

Relationship management and business controls were kept simple by a narrow geographical spread. The vast majority of institutional equity brokers relied on British investors in British securities for almost all of their income. In 1980, overseas investors accounted for only 7 per cent of total turnover in British equities but in the late 1970s a small group of brokers began to serve US investors out of London. John Holmes, then a partner at Hoare Govett, was one of the first to sense the potential of this market: 'In the summer of 1979 I saw clear signs that the Americans would soon be buying more international equities and took a trip to New York to see. I met a few people and when I got back began to cover them out of London. Things built up nicely and in 1982 I went to New York and we built up a staff of about thirty, including corporate finance people and the back office, to service Americans interested in buying UK shares.'[6] Other firms had come to a similar conclusion and a small community of expatriate brokers had developed in New York by the early 1980s, supplemented by a few interested American brokers. The business was simple to run, being agency only, and largely consisting of existing employees who were trusted and well-versed in the firm's ways and values.

A few firms specialized in Far Eastern equities, such as Vickers da Costa, but these were also usually staffed by expatriates known to the partnership. As such they were merely an extended arm of the family and posed no new cultural or control issues. There was a small circle of experts in South African and Australian gold mining shares but these were usually London-based. At this stage in Japan, no foreign firm had been granted membership of the Tokyo Stock Exchange and operations there were through representative offices only, as they were in the handful of Asian offices operated by a few British brokers. The lack of local stock exchange membership kept things simple with no major regulatory or capital issues and no risk positions to be monitored.

Europe was also covered out of London if it was covered at all. The equities culture was not well developed on the Continent and local markets were generally thin. The European departments in the British brokers were small, fringe operations staffed by a mixture of genuine European enthusiasts, those who had not quite made it in UK broking, language graduates or those with a European family background. A few of the analysts in UK equities such as Keith Brown, Greenwell's banking sector analyst, kept a weather eye on developments in Europe, but the quality of investment research on European companies was generally very poor.

Although by the early 1980s the horizons of London's brokers were beginning to broaden, travel was still rare. The leading analysts took annual trips to the US to visit subsidiaries and competitors of the companies that they followed, but these were considered something of a luxury and had to be defended in front of cynical colleagues and parsimonious admin partners. The circuit of visiting foreign investors in British companies, especially in New York, had yet to be established.

The absence of an international business of any scale helped keep the back office simple. Because most equities that were dealt in were British, settlement and banking arrangements were straightforward and firms did not carry any currency risk. At every level – management, sales, research and back office – the absence of an international dimension helped ensure focus on the domestic business but restricted the experience and skill set of the London broking community.

LEADERSHIP RATHER THAN MANAGEMENT

The simplicity and scale of the business carried out by the London brokers meant that they required leadership rather than management. This permitted a very lean management structure which was in keeping with the inclinations of the type of person likely to have got on in broking and with the financial needs of a partnership. In a typical firm of thirty partners and 270 staff, only two partners would be in full-time managerial capacities. The senior partner would act as the chairman and chief executive and the administrative partner would be the equivalent to a finance director and chief operating officer. Each would be backed up by a senior administrator, usually at below partner level. These two partners would deal with the full range of administrative and regulatory matters. Liaison with the Stock Exchange was a time-consuming task and there were essential matters like pay, pensions, accounting, office facilities and staffing to be organized. The settlements area or back office usually reported to the administrative partner and would be run by a senior clerk. In time, and especially as settlement became more complex with dual capacity and the increasing internationalization of the business, the heads of the back office might become junior or salaried partners.

There was very little committee work in the pre-Big Bang brokers. There would be a weekly partners' meeting, often over lunch on Friday or over drinks after work on Thursday. Meetings late on Friday were not held since they would interfere with the trek to the country. Meetings generally were held in low regard and not viewed as being real work. 'He spends all his time in meetings' was one of the most damning comments that could be made about an individual. Goldman Sachs is regarded as one of the best managed of the modern investment banks. Its one-time senior partner Jon Corzine felt it appropriate to explain some management changes introduced in 1996 with the preface 'I'm a trader and I hate meetings'.[7] Whether or not Corzine really hates meetings is not the point; the fact is that the head of the world's leading investment bank in 1996 knew what chord to strike with fellow investment bankers: I hate meetings. And by implication, real work is done on the trading floor, with the client, over the telephone, at lunch or wherever. Anywhere but at meetings.

It is not surprising, therefore, that in the broking firms in London in 1983 meetings and management were kept to a minimum. The partners' meeting would focus on the week's results and would be of intense interest to those present. The partners had unlimited liability to the firm's debts and the partners were not paid a salary but were allowed to take drawings from the year's accumulated profits. The Stock Market collapse of 1974 caused by the oil crisis was still close enough for partners to have vivid memories of personal financial losses and the prospect of bankruptcy. It was that experience that caused the partnerships to be so lean financially and to be thin on management. Non-productive overhead was to be frowned upon since it could make the difference between profit and loss in a poor year.

As a result of being based on trust and personal contact and, because of the anti-management culture, there was very little formal management in the old City. 'Seat of the pants management' best describes the style of 1983. Although at one level the firms were tightly run by administrative partners charged with protecting the partners' wealth, management in the operation of the business was frowned upon. Broking was held to be a flair business which too much management would stifle. Appraisals, formal targets and training for staff were still in their infancy as far as stockbrokers were concerned. Few had a personnel department. There was a distinct feeling that management did not matter and that what really counted was writing tickets. Ticket writers not pen pushers were the heroes of the day. Management was for wimps or for those who had not quite cut the mustard as brokers.

The anti-managerial culture that still prevailed in broking in the early 1980s in London meant that many of the skills that would soon be required to manage larger, risk-carrying and international business were missing. The broking community simply did not contain enough people with the basic human resources management skills to sustain and control organizations which were to become too large for paternalism and personal relationships to be the binding forces. A similar skill shortage prevailed in risk management where there were not enough jobbers to go round, with an even worse shortage of senior risk managers. Basic administration skills were also in short supply so that record keeping and process – dismissed as red tape in the smaller partnerships – were not part of the prevailing culture. This can be described as instinctive and short-term rather than considered and long-term.

Ironically some of the management skills that were lacking in the brokers were present in the merchant banks and commercial banks that were to buy the brokers. Despite their more staid and conservative appearance, the merchant banks were more international and more entrepreneurial than their broking counterparts. There was a buccaneering spirit which saw them open up overseas offices in Latin America, Asia and the United States, giving them some experience of running foreign businesses. They had some risk management experience through the underwriting system and from diverse businesses such as Eurobonds and corporate lending, and as larger organizations they had better developed human resources functions. The commercial banks had even more experience of administrative procedures and risk management. To understand why the merchant and commercial banks were not able to graft this on to the brokers they bought requires an analysis of the prevailing cultures and attitudes that existed in the City.

4

Shoes with Laces, Trousers with Braces

The Chancellor's Stock Exchange Christmas Carol

Come, my friends and stand by me,
My words are not hollow
Though the winter bitter be,
Gentle spring will follow
Christmas is the time of hope,
Hope is what I'm stressing
Brokers, jobbers one and all.

Sung by Sir Geoffrey Howe at the Stock Exchange Christmas lunch, 1981, accompanied by the chairman's son, Adam Goodison, on the guitar.[1]

'Gentlemanly capitalism' was a phrase coined by the historians P. J. Cain and A. G. Hopkins and revived by Will Hutton. It describes a culture and a style of business and captures the tone of the twilight world of the pre-reformation City.[2] Although the City's values were being challenged by the early reforms of the Thatcher Government and by the more aggressive mood that was sweeping the country, in 1983 the predominant culture was traditional and class-based. The City's institutions and values reflected three of the pillars of conservative England: the public school, the gentleman's club and the country house.

Stockbroking had originated with the private client. Firms provided advice to rich individuals and families and were staffed with people who were at home in such company. The institutional departments that had grown to be the dominant force were put together by people who came out of private client firms and who shared the same background and networks as the private client brokers. Merchant banks

33

were, if anything, even more public school based. The corporate finance departments included more graduates than the brokers but Oxbridge and the public schools predominated.

The jobbing firms were run by a mixture of public school boys and senior dealers who had moved up the organization on merit. Many of the dealers came into the City via the East End and Essex where there was a tradition of working on the market floor but, as we shall see, they adopted the style and values of the public school boys.

By 1983 graduates had begun to work their way up broking firms, especially in research, but quite often they also came from the public schools. Grammar school boys and girls, especially from the North of England, were relatively unusual in 1983 and had some work to do to gain acceptance. A bright graduate from Burnley at one broking firm in the early 1980s was always known as 'Burnley', his accent gently mocked, and he never lived down the day he referred to the lunch duty roster as the dinner list.

City gents had very little idea how ordinary people lived. A well-meaning merchant banker at a staff Christmas party, on hearing that one of his typists lived 'on an estate in Romford', replied, 'How splendid. Do you keep horses there?' A few weeks ago I overheard an exchange between two corporate financiers which showed that things have moved on, but not by much: 'None of the secretaries can come. They're all in Southend and I'm in Wiltshire. We're getting outside caterers in, otherwise Jenny and I will be cooking and waiting all evening. As it is, we'll be free to chat. Rounders is such good fun, everyone can play. Even the secretaries.' The grip of the public schools on the broking and banking fraternity was evident to anyone who spent more than a few hours in the City in the early 1980s. From *City Lives*, the published anthology of City stories from the National Life Story Collection, it is possible to glean the educational background of fifteen senior figures from banking, broking and jobbing in the late 1980s and early 1990s. All thirteen males had been to public school, seven of them to Eton. One of them, Michael Verey, explained how Eton set the standards for the old City: 'During my time in the City, those who hadn't been to Eton were striving for Eton standards and the Eton ethos dominated from Kim Cobbold, Governor of the Bank of England, downwards. Good Etonian standards means a total trust

– if you say you'll do something, you'll do it.'[3] The Stock Exchange motto, '*Dictum meum pactum*', 'My Word is My Bond', reinforced this.

The atmosphere in the City, especially in the Stock Exchange itself, was reminiscent of jolly japes at boarding school, the officers' mess or the junior combination room of an Oxbridge college of the 1950s. This is illustrated by an account of life on the Stock Exchange floor from Jane Partington, one of the first female dealers to work in the market, an account that also shows the sexism which the few females to succeed in broking had to endure: 'The girls all got given nicknames by the men – I was the Night Nurse, there was Sweaty Betty, Super Bum, the Grimsby Trawler, the Road Runner, Stop Me and Pick One . . . If you were dressed in red from head to foot they'd call you Pillar Box all day and try to post letters . . . They'd sit ripping up newspapers and sticking it all together and then creep about and clip it on to your skirt so you'd walk off and have a thirty yard tail behind you.'[4]

Merchant banking owed its origins to advising corporates and it was traditionally staffed with those who felt comfortable dealing with senior business people. They were hierarchical and deferential. Clients visiting merchant banks were received like visitors to a country house. The meeting rooms were adorned with classical paintings. Tea and coffee were served by deferential butlers. The style of catering was old-fashioned English. Like the public schools, there was a strict hierarchy more obvious to those in the know than to outsiders. The standards set by the merchant banks were imitated by the brokers and jobbers.

Everything from the way people dressed, spoke and ate to the buildings and rooms in which they worked was derived from the standards of the English upper and upper middle classes: the gentleman's club lived on. The City lunch was still in its heyday in 1983. Waitresses dressed in black and white outfits or traditionally clad butlers presided over panelled dining rooms hung with classic hunting scenes. Client lunches were preceded by sherry or gin and tonic, accompanied by French wine and followed with port and cigars. It was not done not to drink. Perrier water was rare in the City in 1983.

Just as City lunches followed a standard form, so too did dress. The number of professional women in the City was very small so it was a dark-suited City. The only colours permitted were blue or grey, the only variation the width and thickness of the pin stripe. Brown suits were not worn except by the clerks. Socks were dark and shoes were black. Shirts were plain or striped, never check and the button-down collar was for Americans. Braces were still for the old school, not yet having had their yuppie revival. Ties were silk, plain or patterned but pictures on ties were not known and polyester was for the back office, the clearing bankers or the insurance companies. Jewellery was not worn except for a signet ring on the little finger and then only for the very grand or the highly aspirational.

Outside the office, the country weekend was common. This did not mean that everyone had a farm in Gloucestershire, although some did, but that among the senior partners who set the codes the talking points would be shooting and fishing, and many of the young salesmen spent only Monday to Friday afternoon in London, preferring to spend weekends in the country with family or friends.

The predominant winter game was rugby and, although some followed soccer and played in such competitions as the Arthur Dunn Cup for public school old boys, soccer had not yet been through its Sky-inspired boom. Soccer was for the jobbers, the back office and the young generation of graduate entrants. The senior City preferred Twickenham to Wembley and billiards to snooker. Summer games provided a unifying influence with cricket avidly played and followed. It was a noticeable feature of the summer of Botham's Ashes that the Stock Market went better whenever the Australians were receiving a hiding. The Stock Exchange ran many sporting societies with very well organized teams following the public school tradition of the Easter and summer tours complete with ties, colours and dinners.

The jobbing firms straddled the City's class divide. The jobbers were run by a mixture of public school boys and quick-minded men from a variety of backgrounds. The classic jobber is the East End youngster with an eye for a bargain. However, those who made it were highly intelligent and commercial and as likely to come from the London suburbs as the East End. Mike Geering, later head of equities at James Capel, joined the firm in 1972. His father owned a butcher's business and wanted his sons to follow a professional career, 'and not work the hours he had worked going to Smithfield at the crack of dawn. So I came into the City, get up at five every morning and come to work near Smithfield.'[5]

The bright, razor-sharp young men in jobbing from more humble backgrounds were quick to adopt the public school ethos in dress and recreation. The dress code was identical to that of the senior stockbrokers and merchant bankers and the lunches followed a similar although reputedly more alcoholic pattern. Upper-class recreations of the 1960s and 1970s, such as shooting and skiing, were taken up by the young jobbers looking for outlets for their high disposable incomes. Client areas in the jobbers' offices were just like the brokers'. To the first-time visitor it was difficult to distinguish between the brokers, merchant bankers and jobbers, all being staffed by identically dressed people located in country house lookalike offices.

In time I learned that the shoes (always black, never brown) were a good guide to what people did. In the early eighties, the following held good: lace ups with leather soles and either toe caps or brogues – merchant banker or very senior partner in broking or jobbing; other lace ups – agency dealer; tasselled loafers – well-bred broker or American; other slip-ons – ordinary broker or jobber. Other useful signs were tie pins (small pin and chain connecting both parts of tie and shirt – analyst; 24-carat gold pin holding front of tie only – merchant banker) and cuff links (gold oval disks – merchant banker or very senior broker/jobber; swivel-backed – the rest).

People in the City not only looked like gentlemen, they worked like them, too. The City in 1983 is generally believed to have been more fun than in the post-Big Bang era. Whilst some of this is probably down to rose-tinted nostalgia, there are good reasons for believing that the earlier era was more enjoyable and less intense. Jobs were simpler, more manageable, less stressful and people worked less hard. The gentleman capitalists worked gentlemanly hours.

The Stock Market did not open until 9.30 a.m. and, although preparation for the day began before then, the morning meeting between salesmen and analysts rarely began much before 9 a.m. and often not before 9.15 a.m. Commuters from the suburbs in 1983 were leaving home at around the time they would be starting work in the early 1990s. Jobbers left the market floor at 3.30 and, although there followed a period of after hours dealing, the intensity had gone at 3.30 and most were on their way home by 5.30.

The more enjoyable aspects of the old City included a tolerant attitude to alcohol: 'On the Stock Exchange floor you were expected to go across to the bar and have several drinks at twelve o'clock in the morning and then have a heavy lunch. There was a lot of drinking in the lunch room. Some people were known to enjoy several glasses of brandy after lunch, having had two gin and tonics before and several glasses of wine. That was pretty standard.'[6] Nick Durlacher recalls, 'The Stock Exchange could very fairly be described as a club and people in the club fairly understood who was good and who was bad and who drank too much and who didn't. There was always a sort of machismo that if you could hold your drink then you were somehow a better man than your neighbour who couldn't.'[7]

Whilst it may be very interesting to note that chaps in the City had either been to public school or behaved as though they had and that they made their offices look like country houses, did it really matter? Had the City remained as it was, sheltered from competition, the answer would have been no. But the City did not stay as it was and the old guard was shown up to be uncompetitive in its work ethic, not flexible enough to cope with radical change, and so imbued with class attitudes of superiority that it would not take help from those who could have given it. It is impossible to prove that this was all down to the public school backgrounds of the senior people in broking but the traits of hierarchy and arrogance that were common in the City in 1983 coincide with the values of order and self-confidence that were taught at the schools attended by most senior brokers.

The different social backgrounds of the brokers and the commercial bankers that bought them was a factor in the cultural differences that beset such marriages. The clearing banks were dominated by grammar school boys and were totally different in style and values. The clearing bankers tended to have had a grammar school rather than a public school education. More of them came from the English provinces, the North and Midlands, than the merchant bankers who were from the Home Counties, Gloucestershire or Edinburgh. Out of the hundreds that I know I can think of only one or two senior merchant bankers and brokers with regional accents, in contrast to the clearing bankers where regional accents are common. In addition to speaking differently, they lived in different places. While the clearing bankers travelled in from the suburbs, the senior brokers and merchant bankers more often lived in London, except at weekends.

The social divide was exacerbated by a contrast between the work ethic of the clearing bankers and the gifted amateur approach of the other side. Clearing bankers were trained to keep records, fill in forms and to follow the procedures manual. The merchant bankers and brokers dismissed this as bureaucracy. As a result of all these factors, the two groups moved in totally different circles and did not much like each other. This became a serious business issue when clearing banks tried to build investment banks.

THE CITY IN 1983: SUMMARY

The simplicity of this world was beguiling. It was fun to work in, competitive without being over-complicated but it was a very poor training for what was about to occur. The single dimension between the firm's interests and those of the client was about to be complicated for jobbers, banks and brokers by the proliferation of products offered and geographies served. Management was not used to dealing with technology, change or the need to work at inter-personal relationships in larger firms. No one in the old City was prepared for a world in which the computer replaced the handshake.

The merchant banks, bigger, more complex, more risk aware and more international, were theoretically better placed to handle these new dimensions. But they too were class- and attitude-ridden. They had not yet grasped that, in a world where paternalism no longer worked, the anti-managerial attitudes of the armed services and the public schools would not be sufficient to bring the best out of people.

The new entrants to the City had a more promising managerial skill set. The clearing banks were structured, risk experienced, complex, international and, above all, large. But they too were handicapped by a value system which put time serving above merit and in which sound decisions could be marred by bureaucratic procedures. As grammar-school-based institutions, their senior managers lacked the nerve to challenge the overbearing, instinctive and usually misplaced self-confidence of the public school boys in the merchant banks and brokers.

As events were to prove, the other newcomers to the City, the foreign banks and brokers, were best equipped to cope with the many changes that were to occur. They had the size, experience and flexibility to adapt to the new world. They were unencumbered by class-based historical experience and given no discouragement by the UK authorities. In fact, by imposing so many changes on a City that was manifestly unfit, the Government, the Stock Exchange and the Bank of England effectively ensured that only the foreign firms would survive.

PART TWO

**RIDING BIG ELEPHANTS,
1983-6**

5

Laissez-faire

Soon after I entered the City in 1978 I became aware that it could all go wrong. The other junior analysts and salesmen talked knowingly about a case being mounted against the Stock Exchange by the Office of Fair Trading, how this would lead to lower commission rates for brokers and how we would all lose our jobs. The partners never wanted to talk to us about it which confirmed our suspicions that something serious was going on.

But one day in 1979 the mood lightened. Mrs Thatcher was elected Prime Minister. The partners brought round bottles of champagne at 11 a.m. and we all stopped work to celebrate. I felt guilty: I had not voted Conservative but I dared not admit it for fear of being branded an outcast; and I had not yet learned to be comfortable pretending to be pleased about something I disliked. After a few minutes one of the other junior analysts, a young woman, had the courage to say what I had been thinking and was given the cold shoulder. After that, she never lost the reputation for being 'difficult and a bolshie' and probably set back the cause of women in Fielding Newson Smith a long way. From her treatment I learned that, even if you did not think like them, you had to act and sound like them so I drank the champagne and looked as pleased as punch.

I asked another analyst, a partner and a Tory so loyal that he was rumoured once to have broken through a picket line to empty Ted Heath's dustbin, what it would all mean: 'It's extremely good news. Lower taxes, no exchange controls and a sympathetic hearing in the court case. That's all you need to know.' Like much of his analysis, there was a lot of truth in what he said but he was inclined to overlook the risks.

In the short term, his confidence was well placed as the new Government appeared to demonstrate that it was in tune with the City. One of its earliest reforms was the abolition of exchange controls in 1979, opening the way for UK investors to invest directly in foreign shares and something that the City had long been advocating. Equally popular were the reductions in tax rates that were announced in successive budgets. Clearly the City's high earners benefited, but the tax cuts were equally important as a signal that wealth generation was back in favour. The City had been miserable under the Labour governments of the 1960s and 1970s. The unions not the City had the Government's ear. Making money was considered immoral in Socialist Britain. The public sector, not the private, was where sympathies lay.

THE STOCK EXCHANGE REFORMS

The third of my colleague's predictions, that the case against the Stock Exchange would be sympathetically dealt with, came true in part but not until 1983. The Stock Exchange had been required to register its rules and regulations with the Office of Fair Trading which had then identified several practices as 'restrictive'. These included fixed minimum commissions on share bargains and single capacity, the compulsory separation of jobbing and broking functions for Stock Exchange member firms.

These matters were referred to the Restrictive Practices Court but it became obvious that major strategic issues were involved and that a court was not the best place to work them out. Cecil Parkinson, then Secretary of State for Trade and Industry, and the then Chairman of the Stock Exchange, Nicholas Goodison, embarked on negotiations that ended with an announcement on 22 July 1983.

The terms of the initial agreement were that the Restrictive Practices Court case would be dropped if the Stock Exchange reformed itself by the end of 1986. A subsequent letter from the Stock Exchange to its members in September set out the two central pillars: fixed commissions would disappear within three years and outside ownership would be permitted within the same time scale. It was soon evident that dual capacity was a likely consequence of negotiated commissions since agency brokers would need alternative sources of revenue to survive the squeeze. As early as October 1983, Alex Fletcher, the Minister for Corporate and Consumer Affairs at the Department of Trade and Industry, made a major speech in New York: 'It was made clear to us – and experience in New York was one of the arguments – that the maintenance of single capacity might not be possible once commissions were negotiable'.[1] This was confirmed in April 1984 when a Stock Exchange discussion paper on Big Bang was published and 27 October 1986 was set as Big Bang day.

During the next three years, a framework for the detailed operation of the new market was established. The Stock Exchange rulebook was revised, introducing conduct of business rules and abolishing minimum commission rates. The old structures began to crumble as the City prepared for Big Bang. In October 1983 the Stock Exchange announced new rules to allow member firms to trade on a dual capacity basis in foreign securities and another step came in April 1984 when negotiated commissions on overseas securities were allowed.

SELF-REGULATION

Following a number of collapses and frauds in the late 1970s and early 1980s, the Government turned its attention to regulation. In 1981 Professor L. C. B. Gower had been commissioned to review the regulatory framework and this report gave rise to a Government White Paper in 1985 and, eventually, the Financial Services Act of 1986.

The Securities and Investments Board (SIB) was created to oversee financial and investment business in the UK. Self-regulatory organizations (SROs), reporting to the SIB, were to authorize participants in the industry. An unwelcome side issue facing the Stock Exchange was a plan by 187 Eurobond houses in London – mainly foreign banks and brokers – to form their own SRO for bonds and equities to be called the International Securities Regulatory Organization. Eventually, ISRO merged with the authorization/regulatory side of the Stock Exchange, forming the Securities Association. The Securities Association authorized and regulated trading in domestic and international securities and the Association of Futures Brokers and Dealers authorized and regulated trading in financial futures and commodities. Beneath them were recognized investment exchanges, which for equities was the International Stock Exchange encompassing the old Stock Exchange and a number of foreign banks and brokers who had not previously been members. This meant that the immediate authorities over the broking industry remained the same and that practitioners retained considerable influence; in other words, the industry would remain self-regulating.

The City criticized the new regulations roundly for being too bureaucratic. The view of Sir Adam Ridley, a former special adviser to the Chancellor and a director of Hambros Bank, was typical: 'The regulations are so complicated that the whole thing threatens to be a bit of a shambles. It is as if the Highway Code, instead of stating general principles, said what has to be done at every junction and intersection in the country for each of seven classes of vehicle.'[2] But in reality, as the Lex column spotted, broking had got off lightly: 'Self-regulation lives on', albeit shackled by a regulatory framework, and with a restricted role for the Bank of England. 'But under the pressure of lobbying from City and other financial institutions many of the new rules have been hedged with so many exemptions that the investor will often do better to rely on the current law.'[3]

This was a solution born out of the old City. Chaps would be trusted to behave under the watchful eye of benign authorities. This had worked reasonably well in the old world of small, well-defined, interconnecting circles where everyone knew everyone else and deals were done face-to-face. But it was not appropriate for the more complex structures which characterized modern investment banks, nor for the imminent growth in diversity of products traded and risk carried.

IDEOLOGY AND FEAR

The reforms to the Stock Exchange and the regulatory system that were put in place between 1983 and 1986 were shaped by two forces: the ideological beliefs of the Thatcher Government and a fear that London would be passed by as Europe's financial services capital.

The core belief was that industries would benefit from being exposed to competition and that Government interference should be minimal. During the House of Commons debate on the Financial Services Act, Norman Tebbit, the Secretary of State for Trade and Industry, described the Government's task in financial services, as in other sectors, as being to create an environment in which industry could respond effectively to the challenges brought by 'modern technology and intense international competition. This is best done by allowing market forces to operate responsibly but without unnecessary constraints, in a way which promotes efficient and competitive business.'[4] It was believed by influential politicians such as Nigel Lawson, the Chancellor of the Exchequer, that unless the City was exposed to the invigorating effects of competition London would become a backwater in the global, highly competitive securities market.[5]

The conviction that competition would sharpen up the City was entwined with a fear that, unless foreign firms were given easy access to the City, they would set up a rival market elsewhere. The Chairman of the Stock Exchange recalls this as being a strong influence on his thinking:

The most important thing was the opening up of the Membership at the right moment to the overseas securities houses, because it seemed fairly obvious that the London Stock Exchange would not capture the business in overseas securities – and might even lose business in securities like BP and ICI that were traded freely in New York and other places – if it did not bring into the community the houses that were able to compete outside the Stock Exchange.[6]

Fear of losing out to an offshore market and the ideological belief in competition produced a lightly regulated regime in which all were welcome to participate and where no constituency would be given a special advantage.

PROBLEMS IN THEORY AND PRACTICE

The market forces theory might have had a chance of working in broking if the competition were all starting from the same point. But Wall Street had been through deregulated commissions in 1975 and the American investment banks had over a decade's experience of the system towards which London was moving. This gave them a huge advantage and meant that the level playing field in which the Government believed was in reality tilted towards Wall Street. The Government and most commentators were so worried about the foreign firms setting up a rival market offshore, and so confident in the doctrine of free market competition, that they overlooked the global nature of the industry and underestimated the advantage conferred by Wall Street's experience.

Minimal Government intervention was also damaging when it came to the regulatory system which suffered from errors in design and implementation. From the beginning, the regulators were under-resourced which meant that they could keep only a superficial watch over the firms they controlled. The Securities and Investment Board could only pay salaries to its staff in its early days out of a Bank of England loan. When the Stock Exchange increased the size of its surveillance department in January 1986 it moved from five teams to eight, and from twenty-six inspectors to forty, a step forward but nothing like enough to keep pace with the changing scale of the industry.[7]

There were also weaknesses in the reliance placed on practitioners. Sir John Craven, once chairman of Morgan Grenfell plc and a member of the Securities and Investment Board, cast doubt over the whole system: 'The idea of having a board made up of practitioners in the financial services and investment industry and then having a staff who do the work has not, in my opinion, worked because the non-executive director, going in once every three months to a board meeting, just gets a quick sort of photograph of what the concerns are. One is not involved in the affairs in the way in which the public thinks we are.'[8]

Other mistakes included the changes that were made in the qualification required of practitioners. Previously it was possible for brokers to speak to clients without a qualification but to become a Stock Exchange member required passing all four parts of the Stock Exchange examination. This was quite a stiff test. My own experience in requiring three attempts to pass the taxation paper and failing one of the other papers was not untypical. Because all partners needed to be Stock Exchange members and all brokers aspired to be partners, the examination was widely taken so that there was a good seasoning of well-qualified brokers throughout the City. The Stock Exchange examination was replaced by the registered representative qualification, which is a requirement for any broker wishing to speak to clients about investment business. The introduction of a compulsory qualification was a step forward but the lowering of standards to a multiple-choice test further contributed to the lack of rigour that was coming to characterize the City.

There was confusion about the lead regulator. The Bank of England was the lead regulator for banks, including those with broking arms. The Securities and Futures Authority became the lead regulator for their UK-based broking businesses. Overseas broking operations have different lead regulators depending on the country where they operate. To overcome this complexity a well-staffed lead regulator is required, together with a clear definition of who is doing what to whom. Instead, the pressure on resources meant that the regulators have allowed gaps to exist between them leaving dangerous areas to be unsupervised.

THE ALTERNATIVE AMERICAN MODEL

The weaknesses in the British regulatory system contrast with the American regime. The radical changes that were set up in Big Bang required a tough independent regulator on the model of the Securities and Exchange Commission in the United States. There was support for this at the time, usually from those outside the City. For example, Peter Shore, the Shadow Trade and Industry spokesman, called for the US model, demanding 'the establishment of an SEC to regulate the self-regulators'.[9]

The key difference between the two systems is rigour. The SEC is more deeply staffed than its UK equivalents. It sets more stringent operational hurdles for the firms it supervises. It requires more qualifications from practitioners, graded for various levels of seniority and responsibility and there are no exemptions. After a long and distinguished career at the Bank of England and as chairman of the SIB, Sir David Walker joined Morgan Stanley in 1994. He had to study part-time for several months before sitting – and passing – the required professional examinations. The SEC is unambiguous in its reach and there is total clarity as to its responsibilities. Above all, it breeds a culture of control and compliance amongst the firms it watches over.

TOO OPEN, TOO SOON

The City's ways and institutions in 1983 were so different to what was planned that careful preparation by the official agencies – the Stock Exchange, the Bank of England, the Department of Trade and Industry – was required. Their preparations focused on the mechanisms of the new market and not on the ability of the new firms in that market to manage change. By failing to introduce gradual change and by permitting self-regulation, the authorities exposed the City's limited range of managerial experience and limited international experience.

The old City was ordered and hierarchical. Every firm had a clearly defined set of relationships with its clients and with the other firms that provided services and competition. Firms were prevented from breaking out of these boundaries by rules and customs. Suddenly, most of these relationships were thrown up in the air by Big Bang and, when they landed again, were very different. The City's response to this new landscape was hindered by its lack of experience of institutional change. It needed either a period of protection while it adjusted or help in raising its standards.

The regulatory system has been regularly criticized in the press and by politicians for failing to bring successful prosecutions for inside dealing and fraud but this misses the real problem. The failure of supervision in London is not to do with the City being perceived as an unethical place in which to do business, but the failure to set up a tough regulator like the SEC allowed the brokers to persist with the informal controls and seat-of-the-pants management that were to prove inappropriate to the more complex world they were about to enter. The requirement to meet the kind of detailed reporting and control criteria which are compulsory in the United States might have forced the British firms to develop the structured management systems and risk monitoring systems that would have increased their chances of success.

The brokers and jobbers decided that independence was no longer viable well before the City's new structure was finalized. They decided that securities firms, in the words of David Lloyd, the senior partner of the medium-sized broking firm L. Messel, would need 'a big elephant to ride'. A few took a different view but even amongst these the vast majority of partnerships could not resist the chance to cash in. For on the other side of the table were many large financial institutions trying to buy brokers and jobbers as a way into the new world of investment banking.

6

Eager Buyers – European Commercial Banks

With long-term margin pressure on their core lending business, especially in the large corporate sector, the clearing banks had long been interested in merchant banking as a means of diversification. They were looking for ways of moving up the value chain from the tactical provision of credit to advising on corporate strategy. Barclays, Lloyds and NatWest had all started their own merchant banks but, as we have already seen, none of them featured prominently in the top ten rankings in mergers and acquisitions, rights issues or flotations. In 1985, the Royal Bank of Scotland bought Charterhouse Japhet, ranked seventh and ninth in flotations and mergers and acquisitions in 1983, out of Charterhouse J. Rothschild and Midland owned 60 per cent of Samuel Montagu, which was in the top ten in each category. But, as a group, the clearers did not have a strong position in merchant banking in 1983.

The Stock Exchange reforms required them to review their position. Would there be a new model of integrated investment bank, combining merchant bank and broker? If so, was this a chance to close the gap on the established merchant banks by moving quickly? Barclays, Midland, NatWest, HSBC and the Swiss bank UBS came to the conclusion that this was too good a chance to miss; only Lloyds took a different view.[1]

Lord Camoys, chief executive of Barclays Merchant Bank, initiated a strategy paper from his holiday in Ibiza the day he read about the Stock Exchange deal with the Department of Trade and Industry. Barclays had been blocked in the past from finding a way into the Stock Exchange under the old system so for Sir Timothy Bevan, Barclays' chairman, 'Big Bang was a good thing. It just seemed to me that there ought to be some way we could bring a securities operation into the bank.'[2] Camoys wanted Barclays to follow the US model investment bank: 'Now we have the chance to crack right into the middle of the merchant banking business. If we choose, we can actually buy a broker and a jobber and form a real American-style investment bank – not an old style merchant bank.'[3] At Midland, Geoffrey Taylor, the chief executive, spoke of 'implementation of the group strategy for the development of a fully integrated domestic and capital markets capability'.[4]

Lloyds took a different view. It regrouped its merchant banking activities into Lloyds Merchant Bank in 1985. But for reasons explained by Richard Fortin, a director of Lloyds Merchant Bank, it did not follow the rush into broking: 'We're not prepared to pay enormous sums for two-legged goodwill. Probably the best time to get into equity distribution is after Big Bang, when we believe strains will appear in some of the houses.'[5]

THE CLEARERS MOVE IN

Once they had decided on their strategies the clearers sized up their options. At Barclays, Camoys and Andrew Buxton, then managing director of Barclays' UK operations, compiled a scorecard for the various brokers and decided to aim high: 'We decided that we would go for the high ground as quickly as possible because we knew by then that others were coming in. There was Warburg and there were the Americans and the competition was fierce.'[6]

Cazenove emerged as the most desirable broking partner but was determined to remain independent. Rowe & Pitman, another leading corporate broker, was already linked to S. G. Warburg. De Zoete & Bevan had good all-round strengths in equities, fixed income and corporate broking and, although it was not a leader in any of them, it was high enough up every league table to be Barclays' next choice and a price of £50 million was agreed in the winter of 1983–4. Barclays appreciated that top quality jobbing skills would be necessary to supplement the broker. Akroyd had already linked up with Warburg, but Wedd, the other leading jobber, were already close to de Zoete.

Barclays agreed to pay £100 million for Wedd in March 1984, double its opening shot, and announced its acquisitions that month.

In contrast to Barclays' strategy of aiming high, NatWest tried to buy small and build. It was the first of the clearing banks to make a move when, in February 1984, it took a stake in Bisgood Bishop, a medium-sized jobber with particular strengths in the Unlisted Securities Market. For a bank of NatWest's scale, a jobber focused on the smaller end of the corporate sector was not an ideal fit. Five months later NatWest announced that it was to take a 5 per cent stake in Fielding Newson Smith, a medium-sized broking firm which did not appear in the top ten in any of the league tables. The total purchase price of the two companies was about £30 million.

Midland had also decided its investment banking strategy. In February 1985, it was announced that Samuel Montagu was to buy a stake in W. Greenwell, one of the leading gilts brokers but only a medium-sized player in equities. In July, Midland placed its bet on investment banking rather than asset management when it repurchased its stake in Samuel Montagu for £98 million and sold its stake in Montagu Investment Management for £45 million.

HSBC scooped the pool in equity broking through the acquisition of James Capel for £100 million. Capel was the largest (1300 employees by the time of Big Bang) and reputedly the most profitable of the UK broking houses. It had regularly topped the research rankings for some years and had the reputation for being innovative, imaginative, and forward looking. The driving force was the senior partner, Peter Quinnen, and the firm had built up a very powerful position with the institutions. Although substantial sums were reportedly set aside for market making when the deal was first done, it was decided to start out as an agency broker: 'We felt that if we wanted to go into market making, we could grow a team organically. People have been paying too much for jobbers without realizing that the goodwill they are buying arises only from the jobbers' dealings with the counterparties and not with the clients – and all the counterparties will be changing after Big Bang.'[7]

An insider recalls that Union Bank of Switzerland's debate about whether or not to follow the global investment banking strategy as a diversification away from domestic retail and corporate banking was accelerated when Swiss Bank Corporation bought the medium-sized London broker Savory Milln: 'we panicked into a swift response for fear of being left behind'. The first choice, James Capel, was already in talks with HSBC. Phillips & Drew was considered a good second choice with a strong asset management business to back up leading positions in equities, gilts and research. The position in corporate broking was not so strong but was considered to be capable of development and UBS bought Phillips & Drew in 1986.

INCOMPLETE PORTFOLIOS

The portfolios of the broking businesses that were put together by the commercial banks between 1983 and 1986 were incomplete and contained some cracks that were to develop into major faults. None of the banks appear to have been ready for the Parkinson–Goodison agreement, despite the fact that a settlement was rumoured to have been likely for some time. Only when the announcement was made did serious thinking begin and the shortage of available acquisition candidates meant that the banks found themselves being bounced into acquisitions for fear of losing out. Barclays was one of the better prepared banks but, even for them, BZW's sponsored history commented that: 'How much thinking Barclays did beyond the point of deciding which firms they wanted is questionable. For a move which was fundamentally to change the whole company, the double acquisition appears to have been made with relatively little consideration of where it might lead the company.'[8] The same comments applied equally to the other banks.

The failure to think things through to their logical conclusion was to prove one of the events that brought BZW down: 'There was quite a *de haut en bas* attitude from some of the senior Barclays people. The move was seen as being of little significance for the future.'[9] As a result of underestimating the importance of the move into investment banking, neither Barclays nor NatWest spent enough time ensuring that their shareholders or senior managers understood the plan. As the enormity of the challenge emerged, their directors spent a lot of time on the back foot defending a strategy that was going wrong. The pressure would have been much less had it been explained from the start.

Very few of the clearing banks gave sufficient emphasis to the importance of trading. Barclays was fortunate that the partners of de Zoete had already worked out the importance of trading and were in discussions with Wedd by the time Barclays came along:

The abolition of fixed commissions altered the whole fabric of our business because on the new basis, you did not know, even if you put through a mass of business, how much revenue you were going to get. Was the gilt market going to have any commission? We thought, probably not. We didn't know what commission we were going to be able to get out of the institutions. Most importantly, we were very fearful that the institutions would have to come to houses that could execute transactions. Therefore, in both bonds and equities, we needed a trading arm.[10]

UBS also appreciated the importance of trading and gave a senior role in the integration of Phillips & Drew to Rudolf Mueller, the head of securities trading worldwide for UBS. Mueller believed that with UBS's strong trading experience in Europe the firm was unusually well placed to grow trading organically: 'We are not only professional traders we also have a capability of using our distribution to have a wider coverage of the market . . . That makes us different as far as the Americans are concerned in the UK.'[11]

NatWest's failure to appreciate the commitment required to succeed was evident from the first time that its chief executive, Charles Villiers, set out the game plan: 'We are using a building block principle – using constituent parts of the business and building them up.'[12] Fieldings employed about 200 people and with a small jobber, Bisgood, and a mid-range merchant bank, County, it was intended 'to create a Wall Street-style investment bank'. This was a huge underestimation of the size of the task especially since others were there bidding for the same staff and clients with greater parental backing and off a stronger platform.

There was a similar misappreciation of what was required at Midland which bought Greenwell, a top-class gilts broker but a second division equities house. This was an extraordinary choice. Skills in

Government securities were not relevant to the strategy of developing a corporate finance and equities issuing business and, in any case, it was widely expected that profitability in gilts would be squeezed by a commission war. However, this strategic error was a side issue in the mid 1980s compared with Midland's problems at its Californian subsidiary, Crocker National Bank. This was sold in May 1986, two years after it recorded a loss of $324 million, an episode that seriously damaged management's credibility and left it strategically risk averse. The memory of this strategic blunder ensured that Midland was very cautious as the risky nature of investment banking emerged.

By the autumn of 1986 the banks had chosen their strategies and embarked on them. Barclays had bought wisely but had not thought through the implications of what it was doing and had not built sufficient support amongst its senior executives and shareholders. NatWest and Midland had bought the wrong companies to deliver their strategic goals. UBS and HSBC had bought strong brokers, had resolved not to buy jobbers but were hampered by weaknesses in corporate broking. Lloyds had made a controlled low-risk entry and was content to bide its time.

7

Buyers, Builders and Stay-at-Homes: The Merchant Banks

Big Bang prompted the merchant banks to examine their own strategies. They needed to decide whether their existing, primarily domestic, corporate finance business was threatened by the changes at the Stock Exchange and at the same time whether to explore the new opportunities that were being created.

WHY GET INVOLVED?

The fundamental issue for the merchant banks was whether there would still be any independent brokers to distribute new shares issued by corporations and the Government. Under the British system, merchant banks underwrote new share issues and relied on brokers to distribute them. As the shape of the Parkinson–Goodison agreement emerged and outside ownership of brokers became possible, the merchant banks feared that without an in-house broking arm they would be at a competitive disadvantage. They had to form a judgement on whether brokers, once they were owned by banks, would continue to distribute new issues underwritten by other banks that competed with their parents.

A further consideration was the good access to chief executives enjoyed by corporate brokers. By opening up the brokers to outside ownership, Big Bang put into play these prized relationships which could be a back door into a broader investment banking relationship. The merchant banks had to decide whether quoted British companies would prefer to get advice, underwriting and distribution from a single institution or whether they would continue to use a separate merchant bank and corporate broker. If there was any risk of one-stop shopping becoming widespread, the merchant banks would need to safeguard their position by owning their own brokers.

These decisions had to be made against a background where even the traditional British corporate finance market was changing. Contested bids had always been intense and fiercely fought but had been carried out according to a set of rules known as the Takeover Code and administered by the City Takeover Panel. During the surge in bid activity in the mid 1980s, tactics reached new levels of intensity and the rules were pushed to their limit and in a number of cases beyond. The American firms began to appear on the roster of banks advising British companies and Wall Street tactics of market behaviour became prevalent. Some of the UK merchant banks, especially Morgan Grenfell, pushed accepted practices to the limit, further adding to the confusion.

There was much talk of corporates moving from relationship investment banking to transaction banking and the merchant banks had to understand what this meant and how quickly it would happen. In relationship banking corporations appoint advisers and stay loyal to them (except in unusual circumstances, such as a conflict of interest or major changes in personnel at the merchant bank or broker). In transaction banking, corporates are more prepared to give business to whichever investment bank or broker comes up with the idea and are therefore more receptive to cold or warm calls from investment banks. This process was encouraged by the Americans who had experience of it in their home market and who had most to gain from the dismantling of the old relationship system: 'London has leaned heavily on client relationships. Now the market is moving much more to a transactional basis. It is no longer a matter of who you know but what you know and how you do it.'[1]

The American investment banks already owned their own broking firms which gave them superior market intelligence and a deeper research capability and this improved their ability to come up with winning ideas. Major equity issues even for British clients were increasingly involving an international dimension and the lack of a broking arm became a handicap for those British merchant banks competing with the investment banks on big deals. One of the leading corporate financiers of the 1980s recalls: 'All sorts of anomalies were beginning to appear. We could trade and distribute bonds but not equities. The privatisations had international tranches and we were handicapped by not having our own broker. Sure, we could tell the clients that we knew all those nice people over at Cazenove or Rowe & Pitman or Hoare Govett but it didn't have the same ring as saying that we owned one.'[2]

As the merchant banks completed their deliberations, three groups emerged. Warburg, Morgan Grenfell, Kleinwort and Hill Samuel decided to buy brokers or jobbers or both and pursued an integrated investment banking strategy from a strong domestic base. Barings, Flemings and Schroders built from scratch. Rothschilds and Lazards kept their distance from broking, a decision that ensured their survival to the end of the period, but kept them at the periphery of this story.

PITCHING THEMSELVES AT THE CENTRE

The larger merchant banks – Warburg, Morgan Grenfell, Hill Samuel and Kleinwort – believed that they were big enough to add an equity capital raising business to their existing corporate advisory product. This required them to add in-house broking. Although the vision varied from bank to bank, these four firms believed that there was not enough time to build wholly from scratch and that acquisitions of brokers or jobbers or both were required.

Warburg, through Mercury Securities, its parent company, took the lead in building an integrated investment bank and did so wholly by acquisition. The group 'maintained all along that a top merchant bank can succeed in today's huge interconnected financial markets only by pitching itself right at the centre of them'.[3] Capital and global reach were at the heart of it: 'judging by what happened in the US when faced with a similar upheaval in 1975 it is most essential to have a strong capital base and the potential of international coverage'.[4]

Warburg moved early and it went for quality. It already possessed a good position in the Euromarkets and a strong, mainly domestic, corporate finance business. Its acquisition of Akroyd & Smithers, one of the only two jobbers of scale, in November 1984 showed that it was not going to compromise on quality and nor was it going to miss out by being too late. Warburg made its move for Akroyd at a time when many others were still debating whether dual capacity would come or not and when the shape of the new market was unclear. It was a decision that seemed blindingly obvious once it was announced and gave Warburg a clear advantage: 'Very few brokers, for example, already boast any in-house market making capability and many may opt to shun the role of principal or at the most to offer a selective matching service to clients. The firms which have already established links may be in a strong position to take confident decisions on recruitment, market positioning and investment.'[5]

The deal with Akroyd was followed in 1984 with equally decisive moves in gilts and equity broking. The acquisition of Mullens, the Government broker, enhanced Warburg's position in fixed income markets and with the Government. The choice of broker showed that Warburg had identified corporate broking as the most desirable attribute for it chose Rowe & Pitman, which ranked alongside Cazenove and Hoare Govett in the quality of its brokerships but which was just outside the top five in equity market share and outside the top ten in research. Warburg had therefore assembled three strong components for its push into investment banking and had done so at a reasonable cost: £40 million for a stake in Akroyd, £12 million for Mullens and £60 million for Rowe & Pitman. The prices paid compare very favourably with those paid subsequently for lesser firms, and the acquisition of Akroyd for a sum similar to that which Barclays agreed to pay for Wedd was particularly astute.

Under the leadership of Christopher Reeves, Morgan Grenfell had grown from 200 employees and a balance sheet of £160 million in the early 1970s to nearly 2000 employees by the time of Big Bang and a balance sheet of £4 billion. It had a good case to be regarded as the leading merchant bank.

Corporate finance was the powerhouse. Headed by a former Director General of the Takeover Panel, Graham Walsh, the department's reputation was aligned with that of its star player, Roger Seelig: 'Readers of the Sunday colour supplements will be familiar with the flamboyant lifestyle of Seelig, his Palladian house in the Cotswolds, his exclusive circle of friends, his knowledge of fine wines and the radiophone that accompanies him even to the theatre. It goes without saying that he is not universally liked in the City. He is too brash, too buccaneering, too entrepreneurial for the stomach of many a merchant banker.'[6] The firm's tactics were aggressive and there were regular run-ins with authorities such as the Takeover Panel and the Bank of England.

The aggressive development of a securities business by Morgan Grenfell was widely expected. It raised £45 million from shareholders in May 1984 and the *Financial Times* commented then 'Morgan has well-known ambitions to participate in the securities market which will require extra capital and expansion on all these fronts would certainly leave its existing shareholders – particularly Willis Faber – panting to keep up'.[7] In November 1984 it sold a 5 per cent stake to Deutsche Bank for £14 million and came to the market in 1986 'to raise a sizeable sum of money and be able to position ourselves for the Big Bang'.[8]

Its initial analysis was that commissions in equities and gilts would disappear, leaving trading and primary business as the only sources of revenue. It approached Rowe & Pitman and Cazenove to try to secure good corporate broking skills and connections but was politely rebuffed and then turned its attention to its second perceived target, trading. It bought Pember & Boyle, primarily a gilts jobber with a claimed market share of 10 per cent, for £10 million, and Pinchin Denny, an equities jobber in the middle ground between the big two and the rest for £21 million in March 1984.

Morgan Grenfell had no intention of paying goodwill for a broker operating in a business which it believed would rapidly run out of revenue and so it decided to build research and distribution from scratch. Two senior brokers, John Holmes, president of Hoare Govett in New York, and Geoffrey Collier, president of Vickers da Costa in New York, were recruited to develop equities. The vision was aggressive in the true Morgan Grenfell style: 'Morgan Grenfell has a wonderful opportunity to turn itself into an investment bank on a US scale. You can only do that by integrating the operating divisions of the bank. Without the distribution side the corporate finance department cannot survive. And without the corporate finance side you won't make it as a big league player in this market – a broker needs the new issues, the underwriting, the placement.'[9]

Holmes was confident of success: 'New firms capture market share very quickly in a deregulated market place. We hope to get a 5 per cent share in two years' time.'[10] The recruiting programme was equally ambitious, targeting 25 salesmen, 40 research analysts and 50 market makers by September. In sales, this was from a base of just 10 in June and the aim of adding '10 to 15 more seasoned professionals in the 30 to 40 age bracket' at a time when thirty other firms were recruiting was going to be expensive or involve compromise on quality.

Kleinwort entered the Big Bang period on a roll, featuring in the top five for all corporate finance league tables and having secured a reputation as the expert adviser to the British Government after its successful involvement in the British Aerospace, Cable & Wireless and AB Ports privatisations between 1981 and 1983. Its corporate financiers pressed strongly for a move into broking: 'We were already competing with the US investment banks. We were at a great disadvantage not having research and sales when we came up against the Morgan Stanleys and Goldmans. We had won BT and other privatisations so we were heavily involved in equities. In that sense, unlike Lazards, we did not have the option of finding a niche.'[11]

However, Kleinwort's banking and investment management divisions opposed the move, the bank's non-executive directors advised against too large an acquisition, and several opportunities were lost. In November 1983, the board decided to proceed, but with caution.[12]

Kleinwort drew up a list of five potential broking partners, including Grieveson Grant. This firm was already well known to Kleinwort, since Grieveson had asked them for corporate finance advice in helping find a partner. Grieveson ranked towards the bottom of the top ten, with a strong gilts business, a reasonable UK equities position and small international broking operations in Japan and the United States, together with a profitable private client department.

A purchase price of £44 million was agreed which caused Lex to 'increase the wonderment at the prices being paid for City brokers',[13] given that commissions were under threat and that markets were close to the top of the cycle: 'But this is a seller's market and Kleinwort presumably felt that to stay out of the game might seriously weaken the prospects of its own corporate finance and fund management operation.'

The board discussion of 15 November 1983 had ruled out the purchase of Wedd on grounds of size, but the development of trading was known to be essential. The acquisition of a small gilts jobber, Charlesworth & Co., was accompanied by significant recruitment in equities. The Wedd partnership had been divided about the sale to Barclays, some partners fearing the bureaucratic reputation of a clearing bank. Two of the dissidents, Charles Hue Williams and Willie Mellen, both members of the Wedd management committee, joined Kleinwort with two senior traders and four assistants to set up market making. By the time of Big Bang in October 1986, a market making team of around fifty had been built up.

Hill Samuel had decided that: 'Securities markets are becoming increasingly international. Portfolio investors are diversifying outside their borders. Corporations and governments are adopting a more global view when assessing their financing requirements ... these changes would lead to a rapid fusion of the roles of merchant bankers, stockbrokers and jobbers.'[14]

After meetings with the senior partners of Wood Mackenzie a deal agreeing philosophy and the eventual terms and conditions was signed on 4 June 1984. Hill Samuel's chief executive, Christopher Castleman, displayed a realistic analysis of what was achievable: 'It would be lunacy to compete head on in the US market.'[15] Castleman felt that the goodwill being paid for jobbers was too high and Wood Mackenzie had already formed the same conclusion, having hired Colin Mills from Pinchin Denny even before the Hill Samuel deal. Mills built up a small market making team trading as Wood Street Securities until Big Bang.

ALTERNATIVE STRATEGIES

For reasons of scale, expediency or common sense, the remaining merchant banks were wary of broking. Schroders and Flemings decided to build, Lazards and Rothschilds kept their distance and Barings followed a hybrid strategy. None of them believed that there was any need to rush into the acquisition of a domestic broker. Their UK corporate clients told them that ownership of domestic research and distribution skills would not materially affect the banking relationship. The determination of Cazenove to remain independent convinced these merchant banks that third-party distribution of new issues would continue to be available in the unlikely event of 'tied' brokers refusing to handle issues underwritten by other firms.

Barings went so far as to initiate discussions with Cazenove but, when Cazenove gave its customary response, Barings saw no need to be bounced into a defensive acquisition in respect of UK equities. However, it had developed a business in the 1980s advising and helping to arrange Eurobond issues in London for Japanese corporates. It did not have its own distribution team and worked instead with a number of brokers, especially Vickers da Costa.

Citibank's purchase of Vickers left Barings without independent distribution for its Japanese Eurobonds. Barings was not confident in the willingness of Asian corporates to use separate bankers and brokers for these issues and decided that it needed its own trading and distribution team. It began negotiations with the twenty-strong Japanese team at Henderson Crosthwaite run by Christopher Heath and, in May 1984, Barings agreed to pay £5.8 million to Henderson Crosthwaite to buy Heath's business. This was set up as Barings Far East Securities with 75 per cent of the shares held by Barings and 25 per cent by the former partners of Henderson Crosthwaite (Far East).

Robert Fleming was selective in its involvement in broking. Flemings saw no reason to be everywhere and was prepared to be highly specialized in pursuit of profitable opportunities.[16] It displayed an innovative approach to its investment banking operations, combining the approaches of joint venture (with Jardine Fleming in the Far East); acquisition (in August 1985 it announced the acquisition of Eberstadt & Co., a small 170-person strong US investment bank); and organic growth (UK and Europe). Within the UK Flemings wished to be involved in equity broking but had no intention of making an expensive acquisition. Its willingness to break the mould was seen in the autumn of 1984 when it began making markets in leading electrical shares outside the central market, claiming a 9–10 per cent market share in the stocks it covered by summer 1985.[17] Its research was highly imaginative in design and approach and very focused on a few sectors. This was a sensible approach for a medium-sized merchant bank, keeping all options open in case the corporate issuing market went wholly integrated without committing much money to the business.

Schroders followed some of the same strategies, growing from a greenfield site its coverage of UK, European and Asian equities. Schroders' then vice chairman, Win Bischoff, described the advantages of this approach as being 'less capital intensive and you can plan it as you go along'.[18] A total staff of 46 in mid 1984 had grown, by the middle of 1985, to 80 employees with plans to rise to 140 by Big Bang and to gain a securities licence in Tokyo.[19] Having sold its US commercial bank to IBJ in June 1985, it was free of the constraints imposed by the Glass–Steagall Act on US banks owning brokers and paid $100 million for 50 per cent of the US investment bank, Wertheim, in the middle of 1986.[20] This had a sizeable securities component and was, according to the bank's chairman, G. W. Mallinckrodt, 'consistent with the worldwide strategy set for the group two years ago when Schroders decided to develop its securities business'.[21]

Lazards pursued a very distinct, minimalist strategy. In 1993 David Verey, by then chairman, explained the strategy followed by Lazards but equally applicable to Schroders, Flemings and N. M. Rothschild which confined itself to taking a stake in Smith New Court but kept out of operational matters:

Lazard's decision not to buy a broker and a jobber at the time of Big Bang was the right one. As with Warburgs and Kleinworts, once you get into businesses that demand capital usage, there is no amount of money that you can't use. Once you have a great demand for money, it means you have to find people to provide that money for you, which usually leads to a loss of independence of one form or another. The Lazard philosophy is to say that capital is 'bad' and therefore we should have as little of it as we possibly can get away with and concentrate on remaining small but having clout at the same time; that means powerful people.[22]

WHERE DID IT LEAVE THEM?

The four merchant banks pursuing totally integrated investment banking strategies fell into two sub-groups: Warburg and Morgan Grenfell were going full tilt at the global investment banks whilst Kleinwort and Hill Samuel were more focused. The strategy of pitching right at the centre of the bulge bracket was ambitious and in Warburg's case broadcast so widely to staff and clients that a lesser strategy, when the time came to retrench, was not credible. In 1983, when the strategy was first set, the UK merchant banks were much smaller than the broad-scale American and Japanese financial services firms but within reach of the pure US investment banks.

Warburg's equity capital exceeded that of Morgan Stanley and Donaldson Lufkin & Jenrette (DLJ) in 1984 and was only somewhat less than Goldman Sachs. By the time of Big Bang, Warburg's shareholders funds had reached £382 million and pre-tax profits were £98 million. Morgan Grenfell was not much smaller with shareholders' funds of £371 million and pre-tax profits of £82 million.

Unfortunately for Warburg and Morgan Grenfell, the benchmark for the required scale changed while they were building their businesses. Between the time Warburg and Morgan Grenfell laid their plans in 1984 and Big Bang in 1986, the number of staff employed in

Table 4. Market Capitalizations, Leading Investment Banks, 1983, £ million[23]

UK Merchant banks		USA Brokers and financial services companies		Japan Securities firms	
Kleinwort Benson	235	AmEx	4800	Nomura	3278
Hill Samuel	184	Merrill Lynch	2648	Nikko	1356
Charterhouse	171	Phibro Salomon	1392	Daiwa	1219
Mercury Securities	122	E. F. Hutton	779	Yamaichi	1046
Schroders	95	Paine Webber	430		
Total	972	Total	10,049	Total	6899

Table 5. Staffing Analysis of Large US Investment Banks, 1980–88[24]

	1980	1982	1984	1986	1987	1988
Total compensation, $ million	920	1592	2228	3975	4209	4105
Pre-tax profits, $ million	649	1205	1155	2067	693	1433
Employees	15,773	19,922	25,124	38,223	36,201	34,729
Compensation/employee '000	$58	$80	$89	$104	$116	$118
Pre-tax profits/employee '000	$41	$60	$46	$54	$19	$41
Pre-tax profits: compensation	0.71	0.75	0.52	0.52	0.16	0.35

Wall Street's large investment banks rose by 50 per cent and pre-tax profits nearly doubled. This meant that plans that were credible when they were made looked very demanding by the time they came to be implemented.

Of the two leading British contenders, Warburg had moved clearly ahead of Morgan Grenfell. Sales and trading were top quality, corporate connections were good, research had been identified as needing development and the new acquisitions were robustly profitable.[25]

Morgan Grenfell's strategy of building a substantial broker by organic growth required recruitment on a Herculean scale with consequent cost and cultural issues and the absence of a top-quality market making business was a weakness. The head of equities was right to claim 'that as a new player everyone will give us a chance. The name means a lot ... many people perceive us as potential winners', but other commentators had their doubts: 'Investors in Morgan's shares must be aware that to a large extent they are betting blind on an ace that may not come up. The bank is moving into two areas – market making and distribution – of which it has practically no experience. Nobody, not even Morgans, would claim to know what will happen after the Big Bang on October 27.'[26]

Kleinwort pursued a wide-reaching integrated investment banking strategy that stopped just short of the ambitions of Warburg and Morgan Grenfell.

Although it was of comparable scale to Morgan Grenfell (pre-tax profits were £78 million and shareholders' funds £365 million at Big Bang) it was hindered by the absence of top-flight risk management skills and by the debate about the integrated investment banking strategy. The former Wedd partners, Hue Williams and Mellen, were excellent jobbers but there was more to the old jobbing firms than the sum of the parts and a control culture and risk management infrastructure were also necessary. It would take Kleinwort time to develop these, a process that was not helped when Michael Hawkes announced, 'We would love to have had Capels but are content with Grievesons'.[27]

Hill Samuel was realistic in its ambitions and to begin with was generally reckoned to be a promising contender. For about twelve months after the acquisition of Wood Mackenzie, Hill Samuel's integrated investment bank enjoyed an excellent press: 'With Wood Mackenzie on board and market making plans progressing steadily, Hill Samuel belongs to that new category of fashionable bid target, the ready assembled financial supermarket.'[28] Six months later, following a set of good results, it was seen as 'looking a bit of a mouthful' for a predator[29] with £40 million available to invest in gilt and equity market making even after providing for the acquisition of Wood Mackenzie.

Amongst the smaller merchant banks, Lazards and Rothschilds were confident in their 'avoid' strategies and Flemings was embarking on organic growth plans that were unlikely to cause serious damage or to be of strategic benefit. Schroders had similar plans in respect of European equities but the acquisition of Wertheim gave it a mid-range position in US equities with some interesting longer term potential. Barings' entry into Asian broking stood out even at this stage as being opportunistic and tangential to its mainstream business.

By 1986, in committing to follow an integrated broking strategy, all bar Lazards and Rothschilds, had embarked on a path that would cost them their independence. They had different ambitions and different building blocks, but they shared a common vision: the American investment banking model embracing securities distribution and corporate advisory work. This goal would stretch their financial and managerial resources to breaking point.

8

The Americans

Prior to 1983 the American commercial and investment banks had paid little attention to London, regarding it as the 'Siberia of investment banking, a place to banish those the firm wished to forget'.[1] There was hardly any need to be in London. Cross-border business in equities and corporate finance was limited and entry to the Stock Exchange was barred. The Eurobond market had moved from New York to London in the 1960s but the participants formed their own tight community and for many years the investment banks did not seek to build more rounded businesses on top of them.[2]

SIBERIA REVISITED

This changed with the opening of Stock Exchange firms to outside membership and an increase in cross-border investing by American institutions and companies. The second Reagan administration brought a strong dollar, less Government interference in business, and anti-inflationary policies, which created a bull market. US investors found similar economic conditions in the UK under Mrs Thatcher, together with a well-developed equities culture, and when the deregulation of markets was announced in 1983 a number of American banks looked more closely at London.

SEGREGATION ON WALL STREET: GLASS–STEAGALL

America's sell side institutions were permitted to be either investment banks or commercial banks but not both. Following the Crash of 1929, Congress had passed a series of measures to protect bank depositors from the volatility of securities markets. The Glass–Steagall Act and the Securities Act of 1933 and the Securities Exchange Act of 1934 which created the Securities and Exchange Commission were the main pieces of legislation.

Glass–Steagall required that deposit taking and lending had to be separate from underwriting securities or dealing in them. Most commercial banks focused on lending and exited from underwriting but splinter groups left to form new investment banks such as Morgan Stanley and First Boston. A few of the deposit taking banks, such as Lehman Brothers and Dillon Read, went the other way and focused on investment banking. Over the next fifty years the commercial and investment banks developed as separate institutions serving the same customer base but each group with different products.

Like their European counterparts, the US commercial banks eventually faced pressure on margins in their core activities, causing them to search for diversification opportunities. Investment banking was the obvious candidate. The commercial banks were so far behind the US investment banks that even though the most stringent provisions of Glass–Steagall had been gradually eroded their home market seemed daunting. When London deregulated, some of the American commercial banks saw this as an opportunity to create a position in investment banking. The acquisition of broking firms was an obvious first step.

The US investment banks were also interested in London's deregulation. They had benefited from Glass–Steagall in a number of respects. The fact that they were barred from many sectors of the financial services industry forced them to focus on their core business with the consequence that they generally ran it well. The commercial banks, which could have presented well capitalized competition, were kept out, giving them a long period of protection. The regulatory regime was tough, requiring high managerial standards.

This situation had prevailed for a long time, fifty years since Glass–Steagall, and by the time deregulation occurred in London they had developed very deep roots. James Hanbury, who has been analysing the investment banking sector on Wall Street for many years, explains the advantages this gave:

Glass–Steagall gave us a critical incubation period. Prior to the 1960s we learned the hard way and firms regularly went bust. Then we started to manage and plan the business and it got better. There is a self-selection and a management process that is unique to the American firms. The top American firms have been hiring loads of the best and brightest from business school for a long time. They have pulled in an extraordinary amount of talent over twenty-five years and kept and nurtured and trained them until they have taken over the firms. That gave the investment banks great management in depth.[3]

With these well-established structures and a deep-rooted culture, the American investment banks were well-equipped to expand overseas and to take advantage of deregulation. The boom on Wall Street gave them the confidence and financial resources to attack London.

Therefore, in 1983 there were two groups of American institutions casting eyes over the City: the commercial banks and the investment banks. The commercial banks believed they had to diversify out of banking. They had the financial but not the managerial resources necessary to succeed in investment banking so they decided to buy. The investment banks saw globalization coming and regarded London as the building block for Europe. They had the financial resources to buy but preferred to use their experience and managerial talent in organic growth strategies.

COMMERCIAL BANKS

With the need but not the knowledge to enter securities, the American commercial banks were amongst the earliest and most determined of the London brokers' suitors. Security Pacific, the ninth ranked US bank, was the first outside firm to move into broking, paying £8.1

million for a 29.9 per cent stake in Hoare Govett in September 1983, as soon as the rules allowed. This was followed in April 1984 by a 5 per cent stake in Charles Pulley & Co., the sixth ranked jobbing firm, and by the acquisition of further shares in Hoare Govett in July 1984 taking its holding up to 90 per cent. By moving first, Security Pacific avoided paying top prices. The first 29.9 per cent implied a value of £27 million for the whole firm. By the time of the July purchase, competition to buy the leading brokers had increased and the implied price for the whole of Hoare Govett had risen to £78 million.[4]

Security Pacific were followed into London by Chase Manhattan, who acquired Simon & Coates and Laurie Milbank, two medium- to large-sized brokers. Of the American banks, Citicorp made the most aggressive entry into London. Its first move was to buy 29.9 per cent of the London business of Vickers da Costa in November 1983 and a controlling interest in Vickers' overseas operations where there were no restrictions on ownership. The price implied a value of £22 million for the whole of Vickers, a post-tax multiple of nine times earnings 'for the year to end August 1983 but fifteen and a half times average post-tax earnings over the past three years'.[5]

The purchase gave Citicorp control of Vickers' well-established Far East operations but a gap in UK equities where Vickers was weak. This was filled in September 1984 when Citicorp announced that it was to buy Scrimgeour Kemp Gee for £50 million and merge it with Vickers da Costa, forming a unit of 500 staff. Scrimgeour was a powerful UK firm, viewed by some as being the market leader. It ranked second in research, behind only James Capel, second in market share behind only Hoare Govett and had considerable momentum. As a statement of intent, Citicorp could not have been much clearer and it proceeded to round out the investment in broking with organic growth in other activities.[6]

THE INVESTMENT BANKS AND BROKERS

Because of their knowledge and experience of the industry, the US investment banks had the option of moving into London by building rather than buying. Some of the US investment banks held preliminary discussions with the brokers and jobbers, but they all elected to build not buy. They understood better than the commercial banks that the skills and experience of London's brokers would not necessarily be relevant to the new world and were reluctant to pay goodwill for assets that might or might not turn out to be useful. They also had confidence in their own abilities to export talent and to recruit and train local staff.

As builders rather than buyers, the Americans were a major disrupting feature in the labour market in these years. The standard approach was to employ head-hunters and to plunder the 'marzipan layer' of the broking firms. The marzipan layer – below the icing but above the cake – was the senior executives of the broking and jobbing firms, just below partnership level. They were the group with the key client relationships of the future and were rarely looked after financially by the partners of their firms. With London salaries well below those on Wall Street, no cultural hang-ups about paying well and money in the pocket from not having splashed out on a whole firm, the American investment banks were in a powerful position to recruit.

The activities of the Americans and their head-hunters caused a ferment of excitement in the marzipan layer. Calls beginning, 'You won't know me but . . .' were eagerly awaited, discussed and imagined and became an important bargaining chip in salary and bonus negotiations. This was an exciting and glamorous period for the marzipan layer, of which I was a part: we were wanted, we were courted, enormous amounts of money were thrown our way. I was flown to New York by a bulge bracket firm, shown a trading room the size of the whole Stock Exchange floor in London and offered a house in Hampstead as a signing on fee. Only their reputation for hiring and firing at will caused me to turn them down.

Merrill Lynch had been in London since the early 1960s, initially distributing US equities but gradually adding a bond business and winning a substantial share in gilts. It set up trading in 100 global equities in London to form the third leg of the stool with New York and Tokyo. When it decided to add research, Merrill Lynch adopted the highest profile of the US firms: 'Meanwhile in London, Merrill Lynch, the US securities group, is seeking research analysts to join its organization. So far thirty-nine analysts out of forty interviewed at London's Churchill Hotel last week have said that they are willing to attend further interviews.'[7] Alan Lechner, a cultured college professor on Merrill's payroll, was sent over to lead the process. He explained the American way to London's analysts and salesmen. It was different, more glamorous, more corporate finance oriented and more international than the traditional London offering. A few high-profile analysts and salesmen joined Merrill – for example, Tony Church in Chemicals and Bryan Crossley in Banks – but usually the interviews resulted only in the compensation package of the interviewee being raised by his or her existing employer. This is illustrated by the 1984 Extel survey which showed a record number of moves by analysts. But of the eight ranked analysts to have moved, none went to an American firm.[8]

In 1983, Goldman's total London staff numbered around 300. Expansion from this number was led by corporate finance. Goldman Sachs was quick to realize that there was a big opportunity to break into London through the unprecedented wave of corporate finance activity in the mid 1980s. Corporations like Hanson and BTR recognized that stock prices were at a big discount to asset prices and began a wave of hostile takeovers. This gave the American firms an opportunity to break the entrenched positions of the UK merchant banks, initially holding a junior position. As the corporate finance platform was built, a secondary broking capability was put alongside it and, from 1986, Goldman and Morgan Stanley began to attract some good analysts and sales people. Salomon Brothers also began a recruiting effort in London just before Big Bang as it sought to develop an equities business alongside its existing strengths in bonds.

WHERE IT LEFT THEM IN 1986

As a result of the purchases and recruitment between 1983 and 1986, the Americans had made some mark on the London broking community by the time of Big Bang, with the buyers initially making a bigger impact than the builders. Security Pacific and Chase Manhattan had done not much more than to buy agency brokers, add capital resources and recruit market makers but they had a market position and were on level terms with the British commercial and merchant banks that had made acquisitions. Citicorp had complicated its task by buying two brokers. In theory, the fit of Scrimgeour's domestic presence with Vickers' overseas strengths could have created a formidable firm. However, in buying two separate firms, a management which was already very stretched preparing for Big Bang now faced the added complication of integration, especially in London where the two firms overlapped in both the front and the back office. It faced the further problems of trying to build a business to which it was new in a foreign country.

The start-ups were reckoned to face a big challenge 'selling ICI equities to British insurance companies and distributing domestic issues by British blue chips'.[9] Prudential Bache took the lead in recruitment and by the time of Big Bang it had reasonable research and sales depth. Merrill Lynch was next in terms of the number of staff recruited, with about 10 per cent of its total London staff of 1000 being in broking and, in September 1986, Merrill held its first ever full board meeting in London, symbolizing its intention to grow there.[10] Morgan Stanley, Goldman Sachs and Salomon Brothers had begun hiring in the year before Big Bang but their main thrust was still to come.

The American investment banks all articulated a global vision. They were able to bring new tactics and a more intensive work ethic learned in the US during the upsurge of mergers on Wall Street after 1983. They did not meet much competition: 'The British brokers were capital constrained and their industry was suffering a major consolidation. It was a wonderful time to attack, knowing the opponent could not retaliate on your home base.' John Thornton, the Goldman corporate financier credited with building the business in London, was quoted as stating: 'The British disease is that there's always an excuse not to do something.' The British merchant bankers missed the point: 'We fail to see what the American firms add in UK situations but we're not complacent.' Goldman Sachs was described as 'nothing more than high-priced interlopers who produce a massive stream of impractical ideas that have no relevance to the UK market. I give them credit for making a lot of noise.'[11]

The point the City missed was that the Americans were not showing their full hand. The best of them timed their run into London carefully, not making a major effort until corporate finance relationships had begun to be built and then gradually adding research, sales and trading. By 1986 they had made a start but no more than that.

9

The Brokers and Jobbers

Brokers live by arbitraging fear and greed. The seller's fear causes him to sell, creating stock to satisfy the buyer's greed and a deal is done. In the years either side of the agreement of 1983, the broking industry itself experienced the emotions of greed and fear that it normally exploited in its customers. Fear of the damage that might come from lost revenues when fixed commissions were abolished gave way to greed once buyers for the broking firms started to queue up.

FEAR AND GREED

The competition to buy brokers and jobbers was hot. Even the medium-sized firms such as Fielding Newson Smith found themselves in great demand: 'At one time we had six different suitors, all of whom wanted to take us over – they were American firms, a European bank and a London clearing bank.'[1] The large majority decided to sell out, believing that capital and limited liability would be necessary to survive in the new world but amongst the leading brokers and jobbers Cazenove and Smith Brothers decided to remain independent.

During the winter of 1982–3 word began to spread amongst the senior partners of the brokers and jobbers of a deal struck with the Government. The inner ring of senior partners and directors that existed at every firm began to discuss the implications for their business, working parties were established and sometimes consultants were appointed to help with the process. These were important deliberations. Firms had to consider the future welfare of the business and to choose a partner likely to be able to deliver an attractive culture and strategy. These longer term issues were clouded by the prospect of immediate wealth. Many of the partners were at a time of life when short-term gain was more interesting than new challenges and the amount and form of the payout was very important.

The years 1983–4, but particularly the summer and autumn of 1983, were times of ceaseless negotiations. This was an intricate debate, looking into an unknown world where not all the rules had yet been established: 'If you did have a relationship between a broker and a jobber, which would be the dominant part? Was it critical to have the market making and the ability to provide the stock or was it critical to have the client relationships of which we knew very little?'[2] The answers seem more obvious with hindsight than they did at the time. For a generation brought up in a static, domestic environment, it was not easy to make the conceptual leaps necessary to foresee the future accurately.

A few firms sought the help of management consultants or merchant banks to advise them in the process but the culture of broking was averse to 'having loads of consultants marching all over the business which they don't understand anyway'. The one firm that was welcome was staffed by insiders and had good rapport with the brokers and jobbers. Phoenix Securities, a small, independent corporate finance boutique, built a powerful position after it put together the constituents of the new BZW:

The word got round and after that we were inundated with firms saying, 'If you've done that for them, can you do something for us?' We spent two happy years doing nothing but that. Maybe out of thirty significant Stock Exchange marriages that were done at the time of Big Bang, we handled over twenty. There wasn't anyone else who was completely independent who could do it. It got to the point that people didn't want to be seen coming into Phoenix Securities because they were seen as advertising themselves as being for sale.[3]

Once the working parties had heard the advisers, reached their conclusions and discussed them with the rest of the partnership, there began the serious business of looking for a buyer. A mixture of finan-cial, cultural and strategic considerations came into play. The kind of thing they looked for was explained by a de Zoete partner after the deal with Barclays:

They were British, and we felt that if the going got choppy, particularly on the political front, if we had a foreign partner they wouldn't have any need to stay here. Barclays had a very good balance sheet; they were prepared to give the people a lot of autonomy; they were people we felt we could work with; and because they had more than 2500 branches, we felt there was a natural flow of orders coming through – although this proved to be a wrong assessment.[4]

For many thinking brokers the new owner's ability to deliver a long-term strategy were as important as the purchase price. Bryce Cottrell, a senior Phillips & Drew partner, described the broker's reasons for striking a deal with UBS: 'It provided international synergy, the resources from which to take investment decisions from a position of strength in the changing financial climate and the working environment best suited to encourage the best investment work.'[5]

Cultural aspects were considered important, specifically whether the brokers and jobbers would be given their independence and whether the personal chemistry was right. Unlike their future colleagues at de Zoete, the Wedd partners were divided over the merits of Barclays' offer. There was a concern that the clearing bank culture would be bureaucratic and risk averse and some of the partners preferred an alternative from Kleinwort Benson which they considered to be less stifling and more entrepreneurial.

Sometimes people just did not get on. Wood Mackenzie was approached by Exco, a fast-growing financial services conglomerate. There was sufficient interest for Wood Mackenzie's partners and the senior people from Exco to meet at Gleneagles Hotel at a planning weekend in November 1983. John Chiene, the senior partner of Wood Mackenzie, recalls: 'They gave a presentation on the Saturday at our partners' weekend. We met them over dinner that evening and there was no rapport. By the early hours of the morning the partners agreed in the bar that it would never work. I called them to say no on the Monday morning.'[6]

Financial considerations were the most important. The partners debated the amount, the form and the timing of the payments and were surprised at the high value put on their business. A partner of Hoare Govett says: 'We were amazed at what SecPac thought we were worth. Their first offer valued us at £30 million for something we thought was worth nothing. We were not interested in who SecPac were, we just wanted the money. We said thank you very much and put half a million pounds into our trouser pockets. What was £30 million to them? It got lost in their daily sweepings.'[7] A partner of Pember & Boyle, after the purchase by Morgan Grenfell, believed: 'We've been kissed by the Holy Ghost.'[8]

It was estimated that Big Bang created 750 millionaires, most of whom had paid very little to buy a partnership. A partnership at James Capel in the early 1980s cost £25,000 per quarter per cent of the equity, valuing the whole firm at £10 million. HSBC bought it for £100 million. Half a dozen James Capel partners owned 40 per cent of the equity, giving them over £6 million each for something they paid half a million pounds for. BZW had just over twenty general partners; the firm was sold for £50 million, leaving them with over £2 million each after paying something to the senior staff. At that stage the senior partners of de Zoete had each been drawing about £250,000 per year from the firm so the sale represented an enormous multiple of annual earnings. Not all of the money was paid out at once and not all was paid in cash.

Most of the partners were so keen to get their money that they distributed very little to senior employees. They argued that, having carried all of the risk for many years, they deserved nearly all of the rewards. The new owners were naïve to allow this to happen. They did not appreciate that the next generation were as important to revenue earning as the old, especially as millionaires were not going to be as motivated as hungry brokers and jobbers. By failing to distribute the wealth more evenly the brokers and banks played into the hands of the American builders and guaranteed an era of instability after Big Bang. The marzipan layer felt that they had been poorly treated, loyalty to the firm was gone and they had no conscience about listening to the inducements of the head-hunters.

Only a few firms tried to tie in the next generation. Wedd and de Zoete deepened their respective partnerships to over 100 each from sixty-five in Wedd's case and twenty in de Zoete's with the intention of binding in more of the senior executives to the future. James Capel spread 15 per cent of the money received from HSBC amongst the most senior of the non-partners. Other firms made only token gestures. The partners had taken their money and run, looking to their personal future, not the firm's. The new owners overvalued the contribution of the partners, missed the point that the marzipan layer contained the drive and ability to learn new skills, and left themselves vulnerable to subsequent staff defections. There was a great opportunity to create new and binding structures which was missed by the buyers and ignored by the sellers who earned themselves the nickname 'the Generation of Greed'.

It proved difficult to reconcile the conflicting interests of the partners at many of the brokers. The small firm of Scott Goff illustrates this:

It was a very peculiar animal, more a cooperative than a partnership. All the partners, around twenty-five of us, shared everything equally, the senior partner getting half a per cent extra. From 1983, we were aware of what was coming and two of us went to the US to discuss what the Americans had learned from May Day. Partners' meetings got very fraught because the institutional bit was the only part of the firm for which there was any demand. The private client partners were very worried. The business logic of the deal with Smith was very powerful but it was obvious that they were not going to pay a king's ransom . . . The private client partners were very unhappy; they knew they wouldn't last at Smith's . . . Morgan Grenfell approached the institutional side of the firm and would probably have paid us more but it would have been unethical to desert the rest of the partnership. In the end, Smith practically stole the business.[9]

GOING IT ALONE

One major broker, Cazenove, and one jobber, Smith Brothers, chose to remain independent. They were at the extremes of the cultural spectrum, Smith being gritty and streetwise, the epitome of London's jobbing fraternity. Cazenove was well-connected, powerful, discreet bordering on the secretive, and with an effortless style. It was gentlemanly capitalism in corporate form. Outward appearances notwithstanding, both firms had a lot in common. They shared high standards of professionalism, were focused on running and building clearly defined businesses and all members of the firms were strongly bonded together.

Smith ranked third behind Wedd and Akroyd in the jobbing league. Its market capitalization (under £5 million in 1983) was usually less than the value of its net assets. With quality jobbers in short supply, Smith was an attractive target for those firms assembling integrated broking houses.

However, Smith preferred driving to being driven, the chairman, Tony Lewis, believing that 'we have the necessary depth of management and expertise to anticipate and react to future trends'. In December 1983 the merchant bank N. M. Rothschild paid £6.5 million for a 29.9 per cent stake and put in a further £5 million of capital. Rothschilds had decided to stay independent and not to buy a broker and was an ideal partner for Smith to work with as it set about creating an integrated broker around the jobbing skills.

When it bought Scott Goff for £3.3 million, Tony Lewis explained that Smith 'could not stand on its own as a market maker in the new financial markets which are emerging. It is much more logical for us to link with a broker so that we can have an outlet to the agency areas.'[10] Smith's strategic and tactical thinking was excellent. It recognized that jobbing skills were to be at the centre of success in the new market and that it had no need to sell itself. It had existed for years off a tiny capital base making pretty consistent profits and providing liquidity in all market conditions and it was not going to be scared off by loose talk of the scale needed to compete after Big Bang. It also recognized that the prices being paid for brokers were excessive and that, for a firm such as Smith with an existing relationship with institutional clients, it could buy small and then build. The price paid for Scott Goff was far below that paid for other medium-sized brokers and represented excellent value. It is hard to disagree with Ken Taylor's comment that 'Smith practically stole the business', when firms only slightly larger than Scott Goff were being sold for five times as much. Scott Goff were just too small to have attracted widespread interest and Smith correctly assessed not only their vulnerable position but also their potential.

In November 1985 Smith raised £13.5 million in a one-for-three rights issue. The *Financial Times*' comment that this 'scarcely puts Smith on an equal footing with competitors at a time when, like everybody else, the company is expanding its international network and trading aggressively at home'[11] missed the point that Smith's focus and risk management skills offered a viable alternative to the overblown strategies of its competitors.

Cazenove held a unique place in the City. The source of its power was a strong network of corporate broking relationships which it had used to cultivate the ear of the institutions. Cazenove was trusted for its advice and placing power by a large number of chief executives. One of the services corporate brokers like Cazenove performed in 1983 was to educate the market about current trading so that when companies reported results there were no undue surprises. Cazenove's long-established practice of basing its recommendations on verbal advice not written research, together with its excellent corporate list, meant that it was well placed to perform this task. Cazenove's unique role also extended to the Stock Exchange floor where it was used as the arbiter of market disputes between brokers and jobbers. No other broker could have commanded the respect to perform such duties.

Its relationships with institutions were also unique. As the leading corporate broker it distributed sub-underwriting on behalf of merchant banks to institutions. In return for sub-underwriting new issues, the institutions earned useful income and needed to keep in with Cazenove to get their share. According to City folklore, Cazenove were summoned to one London insurance company at the time of Big Bang to be told of reduced commission rates on equity business. The Cazenove partner thanked the firm, pulled out a schedule of that year's business, studied it for a few seconds and said: 'On that basis we will be paying you more for underwriting than you will be giving us in commission. I don't think so.' The rate was not reduced.

Big Bang posed two questions for Cazenove: would there be a continuing role for agency brokers, and how would its relations with the merchant banks be affected by their development of in-house brokers? The answers to these questions would determine whether the partnership structure and independence would remain viable.

The firm was guided through its preparations for Big Bang by joint senior partners, John Kemp-Welch and Anthony Forbes, with backgrounds in institutional broking and corporate finance respectively. Both were in their late forties and had taken over as senior partners in 1980: 'They looked at the structure of the partnership and at how we came to decisions about the business. They brought in a management structure with committees and a proper separation of the business functions. Not all the partners were involved in day-to-day decisions any more.'[12]

As a result of the structure introduced by Kemp-Welch and Forbes 'we didn't have to take a partnership line on Big Bang because the partners weren't invited to give a view. We ran the business through the two senior partners and a few people around them and they determined the future.'[13] The deliberations were helped by the firm's strong financial performance during these years. Nineteen seventy-nine had been a reasonably profitable year, but by the early 1980s 'annual gross profits were running at about twice the 1979 level, by 1984 over four times it and by 1986 almost seven times it'.[14] The corporate finance and institutional side was supplemented by a stock borrowing/lending business and fund management so that less than a third of Cazenove's income was directly exposed to the new dealing system for UK equities.

It is doubtful whether serious consideration was ever given to selling the firm. Although informal conversations were had with most of the merchant and clearing banks in these years, this was always at the request of the banks and was responded to by Cazenove as a matter of courtesy and as a means of gathering information about the banks' attitude to independent brokers. A Cazenove partner recalls 'there were no formal discussions although a whole host of flies were cast over us'.

The senior partnership recognized that the firm 'would have to take a diminished role in the new world unless we were prepared to sacrifice control over our lives. We had no appetite to give up but we equally had no hang up about accepting a lesser role in the world. We did not see London as being the same force in future as it had in the past.

We went to New York and realized that certain activities would be closed to us as a result of our lack of capital. But we were sure we had a future.'[15]

The firm's resolve was hardened by support from the clients:

We were getting significant levels of support from the clients especially in 1985–6. At around this time we decided that we should no longer think of the merchant banks as being our clients but that the institutions and the corporates were our clients. Most of our competitors thought that the role of the corporate broker would disappear. We took a different view although we had no choice. We felt that the role of the broker, the importance of being close to the market, would increase.[16]

That was the key judgement. Traditionally the corporate broker provided pricing, distribution and technical services relating to a Stock Exchange listing. The merchant bank prepared a company for listing, organized the writing of a prospectus and advised on bids and deals. Would the ownership of brokers by the merchant banks jeopardize the viability of independent corporate broking? Cazenove believed so but kept its options open: 'the system seems to us to have served the client well. But that may, to an extent, change over the next period.'[17]

The firm's position was made clear to all staff by Kemp-Welch in a speech at the office party in March 1985:

All of our major competitors – indeed all of the other major Stock Exchange firms – have decided to become part of large financial groups dominated by a clearing, an overseas or merchant bank. We do not believe it right for us to do so. We do not believe it right to sell the goodwill of the firm to a big brother. I can assure you that there has been no lack of opportunity and that opportunity still remains today. In many ways it might have been a safer choice, a softer option, a less demanding, less challenging position to take. But we do not see Cazenove becoming part of the securities division of some large bank only to lose our identity a few years hence . . . securities markets will continue to expand as the mobility of capital increases, and that the services of a strong and independent firm of integrity which has market judgement and market capability of the highest order will be in great demand.[18]

Once Cazenove had decided to stay independent, it had to consider the possibility that it might need more capital. It formed a syndicate of institutions to provide a fifteen-year £32 million variable rate subordinated loan, carrying a return linked to the firm's profits, subject to a minimum rate of 8 per cent. The twelve syndicate members were to have no equity stake, no influence over the running of the firm and would not be able to see the firm's balance sheet, profit and loss account or attend a formal meeting. At the same time, Cazenove put together a second syndicate to provide underwritings for use if corporate clients required.

The *Financial Times* reported Cazenove's syndicate arrangements and devoted a Lex column and an in-depth article on the firm. Comments made by the senior partners reveal the careful planning that had gone into these decisions: 'We have always been convinced there is a major role for a strong independent broker able to give unbiased advice and execution. We are also distinct from our competitors which will be advantageous. It gives continuity to clients at a time when great change is taking place and when we believe personal relationships will become of increasing importance in the new City.'[19]

The strength of the commitment to the partnership and to independence is revealed by a former employee of eleven years' standing:

The firm has been a fantastic success and has survived when other people said they couldn't go it alone. The partners could have sold out at the time of Big Bang and become instant millionaires but they opted not to sell what they regarded as their children's heritage. Theirs was very much the attitude, 'This is not our business to sell.' They cherish whatever it is that makes them so special and feel they should carry on with that tradition which is great and commendable.[20]

POSITION IN 1986

By 1986 all of the brokers and jobbers had placed their bets. They had had to make difficult decisions about a world where little was certain. In the end most of them resorted to money as the final test. Greed overcame long-term planning and crucially an opportunity was missed to build loyalty amongst the senior employees. This, rather than the mistakes that were inevitably made in selecting strategies and new owners that were culturally sympathetic, was to prove the longest lasting legacy of the period.

The independents, Smith and Cazenove, were focused and realistic. Of the rest, most had got it wrong: 'It was a wonderful deal at the time; Morgan Grenfell offered us a good price, they had the right connections, they had plenty of capital, which is what we needed to run as a market maker in the gilt edged market and they were very clever people and could develop the business. The philosophy looked exactly right, although in the event it didn't turn out like that.'[21]

IO

'Trying to Stuff the Whole Lot
into One Big Bag'*

In the period between the Goodison–Parkinson agreement in 1983 and Big Bang in October 1986 the City needed to convert a broad outline into detailed rules and functioning entities. This was a considerable challenge given the scale and complexity of the changes required and the comparatively hazy shape of the original agreement.

The key operational tasks were to design and construct new dealing rooms to house the integrated firms and to build new corporate structures. These were done on time, an achievement which should not be underestimated. Even more difficult, however, were the 'people' tasks: the need to staff up the businesses to meet the aspirations of the owners and to define new relationships both internal to the organization and with clients. Operational and human tasks needed to be done before 27 October 1986, which was Big Bang day, and most firms were not certain enough of their positions to have started before 1985. In practice, the new firms had only an eighteen-month window in which to get ready. It was the human difficulty rather than the physical problem that proved toughest to crack.

BUILDING A BAILEY BRIDGE

The move to a new method of dealing and the formation of integrated firms required an extraordinary amount of planning and work on buildings and information technology. Integration of trading and agency sales required large new dealing rooms and the move away

* Competitor on S. G. Warburg, 1986.

from face-to-face trading to telephone and later electronic dealing required major investment in information technology.

The Stock Exchange knew that time was too short to design, build and install a new share dealing system from scratch. Instead a dealing system called SEAQ (Stock Exchange Automated Quotation) was developed around the existing share price database system. The solution was pragmatic but effective and a similar line was taken with the market makers that would use the system. Stocks were banded into groups according to liquidity, with different obligations for each. This flexible approach ensured that the new trading system would be practical to use for customers and market makers.

Six months before Big Bang, Patrick Mitford Slade, chairman of the Stock Exchange Projects Committee, was warning that 'City firms large and small are in trouble over their technological preparations'. They responded by expanding their information technology and facilities departments to complete the move from the old-fashioned, rabbit warren offices occupied by the partnerships to new state-of-the-art dealing rooms. It was a scale of operation that would have taxed the resources of the old partnerships but which the new owners, especially the commercial banks, were able to tackle. Eighty large offices of over 20,000 square feet were rented and fitted out in the City in the two years to July 1986.[1]

Large amounts of money were spent. The City's revolution involved a lot of technological change as remote dealing replaced personal contact. The cost of the electronics around a single trading position was £30,000 and the new firms each envisaged having an army of dealers. Salomon planned for an initial 300 positions at Victoria Plaza including a trading floor of 13,000 square feet. NatWest Investment Bank planned for over 440, S.G. Warburg for 480, Merrill Lynch for 550. The cost of the dealing positions alone for a firm requiring 500 dealing positions was £15 million even before building costs which was well beyond the range of the small partnerships which characterized the old City.

The move from dealing rooms to trading floor was traumatic for some.

It really spooked me the first time I saw it. I'd been sitting in the same desk for eleven years, next to a window, ten yards from the Gents and being able to shout at and be heard by everyone in the room. The commissionaire and tea lady knew my name and I knew theirs. We were taken to the new place, it was the size of a football pitch with no natural daylight in my bit. The ceiling seemed low. There was no privacy. I felt as though I couldn't scratch my nose without someone watching. We had to use microphones to make ourselves heard. There were security guards on the front desk and machines not tea ladies. It was like moving to another age.[2]

Cazenove and Smith New Court, the independent firms, had to fund infrastructure investment from existing resources and shareholders. This ensured management attention on getting value for money, and prevented either firm from burdening itself with excessive overheads, in contrast with many of the integrated investment banks which were set up in chrome and glass palaces by their new owners.

Cazenove's staff grew from 357 to 436 between 1983 and 1986 and sales, research and dealing moved into new space in Telegraph Street in 1986. Smith New Court's accounts show how capital expenditure rose sharply as it prepared for and moved into new offices. Its initial move was to the offices of N. M. Rothschild but it miscalculated the space that would be required. 'Tony Lewis believed that trading over the phone would never replace the old market floor. The new office space didn't allow for market makers and we were probably in breach of the Factories Act for a very long time. There was not enough kit and we were nearly sharing telephones. There was no air conditioning and it was all pretty unpleasant.'[3]

Table 6. Smith New Court Purchase of
Fixed Assets, 1984–8, £ million[4]

1983–4	1984–5	1985–6	1986–7	1987–8
0.7	1.5	2.7	11.8	9.2

Smith's misjudgement was one of the few it made and had the beneficial side-effect of keeping costs down at a crucial period. The creation of the physical infrastructure for the new firms required practical planning and implementation on a huge scale and required some imagination and vision on the part of those doing it. But it was a problem for which the background of those working in the City provided a good training. The City was practical and task oriented. It was good at applying all of its resources to solving short-term problems. And the fact that its practitioners valued the standards of the armed services ensured that good standards of discipline were applied to what George Hayter, director of technical services at the Stock Exchange, chose to characterize in the military terms his audience would appreciate: 'There is a wide river to cross and time only to build a Bailey bridge.'[5]

BUILDING TEAMS

The new entities had to be properly managed and it soon became clear that a senior management structure much deeper than the old senior partner–administrative partner combination would be required. There was a shortage of managers with international experience. Very few British people had been involved in firms spanning agency broking, risk management and corporate finance.

Neither the former senior partners of the broking firms nor the senior bankers at the commercial and clearing banks were qualified to take the new entities past Big Bang. The new owners of the aspiring integrated investment banks might have supplemented the skills of the senior partners with some of the skills in risk management and big company administration which existed in their own firms. Instead, lacking in self-confidence and susceptible to the charm and arrogance of the brokers who said 'leave it to us', the new owners granted autonomy and independence to their new subsidiaries.

There was a skills shortage in every area. In market making, where there were many new entrants, there was no existing model of how the well-run firm would look. Start-up businesses tended to overstaff in market making as they used the old Wedd and Akroyd structures as an approximation for what might be required. The old jobbers, meanwhile, realized that the new electronic market place would need fewer traders than had been necessary to man the pitches on the Stock Exchange floor and they were not always sorry to see their staff poached by rivals.

Research was another area of intensive staff movement. Combinations like BZW and Warburg that were strong in trading, sales and corporate finance were weak in research and needed highly rated analysts to serve corporate finance. A high ranking in the Extel survey became a target for many of the new firms and, with poor financial results, this was often their only solace. The job of the head of research changed from being mainly about product quality control into a man management role. Recruiting and retention became very important and the heads of research played chess against each other using human pieces. Howard Coates at BZW and Nick Whitney at Warburg were both appointed as heads of research with a mandate to build and were the best examples of the new breed of research director.

Howard Coates was educated at a grammar school in the north of England before going to Oxford University, leaving with a doctorate in chemistry in 1973. He joined de Zoete as one of the firm's first graduate trainees and worked his way up the research department, becoming a partner in 1980 and head of research in 1982. He is quietly spoken, thoughtful and relies on the power of his reasoning to make his points. His reputation in the City is as a builder of consensus:

By the early 1980s we were a better firm than we had been in the seventies and we decided that research rankings would be important. The partnership told me that my job as head of research was to get us ranked and that they knew it would cost us a lot of money. We needed some stars to go with Jack Summerscale [the firm's well-rated telecommunications analyst] and the crucial hires were David Buck from Laing & Cruickshank to cover textiles and Neil Scourse, the number one rated brewing sector analyst from Fielding Newson Smith. These put us on the map and we could then attract other stars and it gave us time to grow organically by hiring and training lots of bright graduates and waiting for them to mature.[6]

Nick Whitney left secondary modern school in 1966 with fifteen GCE O levels and started work in the City as a clerk on a salary of £500 per annum. He is analytical and commercial and was able to get a job in research with Sebag in 1972, and worked his way up the rankings with Cutler & Co., a Birmingham-based broker, Laing & Cruickshank in London, finally becoming a number one analyst by the time he joined Simon & Coates in 1980. He was recruited by Rowe & Pitman as head of research in 1982, the same year as Coates took over at BZW, and became a partner in 1983.

Whitney chooses his words carefully and delivers his views in a logical way that makes it difficult to argue. He has a reputation in the City as a hard man:

Peter Sitwell had just taken over as senior partner. We were ranked first in property and insurance and wanted to extend that to more sectors. The research department fell into two parts. The old-timers, thirty-five+ years old, had come to research out of the back office, were intelligent but cowed by the partners and subservient to sales. The other half were graduate trainees. I was told to shake it up and was given a reasonable budget to do it. All the old stagers were eased out by 1986 and replaced by recruits from outside. I went for the twos and threes rather than the number ones, they were cheaper and more motivated. We took in six to eight graduates every year and kept about half. Once we got to a position around six or seven, I gave it another kick, this time hiring top analysts to put us in the top three.[7]

By the time the votes were cast for 1986 (the results emerged in the 1987 survey) Coates had taken BZW's Extel ranking from sixth to second; Whitney had taken Warburg from seventh to third.

The third area of the broking business, sales, also saw heavy staff turnover with Morgan Grenfell and the start-up Americans especially active as they assembled sales teams from scratch. The losers were the medium-sized brokers belonging to banks with smaller pockets and less commitment than the top firms. There was movement between the leading firms but it was rare for the very best salesmen to switch firms. They needed a strong and reliable flow of ideas to sell from good analysts and they were cautious about changing. A number of second-rate salesmen from the bigger firms were able to join the start-ups and improve substantially their compensation packages in the process, especially in 1986 as the newcomers grew desperate for selling power.

Corporate brokers were even more reluctant than salesmen to change firms. Their clients valued the longevity of the relationship, and they did not want to run the risk of dealing with job hoppers.

Although many of the brokers tried to build up corporate finance they tended to resort to retraining senior analysts and salesmen rather than hiring from other firms.

DEFINING NEW RELATIONSHIPS: RISK

As the new teams were being assembled and bedded down, the brokers faced the implications of integrating sales, trading, research and corporate finance into one entity. There were issues with staff and with clients.

It took the institutional clients some time to adjust to the idea that the broker with whom they had traditionally dealt on an agency basis would now also be running an in-house market making book. As late as 1986, a campaign against dual capacity was mounted by some institutions, led by the chief executive of one of the biggest investors in the London market, M&G. Some of the brokers decided that this created an opportunity for differentiation in the eyes of the client. Sheppards, a medium-sized broking firm, mounted an advertising campaign showing a profile with two faces, one looking left the other right, and with the slogan 'After Big Bang which face will your stock-broker show you? Will it be the face that's offering a genuine opinion – or the one that's thinking of its own book position? That's why Sheppards have taken a positive decision to remain a non-market maker and to continue to put our clients first.'[8] James Capel remained an agency broker for nearly a decade after Big Bang (although a proprietary trading business was quietly added) and Cazenove remained so in all British stocks except those where it was corporate broker. Smith New Court maintained a division between its principal and agency businesses, trading with clients as separate firms, Smith New Court and Smith New Court Agency.

What worried the institutional clients was that they would be encouraged to deal in stock by brokers in order to clear a book position rather than because it was in the client's best interest. Also, the clients were worried that brokers would load their book ahead of anticipated orders and that the clients would get worse prices as a result: 'The informal one-to-one interviews with analysts could become difficult for finance directors to reconcile with the obligation to shareholders and the market at large: if the privileged analyst goes home and tells his market makers to short the stock rather than penning a sell circular to institutional clients, the benefits of it may be too narrowly shared.'[9]

These issues were resolved by a combination of legal and regulatory factors and by the effective operation of competition. The convention between the analyst and the finance director described above would not pass modern insider dealing standards and the law was interpreted much more strictly after Big Bang to stamp out this kind of thing. Firms were also required to make a general disclosure that they might hold a position in the shares being recommended. Conflict of interest between a firm's agency and market making sides was clarified by the best execution requirements and by the need for market makers to be competitive with each other. In a situation where there were upwards of twenty competing market makers, no single firm could afford to get a reputation for making consistently poor prices.

LEARNING TO LIVE WITH RISK

A Kleinwort Benson director accurately summarized the brokers' risk management skills: 'How can an agency broker know anything about trading? He never takes a principal's risk!'[10] Only the Americans had experience of combining agency and principal businesses. Only Warburg, BZW and Smith New Court had a substantial market maker at the core. All of the rest came from an agency background and had no real experience of market making or risk management. The addition of market making teams by acquisition or recruitment brought practical and cultural problems which were first encountered in the approach to Big Bang.

There was more to growing an in-house market maker than just hiring a few people. Effective recruiting was difficult enough given the competitive pressures for the best people and the determination of the existing jobbers to hang on to their stars. But the task was complicated by the need to effect cultural change in an agency environment, to build risk management systems and to combine the management responsibilities of building and running a team with trading a book.

These tasks fell to men who had been good, instinctive jobbers but who had worked in small, stable and highly focused teams and who were generally given no extra training on how to manage. Wood Mackenzie's team was put together by Colin Mills, a senior jobber from Pinchin. Mills was not the biggest name on the Stock Exchange floor but he had very good management skills, cared about people and was a good diplomat, all of which helped to solve disputes between clients and staff. In the event, the appointment of a good manager to run market making proved to be a better policy than promoting the best trader.

Agency brokers needed re-education to work in a risk taking environment. An agency broking firm began the year with revenue of zero and worked its way steadily forward, accumulating income as the commissions mounted. Each successfully executed order was a small step to a successful conclusion of the year.

Contrast this with the position of the integrated broker. An order to buy a million shares at £1 would produce commission of £2000 assuming that the rate of 0.2 per cent was agreed between broker and client. However, if the in-house market maker went short to fill the order and the price moved one penny against him, there would be a mark-to-market loss of £10,000 to set against the commission.

This caused two problems for relationships within the firm. Daily profit and loss accounts, eagerly watched by all members of the firm as a guide to performance, could sometimes show negative numbers. Salesmen felt they had worked hard for an order, 'only for the market maker to throw it all away'. Rumours of the bonuses paid to market makers left the salesmen ready to jump on them if results were poor. One firm's tolerance of a market maker's poor results was seriously shortened by jealousy of the gold Rolls-Royce he was rumoured to own.

Initially market making conditions in 1984 were benign but in 1985, as new entrants bankrolled by rich parents tried to buy market share, there was the first price war. In many stocks, there would now be twenty competing market makers where previously there had been just three or four. Wedd's profits in this period fell so sharply that Barclays renegotiated the terms down from £100 million to £80 million. Conditions remained difficult in market making in 1986, especially in the summer, and even in a leading firm such as BZW trading revenues which had been positive at the end of June had turned £11 million negative by the end of October. Institutional turnover remained high and commissions across the City were buoyant, so that the combination of good agency revenue and bad dealing results created the worst possible tensions in the new integrated firms.

The second cultural problem caused by the integration of sales and trading was that sometimes market makers did not want to transact the orders won by the salesmen. If the aggregate of the firm's books created a long position, the market makers might not want to receive any more orders from clients wanting to sell stock. They were obliged to deal in normal market size but this was usually far below what the larger institutions would expect to deal in. This again created tension between the salesmen who had won the order and whose performance was measured by commission earned and the trader who was measured by his daily profit and loss account. In time, managements inculcated an appreciation that it was the firm's total profit and loss account that mattered and the role of sales trader was developed as an intermediary between the sales force and the market makers, but in the 1983–6 period a process of trial and error operated as the constituent parts learned to live with each other.

GAGGING THE ANALYST

By the early 1980s, research had moved out of the back room to be a front line weapon in the brokers' pursuit of institutional business and was becoming increasingly important in winning corporate finance business. The possession of a ranked analyst and the publication of glossy, in-depth research became a factor in landing privatisation work from the Government and corporate brokerships. Companies appointed corporate brokers on the basis of the quality of research coverage.[11]

When the merchant banks bought brokers, access to expert analysts was seen as a tangible benefit. Corporate financiers in the merchant bank and the corporate broking departments expected positive comment on their clients. In the early 1980s, Steve Plag, Wood Mackenzie's highly rated pharmaceuticals analyst, formed a negative view on Fisons, a client of the corporate broking department. It was not until he moved to BZW and became free of a corporate connection with Fisons, that the full extent of his views was published. Ironically, by the time he was vindicated in the form of poor results from Fisons, Plag was back as Fisons' corporate broker and, once more, not free to comment.

The association of research with corporate finance departments was at least as damaging to objectivity as the ownership of in-house positions was to agency execution. Most of the brokers claim that research is independent of corporate finance and that objective advice is given even if the company being analysed is a client. This is very rarely the case. Chief executives and finance directors apply strong pressure to analysts directly and indirectly where there is a corporate connection. Pressure can be inclusive, with connected analysts being given preferential treatment in the form of private briefings, so that they are made to feel part of the team. It can take the form of direct threats to the corporate relationship, applied through the corporate financier or the head of research, or indirect threats where word is put around the circle of leading chief executives and finance directors that certain banks cannot control their analysts. It is usually the case that the louder the complaints, the more certain it is that the analyst will prove to be correct.

Surprisingly, the conflict of interest between research and corporate finance was not unduly controversial. For whereas it has become accepted that there are limits to the amount a firm is prepared to lose in transacting an institutional bargain, and therefore salesmen do not expect the book to deal for them on every occasion, it is much more difficult for salesmen and analysts to refuse to support a corporate finance deal. This is because the firm's total income on a corporate finance transaction is much larger than on a single institutional bargain and because many banks went into broking in order to sustain corporate finance. Therefore the pressure on an analyst to support corporate finance is enormous, not least because he will probably get a large bonus if the deal is sold well. The practice has developed on large offerings of forming syndicates of connected brokers so that the institutions find it very difficult to get objective advice on the issue being sold. This situation is particularly acute in the United States where the research department is usually seen as a cost to be shared equally between the institutional equities department and corporate finance.

The awareness that conflicts of interest would arise required the regulators to develop rules for every situation and for firms, under the self-regulation code, to ensure that the rules were complied with. This led to the establishment of compliance officers, a new role in London but one which was well established in New York. Richard Sadleir, the compliance officer for Schroder Wagg, described two aspects to the job: 'One is dealing with conflicts of interest, which is how the job was originally conceived, the other with accountancy type monitoring.'[12] Changes to the rules and the fact that the Financial Services Bill had not been enacted meant that firms entered Big Bang with structures not yet firm and such key items as client service agreements not yet written. The US firms, used to operating in an environment where the law and regulations were detailed and enforced, led the way, often transferring staff from New York and supplementing them with local recruits from accountancy or the law.

INTERNATIONAL DIMENSION GROWING

Increasing overseas interest in domestic securities made it impossible for even the most conservative broker to be wholly domestic. By 1984, over half of trading in the leading FT 30 index shares, ICI, Reuters and Glaxo was carried out in New York and foreign appetite for UK privatisations was strong.[13]

The brokers responded to the growth of a cross-border business by opening up foreign offices, initially to serve local investors in British equities but rapidly moving on to sales, research and trading in local equities. UK firms applied for membership of overseas stock exchanges. The long-running dispute between Britain and Japan concerning access to the London and Tokyo Stock Exchanges was resolved when Government intervention won seats in Tokyo for Barings and NatWest's County Bank Asia Securities in return for a banking licence in London for Nomura.[14]

UBS began to develop systematically a securities operation in the early 1980s building out from its domestic market, where it had a strong position in market making, distribution and portfolio management. Between 1982 and 1986 it developed teams of 170 people in London and New York and had applied for a securities licence in Japan. County NatWest spent a lot of time in 1985 and 1986 seeking Federal Reserve Board permission to set up a New York brokerage and won a securities licence to operate in Japan in 1986. Outwardly traditional firms such as Cazenove, who opened a representative office in Tokyo in 1981, joined in the movement towards international expansion and by 1986 every large firm had overseas offices in America and Asia.

The need to internationalize the business added a new dimension to the management task. Local membership required local infrastructure to enable business to be settled. Every Stock Exchange had a different set of rules to be followed. Staff became dispersed across the world, not just confined to London. Management had to spend a lot of time in the air and learned how to work with jet lag. Not surprisingly, there were a number of mishaps. Smith New Court's international dealing subsidiary incurred a loss of £2.9 million in the year to April 1985. Most firms spread themselves too thinly at a time when they should have been concentrating on the challenges they faced in their domestic business but the pressure from new owners to meet grand global ambitions and a fear of being left behind forced them into international expansion.

CONCLUSION

The period 1983–6 saw the best and worst of the City. A lot was achieved that looked superficially appealing but there were some fundamental flaws. In physical form the achievements were most impressive. The new offices were all open on time, the technology worked even if it was a bit cumbersome and expensive and the statutory and legal framework for the new companies was all in place. Gaps in the new firms' staffing levels were identified and filled. As the firms moved towards Big Bang day, sales, research and corporate finance began to develop relationships with each other. The clients began to understand how the conflicts of interest would be resolved. A rudimentary international network was built at many firms.

But this was a case of beauty being only skin deep for management was not in control of the business. The senior managers lacked the experience of running businesses with large risk and international dimensions. Groups of people had been thrown together rather than being integrated into properly functioning teams. Cultural issues and conflicts of interest had not been tackled. There was not the strategy to cope with an emerging 'star culture' or the disorientation that arose from the dismantling of the partnerships.

This was the period which guaranteed that Big Bang would end in failure. Successful organizations need deep roots and these were slow to be established. This is not surprising given the huge number and range of tasks that were required of the small number of individuals putting these firms together. When combined with the lack of experience of the new owners of the integrated investment banks, their fear of upsetting their new acquisitions, the lack of risk management experience on the part of the old broking partners, and the determination of the Government and the regulators not to get involved, it was inevitable that the new organizations would flounder. A consequence was that later on in the 1990s, when the competition became global, the British firms were not well enough established to take their chances.

I I

Seeds of Disaster

In the three years following the 1983 agreement between the Stock Exchange and the Department of Trade and Industry the structure and form of the City underwent a revolution. A new dealing system was established together with a new regulatory framework to police it. New firms were created out of businesses that had been required to be arm's length for decades. Every single person working in broking and jobbing experienced a material change in the nature of his or her job. Relationships with clients had to be redefined. Within firms a new contract between employer and employee had to be created.

As the City approached Big Bang on 27 October 1986 it was in a dangerous state. At a superficial level, everything had been achieved with military precision and the City was ready on time. However, beneath the surface lay major structural faults that were to emerge in the coming years and bring down the edifices that had just been built. The faults fell into four categories: managerial weaknesses due to doing too much, too soon; cultural tensions; strategic errors; and laissez-faire government.

TOO MUCH, TOO SOON

Once the merry-go-round of mergers had begun, the degree of change expected of the City was too great for people to cope with. New skills had to be learned, issues of scale and complexity had to be faced, and the human organization needed to be rebuilt every bit as thoroughly as the physical structures. The senior partner of one leading stockbroker noted very early on that 'The pace of change is too fast. People are not thinking the rationale of these deals through.'[1]

The management skills required to run a small partnership were very different to those needed in managing a firm five or ten times that size. The merger of three previously separate businesses into integrated investment banks made the task of running them much more complicated. Broking firms that consisted of 250 people in 1983 were increased to 600 or 700 by October 1986 and were part of organizations that employed thousands of staff. The old generation lacked the experience and the training to run and build large firms. They tried to run them in the old way, relying on snap decisions and verbal reports rather than meetings and record keeping. This was dangerous given the increase in the number of staff involved, the proliferation in locations and the introduction of trading risk.

The banks had some of the management skills that the brokers lacked but they were slow to get involved. They were much larger than any of the British firms involved in investment banking. They had experience of managing big balance sheets and profit and loss accounts. They had structure and reporting lines and were used to operating matrix management. They kept records, analysed numbers and wrote minutes of meetings and memoranda.

However, the new owners were scared of their new assets walking out and, one after another, promised operational independence to the brokers they bought. Security Pacific 'said that it intended that the day-to-day management of Hoare Govett should remain unchanged'.[2] Barclays regarded BZW as 'a member of the Barclays group rather than being completely absorbed'.[3] HSBC promised that 'Capel's operations will remain autonomous within the HSBC Group'.[4] UBS promised to integrate Phillips & Drew sensitively and to soft pedal the Swiss hierarchical instincts. Barings allowed its securities arm to occupy separate premises and to run the business with minimal supervision.[5] None of the new owners, clearers or merchants, British or foreign, imposed themselves on their brokers.

This was particularly damaging in the area of risk where the brokers were inexperienced and the jobbers had to run bigger positions than they were used to. The Lex column recognized that risk management would be a crucial test for the new owners: 'The main challenge facing

Barclays is to find a management approach to its new business which recognizes the substantial risks inherent in market making and if it goes that route block trading, while allowing sufficient freedom and incentive for de Zoete and Wedd Durlacher to develop their business.'[6]

The bankers' experience of credit risk could have helped the brokers and jobbers as they faced soaring Stock Exchange turnover inspired by Stamp Duty cuts and improving economic fundamentals.[7] The positions held by Smith New Court at the end of April 1986, six months before Big Bang, were five times greater than those held by the old Smith Brothers in April 1983. Increases of this order occurred across all of the market making firms, testing severely the risk management skills and controls learned in less active markets.[8]

Risk management was complicated by new trading practices such as bought deals, programme trading and the growth of derivatives. New York firms were very experienced at bidding for large baskets of stocks unseen in competition with other firms. The skills needed to trade profitably out of such business – hedging, global distribution and tolerance to profit and loss volatility – were only just being learned in London. London houses could not understand how the US brokers could bid blind for such baskets for a commission of ½ per cent or less and still make money. They had to compete to please their clients and sometimes won business but this created a very dangerous situation with the firms carrying large amounts of trading risk which they did not know how to hedge or distribute.

The growth of derivatives meant that a firm's risk exposure could no longer be measured simply by totalling the cash equity positions. During the early 1980s, futures and options on stocks and markets became more available and more widely understood. The FT-SE 100 index was launched in February 1984 and was tailored specifically to the requirements of the London International Financial Futures Exchange to facilitate basket trading. For some firms derivatives became a significant part of the profit and loss account in their own right or for hedging but the systems were not always in place to measure and monitor the risks being run.

The rudimentary nature of risk controls would have frightened the parent banks if they had known about it. Only three firms – Akroyd, Wedd and Smith Brothers – had the experience of running large-scale risk positions but even they had little experience of international trading books or of responding to movements in derivatives markets. Most were overstaffed and traders who had too little to do were inclined to dabble in markets. There was little scientific risk analysis and reporting was rudimentary. Limits were lax and not monitored very carefully. The old agency brokers had no idea what they were getting into, the bankers had been told not to meddle and they did not dare disobey, and the jobbers trying to run new market making firms were out of their depth.

CULTURAL TENSIONS

The creation of large firms where contact by telephone replaced face-to-face meeting reduced personal ties as did the dissolution of the partnerships. This left a void in which the cultural issues that were inevitable when the new organizations were thrown together were allowed to fester.

The paternalistic bonds of partnership still exerted a powerful influence over partners and staff alike in the early 1980s. The managers and owners of the new firms failed to appreciate the need to establish new loyalties and this was a destabilizing factor as the City moved through Big Bang. Haruko Fukada's account of events at James Capel summarizes what occurred throughout the City: 'Selling our firm changed our lives; we were no longer a partnership and the whole ethos changed . . . The effects of the takeover and the sudden expansion of the firm were that there were enormous strains and tensions and the firm became rather divided and by 1987 it was a rather unhappy place. There was no longer the same kind of commitment which prevailed under the partnership arrangement.'[9]

In the old broking firms, career structure was straightforward. The goal was partnership, bringing the chance to share in wealth and the running of the firm. Once this was removed, there was a need to replace it with other goals. Directorships replaced partnership as the senior position but, whereas candidates for partner shared in the liabilities and rewards of the firm and were screened closely for suitability, the criteria for directorships were less closely monitored. The title of director prolif- erated and with that came a devaluation in its status.

Status was dethroned and cash became king. Young brokers had nothing left to go for but a bigger bonus. Most firms, bankrolled by their new owners, were scrambling to strengthen their teams and competed with the foreign start-ups in the pursuit of talent. The established executive search firms such as Russell Reynolds and Spencer Stuart were joined by one-man start-ups looking for a fast buck. The head-hunters were paid a fixed proportion of the candidate's first year's compensation, usually a third, so they were desperate to encourage people to move and for the highest possible price.

Against this background, the new firms needed to work very hard to build loyalty. They needed time to develop shared values. The use of incentive and deferred compensation might have helped but they were unsophisticated in the methods of remuneration they applied. There were a few phantom share schemes in operation but very rarely did deferred cash or equity form a significant part of remuneration.[10] War- burg was unusual in introducing an integrated remuneration scheme to incentivize staff beyond their own unit and this helped it to become one of the first of the new investment banks to develop a culture.

Incentivization had to be managed carefully to encourage inte- gration and break down tribalism. Barings provided a good example of how not to do it. The partners in the Asian securities team it bought from Henderson Crosthwaite would be able to sell their shares to Barings at a price determined by the profits they made. This profit- sharing arrangement encouraged Christopher Heath and his partners to maximize short-term profits rather than develop a long-term business integrated with the rest of the bank.[11]

Very little effort was made to inculcate staff with the culture of the new firms. This led to tribalism, a grouping around old clans and a rejection of the values of the new. The fear on the part of the new owners that, if they sought to impose themselves on the new business, the staff would walk prevented them from establishing control until it was too late. They were taken in by the 'leave it to us' approach of the brokers. The brokers, however, had no idea how to develop loyalty and team spirit in a large organization.

Training might have been a way of replacing paternalism, of re-creating the sense that the employer cared and that something more was involved in a relationship than a contract between the hirer and renter of labour but little was done. The search firm Jonathan Wren's annual survey of City compensation triggered the comment that 'Although numerous bank personnel chiefs now ruefully acknowledge the industry's failure to invest adequately in training over previous years, the problem is too pressing to be solved by raising the training effort from now on.'[12]

This should have been the moment when the established personnel departments of the commercial and merchant banks helped but they were resisted. Brokers regarded personnel as 'overhead' and overhead, the partnerships had been taught, was to be avoided. Furthermore, in the case of the commercial banks in particular, the interface between personnel and the brokers was one of the friction points in the culture clash between them. The commercial banks' personnel departments had been schooled in grades, unions, annual increments for service, and promotion for time served as well as job done. They were paper-based and believed in record keeping and structure and training.

The brokers, by contrast, came from a background that was informal, that paid and promoted by achievement and where training was on the job or not at all. Appraisals were informal, over lunch or just by body language. This was a business for self-starters and those who were going to make it did not need help from personnel. Those who were not going to make it were not worth bothering with anyway. This was the prevailing attitude in broking and, because they had negotiated independence from their new owners, the brokers prevailed over the personnel departments.

Remuneration levels in the clearing banks were much lower than in brokers and merchant banks and this was to prove a source of friction as the businesses came together. This was particularly so in the frequent periods when the brokers were not profitable or were causing the parent companies reputational damage. Even taking average salary levels, which masked some very high individual packages amongst senior merchant bankers, the discrepancy was huge and a great source of potential jealousy. At a senior level, the discrepancy caused real problems and personal jealousy, especially amongst those clearing bankers who did not support the parents' investment banking strategy, and led to open friction. Bankers could simply not understand, and resented, paying subsidiary directors, senior analysts, traders, and sales men compensation packages that were higher than those of the group chief executive. At BZW, at least until Big Bang, there were 'ex-BMB staff, on Barclays bank salary scales, sitting cheek by jowl with de Zoete and Wedd personnel who were about to become millionaires'.[13]

Cultural issues were especially serious at the British-dominated clearing banks: Barclays, NatWest, Midland and HSBC. At Barclays, relations between the clearing and investment bankers were described even in the BZW official history as being at 'daggers drawn'[14] and this was also the case at the other clearing banks. At the heart of this cultural divide was jealousy, exacerbated by the different backgrounds of the clearing bankers and the investment bankers.

Although public school boys were found in the clearing banks, they did not set the culture in the same way as they did in merchant banks or broking. In the clearing banks the culture was more grammar school, more regional than Home Counties, more polyester than silk. The dress code, the manner of speech, the kind of social event that was organized, were all different to those in the merchant banks or brokers. These differences were important once the banks, merchant banks and brokers started to work together because frequently the sides did not like each other. Shortly after HSBC agreed to buy James Capel, a dignitary from the bank visited its new broker. He was horrified by the state of Capel's office which was typical of most brokers in being low cost and basic: 'I'll tell you what,' he announced to the room in general, 'after this, working in our offices will be like working in a palace.' A Capel man shot back: 'That's the difference between brokers and bankers. You work in palaces, we live in them.'

There was a natural tendency for the public school boys at the brokers to lead and for the grammar school boys to defer. This is partly class-based but is also due to the ability of brokers to think quickly and to present confidently. It is a requirement for successful corporate financiers and stockbrokers to sound plausible and confident even when they are on weak ground. It is often said that the first half-hour with an investment banker is more impressive than the second, there being not much of substance behind the confident headlines. As a consequence, despite their superior risk management and experience of running complex organizations, the grammar school boys at the clearing banks failed to grip the businesses they had bought.

The merchant bankers and brokers were very dismissive of the time-serving nature of the clearing banks. The public school values of the merchant banking and broking fraternity did not extend to the old boy network unless a high threshold of competence was passed: if you were no good you did not get on. Whilst the clearing banks were also meritocratic, there did exist within them a time-serving culture which determined that, no matter how good you were, you did not get promoted until you had served your time at a particular grade. And once you had the job you were extremely difficult to dislodge, especially in the early 1980s when the clearers were still gripped by very powerful trade unions.

Further friction occurred over the different approach to record keeping and decision taking. The culture of the merchant banks and brokers, which can be described as 'take decisions on the hoof and write down only the bare minimum' was the very opposite of the committee and record keeping methods which characterized the clearers. Clearing bankers were trained to keep meticulous records and not to take decisions on the spur of the moment or on their own. Memos had to follow a certain style and approval processes could take a long time.

The time taken to approve decisions was held by the brokers to be inappropriate for a trading business. In reality, had they followed the clearing banks' custom in which risk limits were carefully considered and debated, several of the accidents later to befall the new investment banks might have been avoided. The style of the clearing banks, if properly adapted, was in some ways more suitable to a risk business than the informal methods of the merchant banks and especially the brokers. However, the cultural and other issues described here meant that friction and an unwillingness to change, rather than constructive discussion, formed the prevailing mood.

The clearing banks were brand managers and were much less hostage to the 'star culture' than the investment banks. They differed from the merchants and brokers in that the brand name and tangible assets, such as the branch network, were more valuable than the people. The whole system of the clearing bank was designed to reduce tasks to a minimal risk, minimal error process laid down in a procedures manual. The clearing banks were strong on staff training and most of them ran large staff colleges where individuals were trained in the bank's way. If an individual left, that did not matter. The brand rather than the individual was the key asset. This was in great contrast to the merchant banks and especially the brokers where the cult of the individual had always been strong and was now intensifying. Failure to understand this, especially amongst personnel departments, was a great source of tension, especially at bonus time.

Culture clash between clearing bank and broker was not the only source of tension in the new firms. The merchant banks were less bureaucratic than the clearers but even they were too formal for some of the brokers: 'In 1985 Grieveson Grant's partners were amazed to receive office memos in beautifully inscribed pristine envelopes: "We never used a new envelope inside the office. Anyway we hardly ever wrote to each other – we talked!" they asserted. In the cultural struggles that follow mergers, acquisitions and marriages, such issues assume a relevance out of all proportion.'[15]

Within the brokers, cultural clashes occurred between groups of people coming from one firm into another and start-ups like Morgan Grenfell contained tribes from different firms in the City who did not integrate well. There was also tension between salesmen and market makers and analysts and corporate financiers as they learned to cope with the conflicts that were inherent in the new system of integrated investment banks. These inner tensions that were present across the City meant that the new firms would not cope well with adversity.

STRATEGY ON THE HOOF

Adversity would be made less palatable by the failure of the new owners of the brokers to have thought things through or to have explained their strategies clearly to their staff and shareholders. Therefore, when things started to go wrong, the other stakeholders in the enterprise were hostile rather than supportive. The new owners had not been clear enough on why they were buying brokers. Pressure to

THE DEATH OF GENTLEMANLY CAPITALISM

do something quickly while there were still enough quality brokers around caused banks to rush in without considering carefully the long-term implications. Very few appreciated the scale and commitment that would be required. Barings' belief that buying a broker was 'only a small thing' was widespread among other merchant banks.[16]

There was no realization of the risk and reputational damage that could be caused nor of future capital requirements that would be necessary. It was noted early on that

the big clearing banks are determined to play a leading role in the future development of the London Stock Exchange. This is in sharp contrast to the relative caution shown by many leading merchant banks . . . They have been reluctant to be rushed into paying for stock market firms at the top of a bull market at a time when the planning framework for the future has not been at all clear. The risks for the merchant banks would be high given their limited sizes whereas the sums involved are not particularly great for the big clearing banks.[17]

However, the fact that the commercial banks did not appear to be making a very big bet relative to the size of their total assets meant that the subject was not taken sufficiently seriously. As a result, strategy appeared to be more a collection of opportunistic moves than a carefully planned operation.

The shareholders had not been briefed about the risks or costs of the venture and they were not aware of the potential strategic benefits. This meant that managements were frequently under pressure to defend their investment banking strategies which, in turn, resulted in more short-term decisions. NatWest regularly tapped shareholders and the debt market to fund its ambitions in the world's capital markets, most notably with the one-for-one, deeply discounted £714 million rights issue in 1986. But it failed to convince its shareholders of the wisdom of its strategy and came under constant pressure to get out. The merchant banks, on the other hand, carried their shareholders but had not thought through the resources that would be required to achieve their goals.

All concerned were caught out by a step change in the scale that would be required. This arose on Wall Street in 1985–6 when a number of firms began to make structural changes which indicated a growing ambition. Morgan Stanley announced that it was to go public and its announcement followed similar news from three other Wall Street firms.[18] Goldman Sachs agreed to admit Sumitomo Bank as a partner:

Just how right the market has been to worry about the bleakly competitive future of UK merchant banks was underlined yesterday when Goldman Sachs admitted that Sumitomo Bank might be putting $500 million into Goldman's partnership in return for an eventual 12.5 per cent of income. If the deal is done that extra capital will go to Goldman's worldwide business and much of it must be destined for London. A combination of Japanese capital and American aggression presents a fearful prospect to the defending London players who are already fighting off raids on their clients and personnel.[19]

The idea that Hill Samuel was too much of a mouthful for a predator, which was a credible statement in 1985, had been replaced by the view a year later that its resources looked insufficient in comparison with the Wall Street investment banks.

The upscaling of the industry caused some stockbroking partnerships to revise their plans. Quilter Goodison, a firm at the lower reaches of the top twenty but with a staff of 280 and thirty-five partners, including Sir Nicholas Goodison, the Stock Exchange chairman, sold a 29.9 per cent stake in itself to Skandia, Scandinavia's largest insurance group in 1984. Less than a year later it had decided that it needed a substantial bank behind it, and it was announced that Paribas would take control.[20] The Stock Exchange chairman was not alone in being surprised by the pace and degree of change which left a gap between the City's ambitions and its resources.

WHERE WERE THE AUTHORITIES?

The Government ministries and the Bank of England were hung up on a doctrine of non-intervention and were so convinced of the beneficial effects of free market forces and healthy competition that they deliberately remained on the sidelines. The new firms were both allowed and encouraged to press on with ambitious policies, free from close supervision.

The chosen system of regulation was often criticized for being too cumbersome but few realized that the regime was not rigorous enough. One of the few to have done so was Sir John Nott who, as Trade Secretary in 1979, had taken the decision to continue with the restrictive practices case against the Stock Exchange. By the time of Big Bang he was running Lazards and played a major part in their decision to stand alone. He understood that there was more to regulation than the prevention of fraud:

In my view the City was unwise to promote the concept of self-regulation. The Bank of England was even more unwise to promote it. When the next bear market comes there are going to be firms going bust. Politically, no one is going to distinguish between bankruptcy and fraud. The blame is going to descend upon the City self-regulators and certainly upon the Bank for failing to police the system . . . In the end we will have to have a legal authority which will be acting in the capacity of a court.[21]

The model for the legal authority that Nott had in mind was the SEC in New York. It was adequately staffed, had wide-reaching powers, and compelled brokers to follow high professional standards of control. In turn this instilled a degree of professionalism into the management which the laissez-faire system of self-regulation followed in London failed to encourage.

GENTLEMEN TO THE SLAUGHTER

In the three years before Big Bang structural changes occurred in the City that were to change the world of the gentlemanly capitalist into Wall Street. The City's style and work ethic took too long to catch up with the American model. The power breakfast and the sandwich at the desk replaced the port and cigars and the pace, intensity and hours were increased: 'From the point of view of the Brits, the Americans were setting a frightening standard in the City in terms of the hours we were keeping. We would come into the office at seven, which was a good hour or two before most of our English counterparts. We were using London very much as the base of our European business and the Continent was always an hour ahead.'[22]

Michael Lewis gives a similar description of Salomon Brothers' London office in December 1985:

Our Europeans – especially our Englishmen – tended to be the refined products of the right schools. For them work was not an obsession, or even, it seemed, a concern. And the notion that a person should subordinate himself to a corporation, especially an American corporation, was, to them, laughable. The Europeans had a reputation, probably exaggerated, of sleeping late, taking long liquid lunches, and stumbling through their afternoons. The source of this reputation was, as ever, the 41st floor in New York. One New York trader referred to them as Monty Python's Flying Investment Bankers.[23]

The City's pitiful lack of fitness for this new world was summed up by events in Haslemere, deep in Surrey's stockbroker belt. The earliest train of the day in 1986, the 7.15, left Haslemere for Waterloo at about the time the next generation of commuters would be starting work. British Rail saved the day by laying on an extra train at 6.44. By the time the City's work ethic had adjusted to the new world, the Americans had moved in and established a foothold in London.

The exposure of stereotyped gentlemanly capitalists to a new work ethic was accompanied by a breaking down in the old relationships. Staff mobility soared. Money replaced honour and short-term reward replaced long-term commitment. Managerial weaknesses and inner tensions ran through the new firms as they faced the new dawn.

PART THREE

BANG, CRASH, WALLOP, 1986–9

12

Market Overview

Thatcherism was rampant in the late 1980s. The Conservatives won a landslide victory in the 1987 election, unemployment fell, inflation was under control and prosperity, especially in the South, was high. Harry Enfield's character Loadsamoney, a plasterer with too much money, captured the mood of the moment and became the nation's anti-hero.[1] The City, however, was out of step with the country. Scandal, the Crash of 1987 and massive losses saw its public standing move from being a symbol of Thatcherite success to being a byword for excess between 1986 and 1989.

Friday 24 October was the last day of the old system. Phil Leeder, then a dealer with Greenwell's, recalls the mixed emotions on the market floor: 'The Friday evening was a hell of a thrash. It was a festive day, a sad day, the last day of trading as we knew it. People were going round shaking hands, there were lots of tears, and champagne in the hexagons. This was very unnatural, virtually the first time I can remember it.'[2]

Big Bang day itself, 27 October, started out with a great excitement: 'There was a terrific rush to do the first trade. We started at 7 a.m., previously it had been 8.30 a.m. We hoped that the screens would work and luckily they did. It was all new. Competitors like Phillips & Drew with fund management arms suddenly became clients. Clients who had previously spoken to salesmen now wanted a market service and sales trading was born. It took some getting used to.'[3]

For many, however, the first day was an anti-climax: 'On the day of Big Bang a lot of people got in very early and nothing much happened. There had been rehearsals on several Saturdays and there was lots of talk that the systems would blow up. They did go down for a time but in the end the preparations looked like massive overkill. It was all a bit of a damp squib, just a normal trading day.'[4] Others agree: 'My overriding recollection is how smoothly it all went, how well it all melded together.'[5] This created the impression that Big Bang had been a great success: 'more like a carefree transition than the revolution it really was'.[6]

However, the revolution required deep behavioural changes in organizations and individuals. Despite all the planning and practising this realization did not crystallize until 27 October.

We'd just moved into our new dealing room and suddenly we were in this huge place and we weren't a small firm anymore. The main things about 27 October were the systems failures and the fact that life immediately became more complicated. The machines all broke, SEAQ didn't work and questions were asked as to what should be done but that all settled down. That first day was a huge shock. It had all been agreed and rehearsed beforehand but when clients you'd been dealing with for twenty years for a commission of thirty basis points gave you an order and suddenly said that's at twenty basis points or sometimes that's a net order, it was still a shock. Also we had to work with the market making book. It used to be very clean, you got the order, found the best price and dealt. Now you got the order, found the best price and had to persuade our own market makers to match it. Often this caused problems with the market makers because it did not suit their positions.[7]

Initially the strains caused by these complications were concealed by booming business. People were busy, firms were generally in profit and the deep-seated issues did not surface. The Thatcher–Reagan reforms and tax cuts created confidence amongst investors. In the UK the 1986 Budget boosted equity turnover by cutting Stamp Duty and creating an annual Personal Equity Plan allowance. Stock Exchange turnover in equities rose 72 per cent in the year to £181 billion. Corporate finance was also busy with new issues, privatisations and takeovers; acquisitions of UK quoted companies rose nearly £10 billion in 1986 to £16 billion.[8]

Nineteen eighty-seven started with more of the same. Markets rose, corporate finance powered on, privatisations continued.[9] Equity turnover in London soared by £100 billion to £283 billion. The City was euphoric. Big Bang had worked, markets and systems could cope and everyone was a hero: 'It all got ridiculous. People thought they were gods. Huge risks were taken – bought deals, programme trades, derivatives, everyone seemed to be able to get away with it.'[10]

The tone of markets then changed dramatically in the first half of October 1987 when a sudden rise in US prime rates from 8.75 to 9.75 per cent knocked Wall Street. London was slow to catch on, being preoccupied with the sale of £7.2 billion of BP stock planned for the third week of October:

There was a widespread conviction that 'they' would ensure a firm market for the BP sale . . . But any investor who might have been tempted to cut and run on Friday morning [16 October] after learning of the prime rate rises would have found it practically impossible to deal. The previous night had witnessed one of the worst storms in living memory with London and the South East especially hard hit. Falling trees had disrupted road and rail services as well as telephone lines, and most stockbrokers and market makers were unable to get to their offices or even to communicate with them. As a result Friday in London was a non-event for all practical purposes.[11]

The following week was mayhem with London falling 22 per cent on Monday 19 and Tuesday 20 October and markets tumbling in the rest of the world. The investment banks lost £700 million on the BP underwriting and their market making operations made enormous losses in secondary trading: 'The storm on the Friday messed things up, we lost the thread. The Monday was unreal, we had some awful options positions. I was told about them very early in the day and we then worked furiously trying to place stock to ease the situation. The whole day was a blur to me. It got worse on the Tuesday, settled down for a bit and then the real nasties started to emerge.'[12] Some were better placed than others but all shared in the trauma: 'We were lucky, we had a flat book on the Friday night so we had no risk. Gradually during the day, Black Monday, people from the rest of the bank were coming and standing behind us, glued to our screens, making wry comments mostly about their own personal stocks.'[13]

SFA member firms had made pre-tax profits of £399 million in the first three quarters of 1987; in the fourth quarter these were almost totally wiped out by losses of £375 million. Although markets bottomed out in November depressed conditions in equity markets made life difficult for the new investment banks for much longer.

These events caused an enormous psychological shock. Anyone who had joined the City after 1974 had only seen markets go up. The hype and glamour were seductive. Prior to the Crash it had seemed like a certain one-way bet: stock prices only went higher, bonuses only ever got bigger, and jobs were only ever offered, not lost. Fully confident in the future, salesmen, analysts and market makers embarked on extravagant lifestyles with expensive cars and even bigger mortgages. Many of them had invested their savings in the equity market or borrowed to do so. They were faced with paying off huge loans lacking in job security and with no prospect of earning the bonuses they thought they could rely on. When the property market eventually cracked, negative equity in housing added to their problems.

The change in mood was sudden and dramatic: 'The October '87 Crash was a nightmare . . . cataclysmic psychologically for a lot of people. You tend to get optimists working in the City and they can't cope in a crash because it's outside their normal psychological boundaries.'[14] Seasoned brokers like County's Tony Cole believed that the Crash changed everyone's mood: 'The Crash blew it all up. Everyone lost confidence in everyone else.'[15]

Not only was the fourth quarter of 1987 frightening because of the scale of losses that were run up, there was no relief in sight in 1988. Stock Exchange turnover in equities in 1988 fell by a third to £192 billion. Although corporate finance activity remained buoyant and privatisations continued, with British Steel in 1988 and the water companies in 1989, equity brokers faced price volatility, excess competition and falling turnover, leading to more losses. Slender profits of £112 million in the first half gave way to losses of £307 million in the second half as a price war broke out between the market makers. Total pre-tax losses for the year were £195 million from capital employed of over £2.5 billion.

Numbers employed peaked at 25,500 in the third quarter of 1988 and a thousand had left the industry by the end of 1989. Revenue recovered in 1989, especially in the second half of the year, and the industry made pre-tax profits of £504 million in 1989 on capital employed of just over £3 billion.

Table 7. Financial Statistics Stock Exchange Member Firms, 1987–9[16]

Period	Revenue £ million	Costs £ million	Pre-tax profits £ million	Staff '000s	Capital employed £ million
1987 Q1	613	493	120	20	n/a
Q2	785	572	213	20.6	n/a
Q3	716	650	66	24	n/a
Q4	269	644	-375	24.5	n/a
1988 Q1	542	473	69	24.3	n/a
Q2	606	563	43	24.9	n/a
Q3	400	538	-138	25.5	2589
Q4	420	589	-169	24.8	2487
1989 Q1	747	599	148	24.6	2736
Q2	788	676	112	24.4	3238
Q3	885	724	161	24.1	3250
Q4	864	781	83	24.4	3447

But confidence was slow to recover. The market conditions exposed the flawed structures, ill thought-out strategies and managerial weaknesses of many of the participants in Big Bang. The groundwork which could have been done in the stress-free environment of 1983–6, and indeed was done at some of the best run firms, had to be done under pressure between 1987 and early 1990. It was very difficult to take correct strategic decisions under the daily strain of losses, volatility, internal dissension and, in some cases, scandal. Not every firm survived although a second wave of new entrants into the industry ensured that few jobs were lost. Big Bang of 1986 can therefore be said to have been followed by the Crash of 1987 and then by the Wallop of losses, closures and retrenchment at the firms which had been put together so recently. The partial recovery of 1989 did not restore confidence.

13

European Commercial Banks

The European commercial banks suffered more than any other group of banks during the post-Big Bang period. They had gone for the grandest strategies and had thrown the most money at them. Their big cost bases proved vulnerable to tricky markets, forcing them to re-examine their strategies and make mid-course corrections. Midland pulled out, NatWest doubled up its bet and HSBC, UBS and BZW fiddled with what they had.

Many of the senior managers who had put together the first wave of investment banks and brought the brokers through Big Bang did not survive. They were replaced by a younger generation who began to tackle the problems of managing large-scale complex institutions in volatile markets. Some progress was made but, by the end of the period, many of the inner tensions that had been created by the mergers before Big Bang were becoming serious issues.

BUYING THEM TWICE OVER

The banks had paid nearly half a billion pounds to assemble the broking and jobbing elements of their new investment banks between 1983 and 1986. Barclays, NatWest, HSBC, Midland and UBS then spent as much again in operating losses in the three and a quarter years between Big Bang day and the end of 1989. In effect the banks had paid for their brokers twice over by the end of the decade.

Many horror stories emerged. BZW lost £75 million in the Crash; James Capel lost about £20 million in 1987 and £32.4 million in 1988, a negative 21.6 per cent return on capital of £150 million. UBS Phillips

& Drew lost £115 million in the two years to the end of April 1989. Midland's broking arm, Greenwell, lost £6 million in the six months after Big Bang and much more than that over the months of the Crash. County NatWest lost £225 million between 1986 and 1989.

These losses were caused by a mixture of extraneous events and embarrassing mismanagement. The surge in market volumes around Big Bang and through the weeks of the Crash put the systems of the new brokers through a severe test. Most of the new integrated firms failed badly in risk control and settlement, running up enormous losses. The performance of the back offices, who were responsible for settling bargains, was dreadful. This was an early signal of management deficiency at the new brokers, and was especially worrying because settlement should have been a routine administrative matter requiring no great stockbroking skill.

At UBS Phillips & Drew reports in 1987 estimated that back office problems cost the firm £50 million to sort out. Rudolf Mueller explains the situation:

Early in 1987 we realized that the administrative capabilities of P&D were not up to our expectations and later that year got messages from the Swiss Banking Commission via the Bank of England that things at P&D were not good. I was sent over by the Executive Board to take management control. We had to bring in well over 100 people just sorting out the back office problems. There were tens of thousands of open trades, lots of working capital was unnecessarily tied up and we lost a lot of money. I had to remove some people; they were the most inefficient bunch I have ever seen.[1]

Settlement costs also contributed to the huge losses in 1986–7 at HSBC James Capel. At Midland Greenwell, the problems came to a head around the British Gas privatisation: 'The privatisation required a huge amount of physical delivery of stock. The systems were not in place and there was chaos. There were whole rooms full of certificates needing to be sorted out and delivered. I believe that it took Midland a year to clear up the whole mess.'[2]

Before Big Bang the worry had been that falling commission rates would cause financial problems for the brokers. In the event commission income remained healthy for, although institutional commission rates fell from an average 0.45 per cent before Big Bang to 0.25 per cent afterwards, the growth in turnover compensated for this. Stock Exchange turnover in equities, even in the depressed year of 1988, was still double what it had been before Big Bang so that there was actually an increase in the total pool of commission. Poor risk management, operational mistakes and slack cost control proved to be the more serious issues.

The extra work caused by the increase in market volumes was compounded by the problems of integrating the old-style brokers into the banks. The banks did not help themselves. Donald Macpherson was senior partner of Fielding Newson Smith, in his mid fifties at the time of Big Bang, and highly experienced at running a tight, profitable business. Fifteen years later he is still bemused at the approach NatWest took:

NatWest commissioned a report by KPMG on the quality of the controls and profitability of Fielding Newson Smith and it was very complimentary. Dick Fairbarnes was a good commonsense administrative partner and Norma Norton, John Keenan and Brian Hawkins gave excellent support. Inside a year they had all gone. Within six weeks of the takeover that team was unscrambled. County NatWest, in its incredible stupidity, put its own team in. We were virtually unable to trade because we couldn't produce a contract note.[3]

The market crash exposed the rudimentary nature of risk controls in the 1980s. The market makers were natural optimists and believed that markets and stocks go up, creating what Scott Dobbie, formerly chairman of NatWest Securities, describes as 'the incremental effect of a bull market in equities which led us to believe that market making was easy'. Ken Sinclair of BZW, a former Wedd senior partner, backs this up: 'We had a bull market and we didn't notice it in equities. So we kept on not realizing that the profits we were making were a result of the market going up every day. We were running a bull book of about £200 million.'[4] While markets rose, the absence of hedging (laying off the risk through futures overlays, shorting comparable stocks and markets, balancing options positions) was not important. Once the Crash came and markets turned, the poor quality of risk management was very obvious.

At James Capel, the losses were surprising given the firm's status as an agency broker. In the half-year to the end of September 1987, profits were £35 million and one senior HSBC director was gleefully describing the purchase of James Capel: 'We just couldn't believe it. It seemed the steal of the century.' By the end of the financial year, after the Crash caught the firm with large positions in second line equities and convertibles, losses for the year totalled £35 million. Capel was accused by clients of secret market making: 'We had retained positions bought in programme trades in the hope of making a proprietary turn. We learned from bitter experience that holding small illiquid stocks in a falling market could be very expensive.'[5]

The Crash exposed the failure of business controls as well as risk controls at County NatWest and Phillips & Drew in the notorious Blue Arrow affair. Blue Arrow was a fast growing employment and recruitment agency with a Stock Market value of £420 million. In August 1987, advised by County, it bid £800 million for Manpower, a large US employment agency. This was funded by the UK's largest rights issue, raising £837 million. Although the Blue Arrow price fell close to the issue price, it was announced on 29 September 1987 that the issue had been 48.9 per cent subscribed by existing Blue Arrow shareholders and that the rump of shares not taken up had been placed successfully with institutions by Phillips & Drew.

However, the market crash the following month revealed that County NatWest and Phillips & Drew were still holding large amounts of Blue Arrow shares. They had secretly subscribed for shares after the closing of the Blue Arrow offer, taking the subscription level up from 38 per cent from which a placing would not have been possible, to 48.9 per cent, which gave the impression of sufficient shareholder support for the placing to be completed. This episode was to leave Phillips & Drew and especially County under a cloud for a few years, eventually costing NatWest first its chairman and later its chief executive.

Risk control in volatile markets was made harder by a price war. Some of the commercial banks decided to use their balance sheet strength to drive out the competition in market making. Phillips & Drew and BZW were among the leaders in reducing the size and spread of SEAQ quotes. At BZW the senior market makers persuaded the head of equities to show the competition some muscle. Howard Coates was sceptical but the market makers were adamant that it would work and he agreed to let them run it for a while. Bob Cowell, the managing director of securities at Hoare Govett, described the effects of this in the *Daily Telegraph*: 'The last six months have been much more difficult than the previous nine because of cuts in the spread and changes in the size of quoted deals.'[6] There were thirty-two market makers chasing business which used to sustain a handful, with 75 per cent of volume in the hands of the top half dozen. They all lost money during the market making war but the fringe market makers were vulnerable to the policies of the big firms and a number retrenched or gave up, leading to a further concentration.

The squeeze on revenues was accompanied by a rise in costs with increases in headcount, salary and bonus levels, and information technology spend being the main factors. At BZW, for example, the global cost base of the equities division was £50 million in 1986 and was treble that by the end of 1989. There was also a worrying shift between fixed costs and variable costs:

As a partnership salaries were kept very low and there was a high variable element in compensation in the form of bonuses and profit share. The mix was about 25 per cent salary and 75 per cent bonus although it varied from year to year and that was the beauty of it. In a bad year there was lots of room to manoeuvre on costs. County NatWest reversed the ratio by raising salaries and cutting bonuses. Fixed costs skyrocketed and we were hostage to a downturn in revenues.[7]

It was a similar picture elsewhere: 'Midland were uncomfortable with low salaries and high bonuses so they switched the mix. It moved the risk from the staff to the bank. It was a clear indication that they didn't understand the business.'[8]

Aggressive overseas expansion increased costs and caused management stretch. The clearing banks wanted to become global investment banks. The US was the most important foreign market, and the British brokers had established teams in New York selling British equities to American investors nearly a decade ago. After Big Bang, tentative attempts were made to grow in US equities by hiring salesmen, traders and analysts. In Asia, the broking industry was immature and start-ups, sometimes built around small local brokers, were feasible. In Japan, there was a fixation with getting membership of the Tokyo Stock Exchange. In Europe, especially in France, a number of medium-sized local brokers were bought up by the British banks. The banks were having enough problems integrating their domestic acquisitions and did not come to grips with blending in their European business.

BZW embarked on a policy of rapid expansion overseas. Equities moved from having small offices in New York, Hong Kong and Tokyo at the time of Big Bang into the creation of a global network. Expansion occurred throughout Asia and Europe, including a high-profile team hired from Barings and an acquisition in Paris. James Capel embarked on an equally vigorous overseas development strategy and, by 1989, nearly half of its 2400 staff worked overseas. County NatWest opened a network in Asia, including Japan where it was early to gain TSE membership. It bought the Paris broker, Sellier, but had no strong European business into which to fold it and Sellier pursued a policy of polite independence for years. In the US, a team of domestic analysts, salesmen and traders was hired locally.

These initial overseas forays were loss-making and a major distraction for the management. They added an extra layer of complexity on to a management task that was already stretching the executives involved. Extra reports to take; foreign travel; twenty-four-hour trading; a multiplicity of regulators; more staff to manage: the list of additional burdens was long.

The whole period is characterized by mismanagement on the part of the bankers and the brokers. Both sides appeared totally out of their depth. At Midland: 'We had no experience of corporate strategy or business plans. We were required to put in crazy numbers to the board. We were naïve. We were just stockbrokers.'[9] There was a similar story at NatWest: 'Both sides were totally unrealistic. We thought we knew it all and that they were just bankers. They expected us to write reports and turn up at meetings at 10.30 in the middle of the trading day. We saw that as a big imposition, that they were stopping us doing our jobs. It was a big learning process for both sides.'[10]

NatWest's problems typify the cost, revenue and control issues of the early years. Donald Macpherson recalls:

Bisgood, County and Fieldings became instantly out of control. All were growing at the same time, hiring voraciously, expanding into America, Japan and Europe. It was mayhem. The first year of the merger saw staff turnover of 50 per cent. At Fieldings we worried if the staff turn was 5 per cent. It was a period of complete chaos. In early 1987 I went to see Lord Boardman. I said, 'Tom, there is going to be a monumental explosion at County unless you change the management.' He said, 'Donald, we don't behave like that.' I said, 'Tom, be it on your own head.'[11]

MID-COURSE CORRECTIONS

Midland had bought Greenwell primarily for its gilts business and its lack of interest in equities was soon apparent. After comparatively small losses (£6 million) in the first six months after Big Bang, Greenwell announced in March 1987 that it was ceasing to make markets in equities: 'Midland were horrified by the high spend on training, systems and the losses incurred in buying market share.'[12] Whilst agency broking was viable as a strategy for a leading firm such as James Capel and for niche players who had gone positively for such a strategy from the beginning, it was not defensible with staff or clients as a fall back position. A Greenwell's insider recalls the experience: 'We lacked market making skills and management control and we became loss making very quickly. Only the partners were tied in and once salary levels started booming we suffered a lot of departures. We were over-dependent on one client and the equities business declined quickly after March 1987.'[13]

Keith Brown was running Greenwell at this stage:

Once market making had gone we were in survival mode. Could we make it as an agency broker? The weaker you are the higher salaries you had to pay people to stay. The cost base was only half covered by income. It was obvious to me that we wouldn't make it. We were too small, our parent was weak financially and we had no credibility. We looked around for various alternatives and Morgan Stanley were quite interested in buying us but Midland changed its mind at the last minute when Kit McMahon said that it would be too big a loss of face so soon after we had opened up equity broking in the Far East.

It was no surprise when Midland closed the equities business in January 1988 with the loss of 200 jobs: 'It was an enormous shame, we were very sad. This came six months after the talks with Morgan Stanley who would have taken the business off our hands. In the end it cost Midland about £20 million to close it down.'[14]

NatWest's response to 1987, when the investment bank lost £116 million, was to conclude that it had to get more serious about the business if it was to succeed although some bankers wanted to get out. Its predicament was summed up in the *Financial Times*:

County made a false start in the 1986 Big Bang which had left it behind in the investment banking race. In the run up to Big Bang in the mid 1980s, when banks were scrambling to get into the securities business, County held back. Instead of splashing out on big acquisitions, it bought a medium-sized broker, Fielding Newson Smith, and a small jobber, Bisgood Bishop, for a total of less than £30 million. It reckoned that it could build on this foundation. But the first year of Big Bang showed that Big Battalions come out best.[15]

At the end of 1987 NatWest had agreed to buy Wood Mackenzie from Hill Samuel's new owners, the TSB. The cost of the acquisition was reported to be £30 million, the same as the amount already spent on Fielding and Bisgood. The move was designed to give critical mass on the broking side and to bring in new management in the form of John Chiene and his colleagues who had built Wood Mackenzie into one of the leading brokers of the 1980s.

Barclays' mid-course correction was slight after it lost out to TSB for Hill Samuel's corporate finance business and to Deutsche Bank for the whole of Morgan Grenfell. Andrew Buxton, then the acting chief executive of BZW, installed greater financial discipline, including more rigorous expense control, and formalized the management process: 'There was meant to be an equity board but it had never met because every member thought it more important to sell equities than meet to manage the business.'[16] Corporate finance and equities were brought closer together and David Band was hired from J. P. Morgan to be chief executive of BZW in February 1988: 'My remit was to start getting corporate clients and to have people thinking about new issue underwriting and advice. Our origins were secondary market but the clients now were corporate issuers and institutional investors.'[17]

GENERATIONAL CHANGE

The poor performance of the broking firms in the first years after Big Bang, together with the age and wealth of the old broking senior partners, led to pressure for management change. A wave of new, younger managers arrived bringing with it a fresher management style.

At UBS, Rudolf Mueller took over in London to integrate Phillips & Drew in 1988. Paul Neild, UBS's head of equities, left and Hector Sants was promoted from head of research to be in charge of the London-based equity operations at the age of thirty-two. Mueller wanted to make a generational change: 'Sants had been in the US and had not been involved in the problems in London. He was one of the new breed, an investment banking type not an old-style broker.'[18]

BZW's new chief executive, David Band, promoted Howard Coates, formerly head of research, to run UK stockbroking and Nick Sibley, previously head of overseas equity trading, to take charge of all Asian broking. Coates cut the headcount in UK equities by a fifth and focused on the trading losses that were being made. He discovered that customer trades made money, trades with market professionals broke even and that proprietary trades (using the firm's capital to invest in markets) lost money. Once the problem had been analysed, proprietary trading was tightly run and mini-businesses were built around sector teams of analysts, specialist salesmen and market makers. They were responsible for sector profit and loss accounts which were produced monthly and this broke down the barriers between agency and trading and helped mould as well as introduce a focus to the business.[19]

NatWest also decided that a change of management was required. Charles Villiers and Jonathan Cohen stepped down as chairman and chief executive in February 1988 when the full Blue Arrow story broke, later to be replaced by Howard Macdonald, a senior executive from the oil industry. Despite the addition of Wood Mackenzie, County's equities business was not going well, with poor financial results and a declining market reputation. County's failure to place a rights issue for William Low in the summer of 1989, half of which got left with the lead underwriter, S. G. Warburg, did not help. The firm's institutional clients were voting with their feet as were many of the staff.

One of the issues was the leadership of John Chiene, one of the great stockbrokers of the 1970s and 1980s. Chiene had built up the Edinburgh firm of Wood Mackenzie from a small private client firm into a market leader. He was one of the first brokers in Britain to realize the contribution that research could make to fund managers and built a business on the back of it. He recalls these days as though he is reliving a bad dream:

The place was a complete shambles. NatWest knew it was a mess and asked me to start work before the deal was signed late in 1987. I asked for an organogram and asked for a description of what every person did. Too often there was no clear answer, in which case that person was removed. I set up a new management structure, including working parties from each area and with representatives from the existing County business and Wood Mackenzie, and chose the best people for the job.

Blue Arrow was a serious distraction and had to be the top priority after the DTI inquiry was announced. To make matters worse, the market making war broke out. We made profits of about £8 million in the first half of 1988 and losses of about £25 million in the second half. The losses went down badly with NatWest, who questioned the ability of this new man coming in with a fanfare and losing us all this money.

With Blue Arrow and the losses, the staff were leaving. The whole industry was in turmoil, competition for staff was intense and long-term contracts were the norm. I managed to get NatWest to agree to eighteen-month guaranteed employment contracts for middle ranking to senior staff: the securities management committee waived them for itself. Department heads were asked to nominate candidates and a list was built up. Then NatWest changed its mind. The group personnel director was not happy. I remember sitting with him, explaining why we needed it. He kept shaking his head in disbelief and NatWest backed him. I asked them: 'How do you think that leaves me? The ManCo and their senior people have been asked to prepare a list and now you say I can't deliver. How do you think I can manage the place like that?'[20]

I joined NatWest in 1989 and it was clear that Chiene was in trouble. He had always been outspoken, talked a great deal and in a small firm inspired great loyalty from those who knew him. In a large firm, his outspoken views were not popular within NatWest who preferred a more consensual style and were misunderstood by many of the staff who saw only the front and not the depth of thinking behind the words. Most damagingly for Chiene, he gradually fell out with Macdonald, who progressively cut him out of the management in favour of Tim Ferguson.

Ferguson had joined County in 1982 after three years with Hambros and had set up the bank's securities business in Tokyo. He had returned to London at the beginning of 1989 to head up all international operations but had not been admitted to Chiene's management committee which consisted largely of the senior management from Wood Mackenzie. Macdonald and Chiene promoted Ferguson to run the global securities group in the summer of 1989 and, although Chiene was left in position as chairman, it soon became apparent that Ferguson rather than Chiene had Macdonald's support and Chiene resigned. Many of the old Wood Mack senior management also left at the time of Ferguson's appointment. He was given a clean slate to run the business under loose supervision from Macdonald.

Like Chiene, Ferguson had to cope with the backwash from Blue Arrow. He was appointed soon after the DTI report on Blue Arrow in July 1989, a report which aroused widespread hostility to County in the press and at the group head office. It was difficult for the staff to take pride in working for County. The Bank's support was doubted and the place had a losing feel. With Richard Foster, of the management consultants Spicer & Oppenheim, who was already looking over the investment bank for NatWest, Ferguson developed a four-part business plan: staff involvement; customer service; customer liquidity; and proprietary trading. In the final months of 1989, Ferguson, Foster and their team replaced the old management's style of 'leave it to us' with a 'tell us what's wrong and help us fix it' approach. Interviews were conducted with staff at different levels, a sense of involvement was created and morale began to turn. The plan was announced to staff at a meeting after work in January 1990 and followed a day in which seventy-nine people were made redundant.

The plan was entitled 'The Way Forward' and was a radical analysis of the UK securities market after Big Bang. It identified the increased complexity of the institutional clients, many of whom were organized into large teams of portfolio managers, research analysts and dealers. Ferguson realized that, if a broker could work as a team in servicing these clients, the impact would be much greater. He devised the role of account manager and appointed one for each client to coordinate the input and organize team selling. The 80:20 rule was applied to the clients once it was realized that just sixty clients accounted for 80 per cent of institutional turnover.

Following Coates' line at BZW, a distinction was drawn between proprietary trading and the provision of customer liquidity. Proprietary trading means using the firm's capital to invest in markets with the intention of making a profit. Market makers provide customer liquidity to enable the clients to execute business, hoping to make a turn in the process. By separating the two functions, and insisting that the customer liquidity market makers went home with books as flat as possible, Ferguson stopped the practice of 'punting' on markets and stocks. Focus was improved with benefits to the profit and loss account and customer service. A separate team, meanwhile, was put in place to conduct proprietary trading with the firm's capital.

'The Way Forward' had a dramatic effect on the UK equities division. The staff responded to being involved and the customers rewarded the firm for its improved service. Market share doubled from 3 per cent to 6 per cent within a year and trading results turned positive. Ferguson's model became the template for the other large brokers but was rarely implemented so well. Critical to its success was Ferguson's disregard for accepted wisdom and his preference for listening to staff rather than talking at them.

INTERNAL DIVISIONS

The cultural differences between the clearing bankers and the stockbrokers had lain below the surface before October 1986 but broke out once the two sides began to work with each other. The brokers grew exasperated by the red tape of the bankers' processes. The bankers were unimpressed by the cavalier style of the brokers and, when they brought losses and scandal to the parent companies, irritation turned to hostility and spread upwards from the middle management.

Barclays was particularly divided, a situation which took a turn for the worse early in 1987, when BZW's highly ranked banking analyst, Terry Smith, produced a sell note on the parent company beginning, 'There is something wrong with Barclays'. This annoyed Barclays' chairman: 'If you are a family and one of the junior members criticizes you in public, you feel rather bad about it.'[21] But the issues went deeper than the independence of research and a senior Barclays director recalls remuneration to have been an issue: 'Top industrialists like Sir Denys Henderson could never understand the remuneration levels. He used to say, "I have top men, good men, in ICI earning a fraction of these rates. How can you justify them?"'[22]

Lack of coordination annoyed the brokers. Howard Coates hired a new equities team to be based in Frankfurt, not knowing that Merck Finck, a private bank which overlapped with the BZW team, was being acquired by another part of Barclays. He had to return to Frankfurt and break the news to his own team without losing their confidence in the organization they had just joined. This kind of mishap was common in Europe where the corporate banking and broking arms of the clearers were forever bumping into each other.

A lack of support for the investment banking initiative which ran through the NatWest group was kept alive and fostered into a rich seam by the poor results and bad publicity. This occurred at the board level where there were regular debates about the investment bank's future, through the all-powerful office of the group chief executive which initiated frequent formal and informal reviews of the strategy, through personnel, and the bank's senior and middle managers. For NatWest veterans, the loss of the group chief executive and chairman, figures of pontifical stature, after Blue Arrow was shocking and the investment bank was held responsible. Chiene recalls that: 'The bank was run on the basis of hierarchy to protect the leader' so that these senior departures challenged the organization's whole purpose.

The clearing banks felt let down by what they had bought. A former senior partner of Phillips & Drew says: 'UBS did not realize what they had bought. We were an old-style agency broker, dependent on gilts with no depth of management.'[23] Mueller agreed: 'We thought we had bought a company with good management capabilities but they were totally lost after Big Bang. They were unable to cope with risk control and the increased volume of business.'[24] The UK clearers were equally disappointed: 'NatWest suddenly expected us to behave as a big broker. We didn't know how.'[25]

At HSBC, where the bank gave James Capel's management a lot of headroom in this period, the attitude of Peter Quinnen, Capel's chief executive, caused irritation: 'He was in a state of denial. Despite the losses he believed that, while he was still number one in UK research, everything was fine. The complacency of the firm was astounding.'[26]

There were frequent arguments at grassroots level in the banks. At BZW cooperation between corporate finance and de Zoete's corporate brokers was poor. When the two sides did work together on rights issues for Wace and Midland & Scottish Resources, the issues stuck and BZW lost money, and de Zoete resolved to stick to its traditional merchant banking relationships rather than get involved with Barclays.

County NatWest was also showing signs of internal divisions. The component parts of the newly merged County and Wood Mackenzie broking firm fought a tribal battle. Brian Winterflood, the head of market making from County, left to set up his own firm when it became apparent that he was not going to be given the autonomy he expected. The heads of research from County and Wood Mack, Ray Bowden and Ian McBean, both high-quality men of principle, wrangled over the style and look of the research. Would it follow the numbers-based Wood Mack format or the shorter, punchier County style? What colour would it be? Whose layout would it follow? Which analysts would get the upper hand? Similar issues were faced in sales and in trading and were usually solved by a compromise. This was summed up by the eventual colour of the research, which came out as a sickly yellow fudge.

During 1989 and 1990 tensions became apparent at James Capel. An incentive scheme to reward the best performing parts of the business was set up to placate the UK equities staff who were worried that the poor results of the overseas operations would impact on their bonus pool. There were some redundancies which tightened the cost base and gave some reassurance to the UK staff that senior management was on top of the situation.[27]

The investment banking operations of the clearers were thrown together. There was no recognition of the cultural differences between brokers and jobbers, or clearing bankers and merchants, or any combination of these four groups. The cultural differences were reinforced by jealousy. There were no attempts at cross-divisional team building or establishing common values. As a result, a tough, competitive environment was worsened by the rumbling of internecine warfare from within the banks.

A SOUR TASTE

The three years after Big Bang left a sour taste in the mouths of the bankers and brokers. Losses, scandal and stress replaced the optimism that had been present in 1986. Business strategies were in ruins and in one case, Midland, were over. How can the four remaining banks be assessed against their criteria for success?

Profitability was poor across the board. Although calendar year 1989 was a better year the recovery was fragile and NatWest's equities division was still heavily in loss. The brokers had a long way to go to repay their purchase prices and accumulated losses. At NatWest Ferguson's new approach was promising and the new managements at Phillips & Drew and BZW offered a glimmer of hope. HSBC was just facing up to the problem at James Capel and preparing to change the senior management.

Very serious fundamental issues remained at every bank. Relations within the investment banking divisions were fragile with resentment and competition for customers still prevalent. Tension also existed between the brokers and the boards and senior executives of their parent companies and these contributed to poor morale amongst senior management. The overblown ambitions of the banks and brokers also posed a problem. Costs were still too high in the UK and expansion into loss-making overseas operations stretched managerial and financial resources. On balance, the banks and their brokers were sadder and wiser after their experience but still some way off solving their problems.

14

Merchant Banks

The merchant banks were given some breathing space after the crash by three years of frenetic corporate finance activity. However, it became increasingly clear that the merchant banks did not have the balance sheets or profit and loss accounts to withstand the volatility of securities markets. They were targeted by BZW and UBS during the market making war of 1988 and were under the spotlight in the Crash of 1987 with questions being asked about their ability to withstand large trading losses.

TESTING TIMES

It was the scale of their ambition relative to their financial resources that caused the merchant banks difficulties. At the beginning of the period Morgan Grenfell, Kleinwort and Warburg were all of a comparable size. By the end of the period only Warburg had grown significantly thanks to corporate finance and asset management and this enabled it to sustain its pretensions to globalism. Kleinwort was forced to focus on fewer activities, Morgan Grenfell and Hill Samuel failed and Barings and the smaller merchant banks survived by opportunism.

COMMITMENT

Warburg survived the crash, made money in UK equities in 1988–9 despite the market making war,[1] secured number two position in the 1989 Extel survey for research and by 1990 was established as the

Table 8. Merchant Banks' Profits before Tax,
1986–9, £ million[2]

	1986	1987	1988	1989
Morgan Grenfell	82.2	60.1	34.6	54.3
Warburg	98.0	111.1	111.5	187.5
Kleinwort	70.0	51.6	17.7	83.3

leading broking firm in the City. The key to its success lay in trading, Warburg managing to maintain customer liquidity without losing a fortune in market making. This was especially difficult over the Crash: 'The balance between enabling our clients to deal and self-preservation was indeed delicate during those weeks and the improvement in our market share over that period was tangible confirmation of our teams' all-weather ability.'[3] Loss leading tactics 'from participants who are prepared to suffer substantial losses just in order to build market share or merely to maintain a foothold in markets outside their home base'[4] added to the pressure.

A senior Warburg insider explains how the firm flourished despite these conditions:

The profitability of the UK books was very peculiar. Client facilitation made no money, the money was all made on futures contract trading. There was a team of three or four blokes who traded futures. Michael Sargent and Ken Pitcher (the heads of trading) were very good at having a twenty-four- or forty-eight-hour view. In those days there was an informal meeting at 7.45, before the sales meeting, and four or five senior people would sit down and discuss the day. Usually Sargent or Pitcher would have a view and decide on the futures strategy. That book consistently made lots of money, even by the end of the 1980s. There were forty or fifty market makers making no money and three or four of them producing a fortune. There was talk of cutting back on market making and concentrating on the futures but it was too much for the Akroyd old guard to swallow.[5]

Tight control over the trading side was accompanied by strong grip on the delivery of research ideas to the clients. This was led by Nick Whitney, the head of research:

We used a saturation bombing policy. The chances of getting harmony out of fifty talented, temperamental analysts were low so we developed a process that was repeatable. It was a machine-like process that could be delivered by anybody. Although clients said they would prefer to get a small amount of really good research, they in fact paid highly for a large volume of well-marketed research of barely average quality. Most seemed to value a good research service above good research. So we combined acceptable but not necessarily brilliant research and a top-quality service. That way the superstars were less important to us and I refused to pander to them. This caused some problems with a few people but I had hired most of the rest and they were Nick's people.[6]

Warburg had fewer of the internal tensions that characterized some other firms. Sales and research worked well and, with the futures team behind them, the market makers were able to provide excellent liquidity. Tension was eased by a system of parallel accounting so that revenue was recognized by stock (which pleased the market makers and analysts) and by client (which pleased the salesmen). The firm understood the need to build a common culture and develop teamwork, devoting 'an increasing amount of time and money to personnel training and development – the human equivalent of R&D'. Bonuses were not all paid out in cash up front and were deferred over a few years and linked to Warburg's share price. This plan encouraged loyalty and group-minded behaviour so that the firm was more than a loose federation of businesses.[7]

Corporate finance and equities integrated particularly well. Warburg was unusual in finding 'consolidation between the client lists of corporate finance and corporate broking' and at the beginning of 1988–9 primary banking and capital markets were integrated to offer clients a wide range of financing services.[8] The firm successfully managed the research–corporate finance conflict by having corporate finance read all research on corporate clients before it went out and institutional clients knew what they were getting: 'We told the clients that we would not issue sell recommendations on corporate clients. They learned to read the coded messages on house stocks and to rely on the phone call.'[9]

The group understood the importance of commitment: 'We were

able to take a long-term view because the corporate hymn sheet never changed. This was in great contrast to the changing strategies of our competitors. The commitment of the senior managers never wavered publicly whatever happened behind the scenes. We were a calm sea of commitment in an era of volatility. It made it easier to hire and retain staff and gave a great stability of purpose.'[10]

Warburg's success brought with it dangers, especially the stretch to financial and managerial resources. In little over five years, group headcount doubled to 4900 by March 1990. The equities division alone comprised 900 staff, half of them outside the UK.[11] It became increasingly difficult to maintain vigilance over such a vast business but shareholders were assured that what was being undertaken was all very controlled: 'At all times we have to preserve a careful balance between giving free rein to fresh ideas and promising new activities and keeping a tight rein on the management of risk and the control of costs.'[12] However, income volatility is inevitable in a trading business and the inflated cost base was dangerously exposed to a downturn. Management did not prepare shareholders for the fluctuations in results that were inevitable.

FOCUS

The period between Big Bang and the end of 1989 were the Clementi years at Kleinwort Securities. David Clementi joined Kleinwort's corporate finance department in 1975 after Winchester, Oxford, Harvard Business School and qualifying as a chartered accountant. He became a successful corporate financier and played a leading role in the many privatisations in which Kleinwort was involved in the mid 1980s. After the British Gas privatisation was completed, Clementi took over Kleinwort Securities on 1 January 1987. I interviewed him in the Bank of England where he became Deputy Governor in 1997. He is a restrained, donnish figure only occasionally revealing the self-confidence expected of a world-class corporate financier.

His first task at Kleinwort Securities was to resolve problems in the back office. There was an enormous backlog of unsettled business dating back to Big Bang, and Rab Harley was hired from Wood

Mackenzie to sort out the mess. Wood Mackenzie were dismissive of the recruitment, one partner proclaiming that 'Kleinwort have just paid a six-figure package for a clerk' but this was a misreading of Harley and the importance of settlement. The back office had once been the preserve of failed brokers but, as volumes increased and foreign securities and derivatives became more widely traded, professional administrative skills were required. Clementi recognized this and found in Harley an unusual combination of administrative and creative abilities. Harley's efforts are estimated to have saved Kleinwort £30 million in sorting out the mess.

As a corporate financier Clementi was well aware of the importance of research and set about an aggressive hiring programme. He found that 'sales was strong under the leadership of Nick Redmayne, and there was a promising market making team under Charles Hue Williams, but Kleinwort were outside the top ten in research. The firm made a score of senior research hires, often from troubled competitors.'[13] It was generally believed that the key hire was Colin Fell to cover engineering from Scrimgeour since it showed how the balance was shifting away from the traditional leading firms. These twenty analysts transformed the other 400 on the staff and the firm began to make ground, reaching fourth place in the Extel survey for 1989–90 under the leadership of Brennan Hiorns.

Kleinwort's market making was built around Hue Williams' team from Wedd and initially they performed well, avoiding 'significant trading losses and indeed traded profitably' in 1987 despite the Crash. It was one of the few equities firms to do so in London and the new chairman, David Peake, boasted: 'We've traded profitably since the markets cracked. That's a tremendous feather in our cap. Morale in the securities side, after the events of the last quarter, is very high.'[14]

However, Kleinwort was the kind of market maker targeted by UBS and BZW in the price war and 1988 was to prove a terrible year for equities, especially in the UK, and the group, with a profitable first half followed by second half losses of £18 million, taking the year's profits down to £17.7 million.

Kleinwort had no choice but to respond to the profits collapse of 1988. It formalized risk controls, setting up an Asset and Liability Committee in June 1988, but needed to address directional issues. It chose a different strategy to Warburg and resolved to keep the business focused: 'We shall not try to do everything everywhere. Continental Europe, the USA and Japan remain our principal target areas outside the UK.' Several peripheral businesses were closed or sold, cutting staff numbers by 20 per cent during 1989. Equities continued to be developed selectively and 1989 saw an increase in market share in UK equities, expanded coverage in Europe, and TSE membership in 1988.

During Kleinwort's problems in 1988 there were widespread rumours that Kleinwort would exit securities. Clementi denies this: 'There was never any question of that. By 1988 equities was not a peripheral business to us; we were committed to being an integrated corporate finance and securities house.'[15]

Clementi became co-head of corporate finance in October 1989 after nearly three years as head of equities, handing over to Hue Williams and Redmayne. A senior Kleinwort director explained:

Agnew was chief executive by then and it was his decision. Redmayne and Hue Williams were two experienced professionals running their departments and he intended them to run equities. Clementi did a good building job. He changed the old Grieveson Grant culture to a research-based firm and took us towards becoming an integrated investment bank. I think he worked with Goldman and Morgan Stanley in the privatisations and saw how they worked and took us the same way.[16]

FAILURE

Hill Samuel scarcely lasted the opening lap of Big Bang, being flushed out by arbitrageurs. Wood Mackenzie had made a reasonable start to life as an integrated broker but was held back by Hill Samuel's capital constraints and the weakness of the bank's corporate finance department. These weaknesses left Hill Samuel vulnerable to attack and late in 1986 the Sydney-based insurance company FAI began to build a stake in the company which reached 14 per cent by February 1987. By mid year Kerry Packer had built up a stake of 12 per cent and the bank was firmly in play. These speculators believed that merchant banks the size of Hill Samuel would not be able to survive as independents but had sufficient rarity value and asset backing to attract a premium bidder. Under very considerable pressure from the press, Hill Samuel's directors responded to an approach by UBS, went to Switzerland in the autumn of 1987 expecting to have the deal consummated, only to be told that the UBS supervisory board had killed it off.

It turned then to TSB which had just floated on the stock market and which paid £777 million in October 1987 for Hill Samuel. TSB were prepared to take Wood Mackenzie as part of the package provided that market making was closed, leaving an agency broker. Chiene and his colleagues believed in market making, turned down this offer and began discussions with J. P. Morgan and others:

David Band had previously approached me to set up an equities business for J. P. Morgan. Now that Wood Mackenzie was for sale, he expressed an interest in buying the whole firm. Talks went well, we stood down the other interested parties including NatWest, and met one Friday afternoon to rubber stamp a deal. By 9 p.m. we had agreed everything apart from a few very minor issues, and agreed to get together the next day. At 4 a.m. on Saturday they called to say that following a meeting in New York they had decided not to go ahead. With 500 jobs to protect and no better deal in town, we went to NatWest pretty damn quickly.[17]

Morgan Grenfell Securities was brought down by a combination of the Guinness scandal, the Crash and the market making war. The ambitions of corporate finance had been the reason for entering broking but, once it began to lose its reputation as details emerged of its share support operation in support of Guinness's bid for Distillers in 1986, revenue and resolve dried up. This meant that, when the securities business lost £18 million in equities and £4.5 million in gilts in 1988, there was insufficient profit coming from corporate finance to make the group results look respectable. Morgan Grenfell pulled out of securities in December 1988 and sold itself to Deutsche Bank the following year.

Morgan Grenfell's attempt to build equity broking from a greenfield site came close to success. John Holmes and Geoffrey Collier had been recruited from the American businesses of Hoare Govett and Vickers da Costa in 1985 to build the new operation. Holmes was the son of a labourer, a secondary modern schoolboy who had done well at York University and who had got into the City by answering an advertisement in the *Daily Telegraph*. He became an equity salesman, built up a good client base amongst American institutions at Hoare Govett and developed a New York office for them. Collier had a good understanding of trading and was reckoned 'to read the stock markets like the bottom of his glass'.[18] He worked for Vickers in New York using risk capital for American clients who did not like the British 'agency' broking system. At Morgan Grenfell he was responsible for the international and trading side of the securities business. Holmes concentrated on UK sales and research.

Between September 1985 and the closure three years later, nearly 300 recruits were hired, doubling the existing Pember & Boyle and Pinchin Denny base to around 500. Holmes wanted the research to be 'disciplined, controlled and customer friendly' and some innovative products such as a quantitative stock selection system, known as Value and Momentum, were sent out to clients.

The early days were very invigorating and have been described by one employee as 'a wonderful atmosphere to work in. Everyone felt as though they were living a bit of history, were at the cutting edge. We had people from every background, it didn't matter. Black, white or Chinese, grammar school, secondary modern or Eton, everyone got on.'[19]

There was a setback in November 1986 when Geoffrey Collier was caught trading for his personal account using inside information and he was later tried and convicted.[20] Collier had been staying at Holmes' house and, when his host took an early morning shower, telephoned an order to deal in Associated Engineering when he knew that Morgan Grenfell Securities was about to do the same for Hollis Group, a corporate client. Holmes was not involved in the trades and tried to rally the staff: 'I was told on the Tuesday. I was stunned. There was tremendous shock amongst the staff but they were very robust about it. I phoned as many of them as I could in person over the next two weeks to talk things through.'[21]

The Collier and Guinness episodes damaged Morgan Grenfell's

reputation and weakened its management. Yet, in spite of all this, expansion went on, and in December 1986 agreement was reached to acquire C. J. Lawrence & Co., a mid-ranking US securities firm, for $70 million, soon followed by a securities licence in Japan. During 1987, at least up to the Crash, the firm made good progress in its target area, UK equities. In the 1987 Extel survey its research achieved a respectable mid-table consensus ranking of 'fair' and it had a market share in the 2–3 per cent region. Profits of £14 million were made up to the Crash but there was a big exposure to small illiquid companies and around £20 million was lost in the final quarter of 1987.

In 1988 the market making war hit fringe players like Morgan Grenfell very hard. Total losses for 1988 were £18 million in equities and revenues were only about halfway to covering costs of £40 million. But, according to John Craven, it was the trend that was the most worrying aspect: 'The situation deteriorated very sharply indeed from the last week of August onwards.'[22] At the interim stage, the losses were described as 'containable' at £5 million in equities and July and most of August were break even. However, £13 million was lost in September, October and November – £1 million per week. Annualizing this figure and projecting it into 1989, it is easy to see how Craven came to the conclusion that 'A small firm like Morgan Grenfell is not well positioned to stand it.'

On vacation in 1988, Craven decided, 'This business is not going to survive. If we stick with it, it's going to bleed us absolutely dry. And therefore we have to get out of the securities business altogether.' At around this time, in August 1988, their wives out of London, Craven and Holmes spent an evening together having dinner. Over a glass of wine, Holmes told Craven, 'I don't think you really want to be in this business.' Craven was equivocal but Holmes felt that body language and the look in his eyes were very revealing and urged that, whatever decision was taken, it should be done quickly. A strategy review was carried out and it was predicted that the losses would continue until the market turned, projected to happen in 1991. Holmes believes that this gloomy forecast was as important as the ongoing losses in the decision to close.

There followed a process which has since become well-rehearsed throughout the City: preparation of the P45s, organization of outplacement, press releases, handling customers, timing the move for a Friday. In the event, a press leak required an emergency announcement whereby nearly all the staff were sent home and recalled by telephone over the next few days to be told of their terms and outplacement. The closure cost 450 jobs and £37.7 million. The average redundancy payment was £25,000. Craven later learned that 82 per cent of those laid off had been re-employed in the City, that 15 per cent had been employed outside the City and that only 3 per cent had remained unemployed.[23] Craven had founded Phoenix Securities and it is ironic that the man who had put together most of the mergers between banks and brokers should be one of the first to take the decision to reverse the strategy.[24]

Craven believed that the organic growth strategy never had a chance of success: 'But by the time they got around to making up their minds what to do, all the desirable blondes had gone! They ended up buying jobbers Pinchin & Denny, a good firm but only number five or six in terms of size, and brokers Pember & Boyle, which was really a gilt broker and not an equity broker – and equity broking was what it was all about.'[25] Another broker commented, 'To take a zero market share and build a meaningful business was frankly a hell of an uphill task which I don't think that anybody could have achieved.'[26] The hoped-for synergies never occurred: 'Clients of Morgan Grenfell's thriving corporate finance department rarely entrusted the distribution of their new paper to the bank's broking side because, with only a 3 per cent share of the market, it lacked clout.'[27]

OPPORTUNISM

Three merchant banks, Barings, Flemings and Schroders, had gone into broking quietly enough for occasional periods of retrenchment not to matter and both Schroders and Flemings drew in their horns when market conditions got tough after the Crash. Barings continued to pursue an opportunistic trading policy, looking for immediate profits rather than pursuing long-term synergistic goals. Its securities business remained isolated from the rest of the group and drifted into increasingly dangerous areas. Despite the introduction of more discipline and record keeping after Ian Martin was appointed finance director in September 1987, controls were far below what was required for a business as complex and diverse as Baring Securities was running.

Barings' results stand out as being the mirror image of most merchant banks' experience. Whereas its competitors suffered losses in securities but were rescued by corporate finance, Barings' banking and corporate finance profits for the year ending in September 1988 were only £1 million after losing £9 million on its BP underwriting but Baring Securities made £27 million, nearly all from trading warrants, a highly volatile derivative. For the rest of this period, Barings increased profits by expanding into more esoteric areas, opening a futures and options trading business in Japan and Singapore in 1989.

Profits became harder to deliver as the US banks moved into Asia and Japan. With experience in the larger, better established US derivatives markets, they possessed superior risk management and distribution and ate into the margins and market share of regional brokers such as Barings. 'It had been forced to hunt outside Japan for earnings, expanding to Bangkok, Kuala Lumpur, Jakarta, Korea, Manila and Taipei, and now its best bet appeared to lie in repeating in Asia in the 1990s what it had done in Japan in the 1980s.'[28]

By 1988 it had become a large company with 560 employees. It became a member of the Tokyo Stock Exchange in June 1988, attempting to seize the old Vickers da Costa leadership position which was being eroded under Citicorp's management. The character of the company had changed from the small entrepreneurial business started by Christopher Heath into a geographically diverse, risk-taking enterprise but the management infrastructure did not keep up with these developments.

CONCLUSION

In some respects the merchant banks performed better than the clearers during the period after the Crash. They were better managed, more united behind their strategies and more realistic about what they could achieve. Warburg in particular used its financial strength and resilient profits to strive for a position alongside the global investment banks.

Kleinwort narrowed its business spread in an effort to cut costs and improve focus and made a lot of progress as an integrated investment bank over the period.

Despite these successes, the merchant banks as a group had two high-profile failures. Indirectly, equities caused Hill Samuel's fall. It was clear that the bank lacked the scale and the deal flow from corporate finance to succeed in its investment banking strategy. Arbitrageurs would not have been able to alight on it if Hill Samuel had gone the advisory route followed by Lazards and Rothschild. Equities were also a factor in Morgan Grenfell's downfall. The bank might have survived the Guinness scandal if it had been advisory only but the double blow of Guinness and the ignominious retreat from equities fatally damaged management's credibility.

Amongst the smaller banks, Barings drifted into more exotic areas as its original markets matured and Schroders and Flemings quietly reduced their commitment to equities. They had survived but were no nearer realizing any strategic benefits. By the end of 1989, all of the merchant banks had learned that investment banking was harder than it had looked and required more resources than they had ever imagined.

15

The Independents

The tough competitive environment and volatility of markets immediately after Big Bang provided a serious challenge to Smith New Court and Cazenove, the two significant independent broking firms. It was expected that the absence of a large parent company would leave them exposed and that they might not survive. In fact both firms traded profitably over the Crash and showed commitment to their staff and clients. Favourable comparisons were made with the chaos at some of the bigger brokers and Smith and Cazenove ended the 1980s in strong positions.

Ironically, given the general expectation that access to capital was essential to survive, the reasons for the independents' success have much to do with their lack of resources. The need to remain profitable to survive helped to create a business focus. With limited capital they had to monitor risk very closely. This contrasted with the big banks where capital was so readily available that it was treated almost casually and not as a scarce resource. As a consequence the big banks were inclined to run risk positions in the hope that they would come right whereas Smith and Cazenove had to be more disciplined to protect their balance sheets. The same was true in international expansion where the controlled growth strategies of the independents proved more sensible than the aggressive approach of many of the bigger firms.

SMITH NEW COURT

Smith New Court's strategy was to transform a UK-based market maker into an integrated sales, trading and research firm with international reach. Initially the process was led by the chairman, Tony Lewis: 'In management terms, the plc board was a joke. The company was a personal fiefdom run by Tony Lewis, the chairman', a former Smith New Court director commented.[1] In 1986 Lewis recognized the need to broaden the management team and promoted Michael Marks to chief executive.

Marks is a bright and breezy man, but with a serious undercurrent when discussing business. He left St Paul's School, London, after the sixth form: 'It was payback time. My mother had been widowed when I was two and I wanted to put something back into the family.'[2] He joined Smith Brothers (where a cousin was senior partner) in 1959, worked his way up from office boy to red button at the Stock Exchange (red buttons worked under the Stock Exchange floor matching up bargains between broker and jobber) to blue button, running messages on the floor, to become a senior dealer and a partner of Smith Brothers in 1969.

As chief executive, Marks had the task of making the new strategy work by integrating sales, trading and research into 'a balanced, three-pronged approach'.[3] This involved changing the business balance and customer profile of the firm and to begin with the process of building sales and research did not go well:

1986 and most of 1987 were particularly difficult. We questioned whether we had done the right thing. It was almost impossible to hire, the market was roaring and we were regarded as being too small and lacking in capital. Everyone wanted to work for the big firms. Two things changed it: the Crash and hiring Paul Roy. The Crash was very lucky for us. It exposed the cracks that were there in the big firms. On Black Monday we took two decisions: we would cut our positions and we would be there for the clients. We had a record loss on the Monday, our biggest ever, but we slashed the balance sheet and were in profit by the end of the week. In the next few months we did a big market share, built our credibility with the institutions and that helped us attract some good people.[4]

Marks, however, recognized that senior management with experience of running agency research and sales was called for if Smith was to press home its new found advantage: 'Meeting Paul Roy was fortuitous. I was approached by Citibank to run global risk for their equities business, turned them down but was enormously impressed by Paul who was running their agency side. I invited him for a drink, told him I wasn't interested in moving but that I thought he should come and work for us.'[5] Marks and Roy then combined their trading and agency backgrounds to form a close and complementary team and set to work building the new firm.

Big Bang had got off to an embarrassing start for Smith:

27 October 1986 stands out as the day we realized we had made a dreadful mistake. We were seduced by our old chums who told us that the electronic age would never come, that brokers and jobbers would always want to look one another in the eye. They were really talking their own book, hoping that things wouldn't change but we believed them and decided to stay on the old market floor. By 11 a.m. on the first day we knew we were wrong. It was like a ghost town. All the brokers maintained a presence there but the jobbers had moved off and the brokers couldn't deal in a one-firm market so were having to nip off to phone Akroyd or Wedd in their smart new trading rooms. We stayed on the floor for a few months but began to build a new trading room at once and moved up there as soon as we were able.[6]

Initially Smith drew a line between its market making and sales businesses, the latter trading as 'Smith New Court Agency' to remind clients of its independence. This was reinforced in the 1987 accounts: 'It is definitely not an extension of the market making operation.'[7] The former managing director of UK broking, Ken Taylor, describes the agency perspective:

It took a long time for an understanding of the new world to work its way through Smith New Court. Market making continued to cultivate third party business to the annoyance of Smith New Court Agency. Capel and Cazenove were the traditional clients of Smith Brothers and it took them a long time to trust us as much. We used to get very upset if our own market makers called Capel or Caz before they called us and this happened a lot in the early days.[8]

After Paul Roy joined and sales and research were strengthened by hiring, the integration was improved and internal friction diminished. As the institutions became more comfortable with dual capacity, Smith began to acknowledge the connection in its own business and to turn it to its advantage, claiming in 1988 that 'the power of Smith New Court's market making arm has allowed the Agency side to grow through performance. Smith New Court is usually one of the top three market makers in any UK equity in which it trades, offering large lines of stock at very keen prices.'[9] The firm began to see itself as integrated and management encouraged this: 'We never distinguished between trading revenues or commission. We didn't care if the order was won by a salesman, an analyst or a trader, in fact usually it would be a combination anyway. As management we never looked at whether it was commission or trading income.'[10]

The strategy began to pay off and customer perception improved. Although Smith was primarily known as a trading house, research under Mike Unsworth began to rise in the rankings, working its way into the top ten of the Extel survey and reaching eighth position in 1989. The combination of trading skills and improving sales and research won Smith a large share of institutional business. When Scott Goff joined Smith in 1986, Marks made a speech of welcome. Referring to the market share then of 1.5 per cent, he hoped that it would be treble that within two years and, although this hope proved optimistic, market share had moved through 5 per cent by 1990.

With the UK strategy underway, Smith slowly developed an international business. It was one of the few London firms with international experience. It had always traded South African gold mining shares and Marks himself had spent a period working on the floor of the Johannesburg Stock Exchange. This background meant that the firm was internationally minded and it became a member of the Hong Kong Stock Exchange in 1986 and placed Asian equity teams in London, Tokyo, New York and Singapore. A branch office was opened in Tokyo. The firm joined the Melbourne Stock Exchange in 1986.

Smith New Court Europe was launched on 1 July 1987 and a sales, trading and research team centred in London was built up. Carl Marks & Co., an American firm specializing in trading foreign equities for US institutions and brokers, was bought in 1987–8. By the end of the period a rudimentary global framework was in place.

HOW DID SMITH DO IT?

Smith's profits record between 1986 and 1995 shows that the firm had to survive a real crisis in the year to April 1989 when the UK market making war produced a pre-tax loss of £12.6 million: 'The damage was done during November and December when equity markets were volatile, almost hysterical, and destructive competitive pressures within the market made it impossible for a committed market maker to trade profitably.'[11] This was a critical period for Smith and it would have been lucky to survive another year like it. In the event, profitability returned in January, helped by Stock Exchange rule changes making it more difficult for market makers to adopt spoiling tactics when competitors had big positions.[12] Smith was past its crisis and 1989–90 saw record profits.

Smith's story in the years to 1990 confirms the lesson to be drawn from the purchases by BZW of Wedd and by Warburg of Akroyd that market making was the critical element in an integrated broker:

Table 9. Smith New Court Results, 1986–95

Year ending April	1986	1987	1988	1989	1990	1991	1992	1993	1994	199
Pre-tax profits, £ million	6.2	10.3	7.6*	(12.6)	15.1	7.5	18.4	38.7	95.2	3
Staff costs £ million	13.5	32.7	47.0	49.3	53.4	57.7	68.1	93.9	134.2	9
Staff numbers	252	618	937	1074	1049	1144	1168	1199	1293	149

*After BP underwriting loss £8.5 million.

It is widely argued that in the post-1986 deregulated market, institutional placing power, the traditional preserve of the merchant banking and stock-broking community would be paramount. This has not proved to be the case. It is increasingly clear that the methods of the old London market, and the skills of market makers in evaluating risk and in trading on their own account are best suited to the demands of world wide risk assessment and management.[13]

To begin with, the traditional style of informal risk control was maintained, drawing favourable comment from the *Financial Times* which noted the absence 'of formal position limits and risk parameters. Instead Smith's directors control the firm's exposure to the equity market by spending most of their day on the trading floor, watching deals and market movements and shouting instructions.'[14] As the firm expanded, risk management had to cover the overseas locations. This was centred into New York and Hong Kong enabling Smith to 'react swiftly to any sudden change in market positions'.[15]

At the beginning of Big Bang, the general expectation was that Smith's lack of capital would be a handicap. In fact its comparative lack of capital helped to promote focus. Marks believed that 'an excess of capital is as dangerous as a lack of it' and uses the example of the failed BP underwriting of 1987 to illustrate the point:

The share price collapsed below our underwriting price and we cut our position within half an hour. We had to. We couldn't take the chance of a further collapse given our capital position and, in any case, we wanted to be in a position where we could trade with clients and accommodate them and not be worried by a huge existing position. We always prefer to make £100 of profit by making a £10 profit ten times over than by getting one windfall of £100. The next day we were summoned round to Rothschilds by Evelyn, who was troubled by his BP holding, and he asked us what we were going to do with ours. We told him we didn't understand the question; ours had already gone. Now, if we had had lots of capital, we might have been tempted to run the position and got into all sorts of trouble.[16]

The secret was to have just enough but not too much capital and a stable core shareholding group.[17] By 1990 Rothschilds owned 36 per cent, 3i 6 per cent and Carl Marks 8 per cent, taking the combined total up to 49.6 per cent. This avoided the risk that the company might feel it was living a hand-to-mouth existence and gave it the confidence to leverage its capital on occasions to participate in some of the market's major bought deals.

Independence encouraged focus and decisiveness: 'It is the only publicly quoted British securities house concentrating on equities. This goes to the very root of our independent character, because it means we are not subject to the many constraints of decision or of action which inevitably result from being part of a wider financial services group . . . In concentrating on doing the business we know best, Smith New Court readily acknowledges it is a niche player.'[18]

It stuck to its plan with great conviction: 'our capital is wholly devoted towards our equity securities business and related equity products'.[19] The Chairman contrasted the commitment of Smith New Court and some of its more recent competitors: 'Many securities firms have reassessed their commitment to the London market as a result of substantial losses and a changed perception of the volume of present and future trading . . . We have not allowed the changed conditions of the second half of the year to deflect us from our long-term aims.'[20]

High morale was a 'natural consequence of remaining an independent house . . . Unlike many of its competitors in Britain and the US, Smith New Court has had to earn its institutional relationships on its merits as an independent operator.' Although the increase in staff numbers led to 'the more rigorous management structure required by a larger organization',[21] Smith came closest of the major firms to being able to sustain its culture through personal loyalty. It was able to foster a spirit of independence and to build up a reputation of being the little guy standing up to the global bullies. This enabled it to achieve good results in recruitment and staff retention.

CAZENOVE'S CHOICE

In theory Cazenove had much to fear from Big Bang. The institutional and corporate finance sides of its business faced cyclical and structural challenge. As an agency broker, it was exposed to the halving in commission rates. Before Big Bang, with all the talk of integration between jobbers and brokers, some market professionals believed that the new dual capacity firms would not make competitive prices to agency brokers. In corporate finance, there was a risk that the role of independent corporate broker would disappear, being subsumed into joint appointments of merchant bank and broker combined. As late as April 1988, the *Evening Standard* ran a headline: 'Cazenove's choice: a slow death or integration.'

Before Big Bang the firm had decided to build deeper relationships with its corporate and institutional clients. Building on the loyalty of these clients, drawing on the strengths of partnership and, like Smith New Court, turning a limited capital base to its own advantage by remaining focused, Cazenove negotiated the post-Big Bang years very safely. However, in addition to the problems of coping with the new market structure, 1986 and 1987 presented two challenges in the form of the Crash and the Guinness affair.

The Guinness affair had the potential to jeopardize Cazenove's client relationships in the way that Blue Arrow did for County NatWest. In the opening months of 1986 Argyll and Guinness fought for control of Distillers Company. Cazenove had become joint brokers to Guinness in 1985 at the time of its successful bid for Arthur Bell and it worked with Morgan Grenfell and Wood Mackenzie again on the Distillers bid. It was a close contest with aggressive tactics being employed in public relations, shareholder meetings and stock market activity. When the American arbitrageur, Ivan Boesky, was questioned in the US in 1986 in respect of insider dealing offences, allegations were made about a share support operation by Guinness's advisers in the UK.

In April 1988 a Cazenove partner, David Mayhew, was amongst seven people arrested in connection with the affair, and he was subsequently charged with four offences relating to the acquisition of 10.6 million shares in Distillers by a subsidiary or a client of Bank Leu of

Switzerland. Although Mayhew was ultimately acquitted, the affair dragged on for several years but Cazenove's response was decisive, rigorous and public:

As soon as we became aware of the allegations of wrong-doing in connection with the bid for Distillers, we started our own internal investigation. On 15 December 1986 we appointed Simmons & Simmons as our solicitors in these matters . . . nothing in their enquiries has led them to believe that Cazenove was involved in or aware of any illegality. In the light of subsequent events and speculation, it would have been better if Cazenove had not relied on the assurances it received that there was no association between Guinness and Schenley Industries Inc., for whom Cazenove had bought shares in Guinness and Distillers, but had made its own enquiries of Schenley. We were pleased but not surprised by the first conclusion and, although we have always conducted our business in the City on the basis of trust, we accept the second.[22]

This response ensured that the Guinness affair did minimal damage to the firm. It was probably excluded from the BP sale in 1987 on account of the uncertainty regarding the Guinness affair, but even this proved to be a blessing in disguise since the issue flopped. Most of the firm's clients believed Cazenove's version of events and admired the way in which the partnership stood by Mayhew; the firm's reputation may even have been enhanced as a result.

One disadvantage of the affair was that Mayhew was distracted from the firm's business for a long period, spending several hours a day with lawyers. Mayhew is the leading corporate broker in London, valued by chief executives as an impeccable judge of market tactics and likely institutional reaction in share offerings. Until 1986 he had worked from Cazenove's institutional sales desk but then moved behind the Chinese wall to set up a syndicate team. He is in his late fifties, wiry, a cigarette smoker and speaks in a clipped, upper-class accent. He combines this with a delightfully irreverent attitude which he throws into conversations at unexpected moments. He is charming and tough in equal measure; a fearsome adversary and powerful ally, the partial loss of his services for two years was a serious handicap for Cazenove.

Cazenove survived the second unexpected challenge, the Crash, with equanimity. As an agency broker, it was free of large risk positions and traded profitably despite some losses from market making in small brokership stocks. The firm made a point of maintaining client contact no matter how difficult market conditions appeared: 'John Kemp-Welch got all the salespeople together in a back room and told us to keep on the phones, to keep telling the clients what was happening. It was good advice and won us a lot of friends.'[23]

Like Smith New Court, the firm believes that it benefited from the Crash: 'My overriding memory of the Crash was of the preceding months. There was mass hiring, wage inflation and the shape of the market was changing so that capital was becoming king. It was a very worrying period. But the Crash brought it all to a shuddering halt and actually helped us. We seemed a safe haven.'[24]

Cazenove had taken outside advice during its preparations for Big Bang in November 1983 through the consulting arm of Spicer & Pegler, and following the Guinness affair and the Crash they were brought back in to do a further review. Chinese walls were strengthened, research for the institutions was separated from research for corporate finance, and Mayhew's syndicate department was set up. There was no need for redundancies and the firm grew steadily from 488 in October 1986 in London to 620 by June 1991 and overseas from 74 to 116. The partnership grew from 36 to 54 over the same period. The ability to remain on a steady growth trend came in part from the broad balance of Cazenove's business, especially from the more diversified activities in money broking and fund management. Funds under management grew from £2.8 billion at end 1986 to £5.8 billion in June 1991 with a broad spread including unit trusts, charities, pension funds as well as private clients.

Along with James Capel, Cazenove proved that agency broking on a large scale was viable. Its research department was built up to cover the larger companies as well as brokership stocks and market making was carried out in small companies and investment trusts.[25] Modest overseas expansion occurred through a number of small representative offices in Asia, opening in Kuala Lumpur in 1990 and Singapore in 1991. The New York office remained focused on foreign equities. A longstanding South African representation was maintained. The firm joined the Australian Stock Exchange in 1987. Europe was covered out of London and the firm's connections won some corporate finance business there.

The second half of the 1980s were buoyant years for corporate finance activity in London. Cazenove was able to retain its corporate broking clients as there was little appetite amongst corporate clients for appointing integrated banks and brokers to both positions. Indeed, Cazenove's stability stood out amongst the chaos that surrounded many of its competitors and it looked a better and better choice for chief executives in this period. In 1989 it was involved in a string of rights issues including those for BICC, Enterprise Oil, Lasmo, Pearson and Reuters. It was involved in defending Consolidated Gold against Minorco, BAT against Hoylake and Rowntree against Nestlé. Apart from missing out on BP at the height of the Guinness scandal, it was involved in all the major privatisations such as British Gas in November 1986 and the water companies at the end of the period. The corporate finance revenues played an important part in maintaining Cazenove's profile as a firm that had to be listened to and in protecting profits from the worst ravages of the commission squeeze and volatile markets.

POSITION OF INDEPENDENTS, 1990

During this testing period in the market between 1986 and 1990 the combination of the strength of the existing business and judicious development ensured that Smith and Cazenove fared better than most. They entered 1990 in a strong position. They had shown that they could survive the most adverse market conditions that most working brokers of the day had experienced, which improved their credibility with staff and clients. The process of digging deep and succeeding against the odds had created a strong camaraderie which, in the case of Cazenove, was reinforced by the bonds of partnership. Smith was not a partnership but it was a very close company and during my interview with Michael Marks he often referred to his colleagues from Smith as 'my former partners'; it is clear that the partnership spirit had also existed there.

Smith and Cazenove had succeeded by focus. The fact that they did not have enormous capital resources to bale them out of trouble helped to prevent them from overreaching. Risk was carefully monitored and controlled. Expansion was moderate and was for achievable business reasons rather than being undertaken as a pleasant diversion from the problems of the existing business. Both firms had established themselves as viable, well-run businesses that had adapted well to the new world.

16

The Foreign Banks

As the shape of the new market emerged, the foreign banks became less of an amorphous invading army and it became possible to identify groups pursuing distinct strategies. It also became clear that events in their home market were as relevant to the UK strategies of the foreign banks and brokers as to what was occurring in London.

There were three non-European groups trying to build broking in London: the American commercial banks who had proceeded by acquisition, notably Security Pacific, Citicorp and Chase Manhattan; the American investment banks such as Goldman, Morgan Stanley and Merrill Lynch; and the Japanese. The American investment banks divided into two groups, one chasing a trading strategy, the other putting corporate finance first. The Japanese were discouraged by the Bank of England from buying brokers and so tried to build full service brokers on the traditional British model.[1]

Between 1986 and 1990 the resolve of the American commercial banks was tested by the Crash and the growing pains of the new system in London and most of them retreated. Whilst the Japanese enjoyed a favourable domestic market for a few more years, they panicked and failed to press home a moment of advantage. For the US investment banks, a sudden downward shift in profitability on Wall Street made them much less expansionary than they had been. During the first half of the 1980s the large US investment banks had earned a return on equity ranging from 31 to 57 per cent. With inflation tumbling to below 4 per cent this represented an attractive real return. In 1987 the Crash took the return earned by the large investment banks down to 9 per cent. It recovered to 18 per cent in 1988 and dropped back to 9 per cent again in 1989. Numbers employed, having risen steadily to over 38,000 in 1987, went into retreat, slipping to 33,451 in 1988 and 32,057 in 1989.[2] Against this background the expansion strategies in London were vulnerable. World markets were thought to be entering a more bearish phase and confidence waned. Cost control became more important than ambitious plans for revenues and loss-making foreign operations came under the microscope.

SECONDARY

The leading American investment banks saw secondary equities purely as a support for corporate finance. They put most of their efforts into winning business from corporates and regarded stockbroking as a means of executing that business, not as a means of winning it. Their equities teams needed to be good enough to distribute primary offerings and give research support to corporate finance but they were not regarded as profit centres in their own right.

The strategy of organically growing equities in support of corporate finance was pursued by Goldman Sachs and Morgan Stanley. Goldman set up in London in 1969 but, as late as the early 1980s, the London operation was still not seen as being very important.[3] Then in the mid 1980s, as corporate finance activity in the UK picked up, Goldman and other American firms saw an opportunity big enough to send over some of their star investment bankers. Equities businesses were assembled to support the emerging corporate finance teams.

Drawing on long experience of contested takeovers in the US, particularly after the upsurge of mergers on Wall Street in the late 1980s, the American investment banks were able to bring new tactics and a different, more intensive work ethic. Initially they worked alongside or junior to the traditional merchant banks but they used this position to impress and to build relationships.

Goldman was in the top ten M&A league tables by 1987 and the strategy of building a broad investment bank in London was gradually stepped up. The proportion of British staff rose and the firm looked more like a top quality bank than a collection of expatriates enjoying a few years in London. Goldman was a successful recruiter of top quality British graduates and it tried to hire the highest calibre of the next generation from competitors. The firm set new standards in the thoroughness of staff selection, subjecting candidates to previously unheard of layers of interviews, and involving a generous quota of senior management in the process.

The equities business had a comparatively low profile build but it was always with a focus on quality people and a prominent role for Gavyn Davies and David Morrison, the strategy and economics team. Trading was selective in terms of the times and places when capital was committed but was punchy on the very big deals. By 1990 Goldman had established a presence in the secondary market, a leading position in UK corporate finance and topped the cross-border league tables. It was also developing strongly in Continental Europe from the London base.

Morgan Stanley applied to join the London Stock Exchange in September 1986 and appeared to be set on an organic growth strategy. In 1987, however, before the Crash, it tried unsuccessfully to buy Greenwell Montagu Securities from Midland Bank. Midland's rejection of this approach caused a number of senior Greenwell staff to leave, including the head of equities and banking research guru, Keith Brown, who joined Morgan Stanley. Having flirted with acquisition, the firm returned to its organic strategy. From Stock Exchange memberships in London, Zurich, Frankfurt and Tokyo it sought to build a position of domestic strength and then develop cross-border flows. It began market making in the summer of 1987 in London, beginning with around twenty blue chip companies and gradually built up a sales trading and research staff.

Keith Brown joined Morgan Stanley in February 1988 and was initially struck by the quality of the people and the operation:

I realized what a lot of rank amateurs we and the rest of the UK houses were. Morgan Stanley had a tradition of investment banking, built up over a long period. Investment banking was a core and a serious part of their business. They understood equity markets, how to operate in a free market and above all how to approach the corporate sector. They understood the value of financial disciplines and how to reward and evaluate staff. They followed a pan-European approach and understood that events in one market can influence another. They were about the first to do this in London.[4]

In January 1989, John Holmes moved to Morgan Stanley after the closure of Morgan Grenfell Securities. He was responsible for the team selling international equities outside Japan and the US and remembers that it was quite small-scale, a team of ten to twelve selling to the UK and Europe: 'There was great attention to detail. The compliance culture was strong, so was cost control. The focus was totally on investment banking, not just securities. The quality was excellent. I looked around the office and thought, They're all good.'[5]

LEADING WITH THE BALANCE SHEET

Whilst the other large US firms shared the objective of Goldman and Morgan Stanley in building an all-round investment bank, they did not all have the strength in primary markets to lead with corporate finance. Therefore they put more emphasis on trading to create a broking business and tried to migrate into broader investment banking from the late 1980s. Merrill Lynch and Salomon were the leading firms in this group.

Merrill Lynch had a team in London selling US equities in the early 1980s. The expansion into Europe was by Lechner's recruiting efforts in research and supplemented by aggressive use of capital to win institutional broking orders. The international trading team was headed by Jim O'Donnell and it faced a tough time initially: 'The head traders at the clients in London wouldn't take a call from Americans. Eventually I told one of them, "Thanks a bunch. I've just been fired and I'm on my way back to the US." A huge order came in that afternoon and we've been friends ever since.'[6] At this stage the culture at Merrill Lynch was still very American, with no real understanding of international integration. In 1986, the London international team was getting no accounting credit for its revenues. These were being credited to the US business and to domestic US salesmen for bonuses. At one stage New York management wanted to retrench in London because, on this accounting basis, international business in London was not profitable. These political issues and misunderstandings made some of the American firms frustrating places to work in and, as this reputation spread, the initial glamour of working for the US investment banks was replaced by a more cynical attitude.

This was fuelled by periodic cutbacks on their London operations when profits at home came under pressure and the US investment banks were tainted with a 'hire and fire' reputation. The closure of Drexel Burnham Lambert's business in London in May 1989 was a major contributor to this. Jim O'Donnell had moved from Merrill Lynch and by January 1988 was running international sales and trading for Drexel:

During 1988 we hired quite a few analysts, for example, Nick Knight, to do strategy. We moved a number one ranked US analyst from New York to run research. We were buying and selling some very big blocks to get in with the clients using lots of capital. We had no formal limits or risk controls. We were doing huge business. Then in May 1989 I got a sudden phone call to take the next Concorde to New York. They told me that the firm faced a crisis and was reducing from over 10,000 employees to 5000. All overseas offices would be closed and I would have to fire everyone in London. By the time I got back word had spread. The head of research who was due to help me disappeared for the day so I did it all on my own, eighty to a hundred people, I guess. It was devastating. That was a sad day.[7]

Salomon had started an aggressive hiring programme in London in 1985 and 1986, targeting top analysts and salesmen at the leading UK brokers and offering premium packages for those willing to join. Problems in New York brought the London expansion to a halt even before the market crash. Salomon's total headcount trebled to 6500 between 1982 and 1987 and rose by 40 per cent in 1986 alone in a globalization binge. Revenues suffered when the US bond markets turned in 1986 and the cost base was very exposed. In the middle of October 1987, 12 per cent of global staff were made redundant as part of a cost saving programme. Of the 800 jobs to go, 150 were in London and included salesmen and traders as well as back office staff.[8] Many of these had only just been hired and the episode was very damaging for the reputation of Salomon and the other American firms in London.

COMMERCIAL BANKS: THE SAME
THE WHOLE WORLD OVER

The poor performance of the American commercial banks in London showed that the British clearing banks did not have a monopoly on mismanaging brokers. The first of the American commercial banks to take a stake in a London broker was Security Pacific but its acquisition of Hoare Govett seemed at odds with the management style espoused by the chairman, which he characterized as 'crawling before they walk' and 'never betting the company.'[9] It was therefore not a surprise that they were amongst the first to flinch in the post-Big Bang storms, buffeted by losses in the Crash, the BP underwriting and the market making war.

Hoare Govett was particularly badly hit over the Crash: 'I remember the shock and the horror of it all vividly. Our risk position was so bad that people were scared to answer the phones for fear of getting an order that would make it worse. After the fall the natural instinct of the market makers was to buy, so they did and it fell again. We lost millions on the first day and it just got worse. People were stunned.'[10]

The Crash traumatized SecPac and broke the aura of success that had surrounded Hoare Govett:

It was chaos and the whole thing was quite beyond us. There was very little discipline in the market making side, they regularly broke their limits and argued that we didn't understand, that their business was different to ours. There was no sophisticated risk management, they were just punting. They never integrated with the rest of the firm, they sat in the same room but just did their own thing. Hoare Govett should never have gone into market making; we should have copied Cazenove and stayed agency, playing off the corporate list.[11]

There was a round of downsizing in the middle of 1988 and then, at the end of the year, the decision was taken to withdraw from gilts, Eurobonds and Japanese equities. SecPac's round of cuts drew a scathing comment from the Lex column: 'Yet another London broking firm expensively acquired and expanded is being more expensively reduced to less scope than it started with . . . each of the three shows signs of mismanagement as does the fact that all three were subjected to a half-hearted trimming six months before closure.'[12]

Although Hoare Govett's corporate broking franchise remained strong, the progress being made by Warburg and BZW meant that its position as London's leading broker before Big Bang had gone by the end of the 1980s. SecPac's obvious lack of comfort with broking spread to the staff: 'Once we worked with the SecPac people it was obvious they had no idea what they had bought. They knew very little of life outside California, let alone about investment banking.'[13] A director of Hoare Govett formed a similar view:

SecPac did not have a clue. We were sent a relative of the chairman to look after us. The more they saw the less they liked. We got left with some BP underwriting and SecPac came rushing over wanting to see the minutes of the risk committee and to understand how we had decided to take the position. Richard Westmacott, our senior partner, told them that he had taken the decision and that's the way we did things. We were rather arrogant in hoping for all the capital we wanted and none of the interference. They had problems of their own in America and clearly wanted rid of us.[14]

In 1989 discussions began with a view to the staff of Hoare Govett taking a stake in the company. The other American commercial banks went through a similar experience to SecPac with their London broking firms. Chase Manhattan had bought two brokers, Laurie, Milbank and Simon & Coates. In January 1989 it closed its entire equities operations with the loss of 135 jobs. A greater shock came with the effective closure by Citicorp of Scrimgeour Vickers in January 1990 with the loss of 215 jobs.

Scrimgeour Kemp Gee had been, with James Capel, the leading institutional broker in the run up to Big Bang. Its aggressive business methods had earned it the nickname of 'Scrimgeour Ramp Gee' and it was widely regarded as being ideally suited to the new environment. But its lack of risk trading skills meant that the prowess of institutional sales and research simply brought in business on which the firm lost money through market making. In 1988, after Smith New Court head-hunted Paul Roy from Scrimgeour Vickers, Citicorp brought in

Nick Whitney and Ian McLean to run the London broker. Whitney had been very successful as head of research at Warburg and McLean had been head of sales at County NatWest until he resigned when Tim Ferguson was made chief executive there.

Initially Whitney and McLean were given three years to get the business back into profit: 'But we were culturally unprepared for the politics. People would tell you what you wanted to hear even if they never intended to deliver.'[15] The most pressing problem was the level of losses, which were running at over £1 million per month in 1989. Infrastructure spend over Big Bang had not been written off as incurred but had been capitalized, saddling the business with a large depreciation charge: 'We had to treble revenues to get a profit. We weren't allowed to pay bonuses until we made profits so we couldn't hire or retain staff. Citicorp wouldn't let us move or change the accounting policy. They had bought the firm for £120 million, invested a lot, and then lost £30 million in 1987 and 1988, or more like £50 million on a proper accounting basis.'[16]

When it came, the end was sudden. John McFarlane, the bank's senior man in London, asked the management team one day, 'Should we close?' Whitney was worried about the write-off Citicorp would incur, but could see no other way out. McFarlane said he would talk to New York. The next thing Whitney knew was when, after a few weeks, in which the matter was not discussed with him again, a closure team arrived from New York. The decision had been taken in New York with minimal input from British management and was very damaging to the reputation of American banks amongst the broking community in London.

THE JAPANESE WALL OF MONEY THEORY

The leading Japanese brokers followed the American investment banks in a building strategy in equities but there was more emphasis on the secondary business than on corporate finance. Coming into Big Bang, Nomura seemed certain to be one of the leading firms. As the largest of Japan's Big Four, it would be well placed to capitalize on the expected flood of Japanese money: 'The Japanese investor's appetite for foreign securities is increasing and is becoming more catholic. For cultural and legal reasons there is a large lagged demand for foreign securities and increasingly for foreign equities. This means that, almost irrespective of what happens to the Japanese economy, there is certain to be a growing flood of yen pouring into New York over the next few years.'[17]

Nomura stressed non-aggression and non-competition in London, arguing that its presence would increase the overall pie by more than the amount of market share it took. It signalled in 1987 that it was serious about building a broking business in London by registering as a market maker in UK equities. However, the Crash of 1987 caused it to slow down its overseas expansion at a time when the quick recovery of Japan gave Nomura an opportunity to press home an advantage: 'Japan's Big Four are suffering from an identity crisis abroad. Are they merely Japanese firms with international subsidiaries, or are they true global firms of the sort that America's Citicorp and Salomon Brothers have tried (unsuccessfully so far) to become? Like it or not they are stuck with being the first.'[18]

The other leading Japanese brokers, Nikko, Daiwa and Yamaichi, also began building up equities teams in London but none made much of an impact. They did not penetrate the inner circle of firms trusted by chief executives for corporate finance advice but had more success on the bond side where their strong balance sheets in the 1980s enabled them to bid competitively on large deals. The Japanese equity market was to a large degree rigged by the major Japanese brokers. Share prices moved with liquidity rather than investment fundamentals and so the brokers had little experience of a research-based, value-driven investment business. As the Japanese economy and Stock Market floundered they ceased to be a threat to London's leading brokers.

CONCLUSION

By the end of the 1980s the reputation of the foreign brokers in London had taken a step back. The overall climate in broking had changed from the super confidence of the first half of the decade to one where job security mattered. The periodic bouts of redundancy and the decisions by SecPac, Citicorp and Chase to abandon strategies they had started only three years earlier shocked the broking community. People became less willing to join the foreign brokers and demanded more of a premium for doing so. Clients also became more cynical about the promises of service that the Americans made.

The UK-owned brokers tried to make capital out of this. They spread the word that, whenever the going got tough, the foreign banks would retrench. Most analysts, salesmen and traders knew someone who had been hired on a big package and laid off shortly afterwards. Scare stories were spread about the foreign banks trying to wriggle out of contracts with employees. It became much easier to recruit from the Americans and the Japanese and, for a few years at least, to turn round staff who resigned to go to a foreign broker.

However, with complacency typical of the City of London at that time, brokers and corporate financiers wrote off all the overseas competition: 'We fail to see what the American firms add in UK situations but we're not complacent.' In corporate finance they were regarded as 'nothing more than high priced interlopers who produce a massive stream of impractical ideas that have no relevance to the UK market. I give them credit for making a lot of noise.'[19] Commentators failed to distinguish between those brokers likely to succeed and those who would retreat. They missed the fact that Goldman Sachs and Morgan Stanley had begun to grow sound businesses in London and to transplant the best of their domestic culture into Europe.

PART FOUR

THE GRAND OLD DUKE OF YORK, 1990–94

17

European Commercial Banks

The Grand Old Duke of York marched his men up to the top of the hill and then he marched them down again. The nursery rhyme was used in the City to describe interest rate changes but sums up the world economic and political environment of the early nineties. Anxiety was followed by euphoria as the Gulf crisis played out, euphoria was followed by anxiety as barriers tumbled in Eastern Europe. The UK was gripped by a stubborn recession and divided by a heated debate over Europe. The political landscape changed dramatically: Major for Thatcher, Smith for Kinnock after the Conservatives scraped home in 1992, and Blair for Smith after the latter's death in 1994. There was a similar pattern of change in the US with Clinton replacing Bush in 1992 and gridlock in an economy suffering from balance of trade problems and lingering recession.

Stock markets were nervous in 1990 but investors began to anticipate recovery in the US and UK from 1991. Encouraged by falling inflation and lower interest rates, equity markets in New York and London powered ahead until February 1994 when a sudden rise in US interest rates brought a correction.

London's brokers entered 1990 still in a state of shock. The optimism and vitality of the Big Bang years had given way to a collective anxiety about the state of their firms. Rumours of closure or redundancy swirled around all the commercial banks and some of the merchants, and all foreign firms, were treated with suspicion. No one regarded their job as safe. The new management teams that had taken over from the Big Bang generation were as yet unproven. Uncertainty filled the air; there seemed nothing people could rely on.

The UK broking industry lost £246 million in 1990 and 3000 jobs were lost, amounting to 12 per cent of the total. There was a glimmer of hope in 1991, when the industry earned a 10 per cent return on capital, but volatility in September 1992 around sterling's exit from the ERM drove Stock Exchange member firms back into loss. The UK brokers recovered in 1993, when Wall Street's boom spilled over into London and claims were made that it was 'a turning-point in the performance of the securities industry'.[1] Turnover and capital raising reached record levels and industry profits topped £1 billion to give a 20 per cent average return on capital.

In the belief that the corner had been turned, and with no option but to pay up if they wished to retain or recruit staff, management reached for the cheque book. By the fourth quarter of 1993, salary costs were 95 per cent above what they had been a year earlier. Average remuneration levels nearly doubled inside a year. Between the beginning of 1990 and the end of 1993 monthly expenditure in the UK broking industry increased from £197 to £347 million and average capital employed rose from £3.8 to £6.7 billion. The operational risks in running businesses on this scale were enormous. A year of depressed revenue would leave these huge costs exposed and jeopardize the existence of some of the parent companies. Such conditions occurred in 1994 when the turn in the interest rate cycle caused heavy falls in bond and equity markets. Inevitably, the London brokers returned to loss.

LOSSES AT THE CLEARERS

The UK clearers and UBS had a terrible time in investment banking in the early 1990s. Their equities businesses were in aggregate loss. They underperformed the other brokers, lost money when the others were in profit and reported the biggest losses when everyone else was in the red. The regular recurrence of losses sapped morale and confidence.

BZW's equities division lost £45 million in 1990, then won a short period of respite before dealing profits halved again in 1994. NatWest Securities lost about £100 million in 1990–91, reduced its losses in 1992, and turned in modest profits in 1993–4. At UBS the equities business was loss-making in 1990 and a senior executive calculated that, by then, adding up the purchase price of Phillips & Drew, capital expenditure including fitting out new offices at 100 Liverpool Street, Blue Arrow and accumulated operating losses, the cost of entry into London broking had been £400 million. In the next three years, equities broke even in 1991 and made modest profits in 1992 and 1993 but ran into losses again in 1994. James Capel had one good year, 1993.

The losses were causing real concern amongst the bankers and Lord Alexander, NatWest's chairman, articulated the private views of many of them early in 1991. When asked about equities at a press conference, he stated: 'This business must be profitable within a year or two if we are to remain in it. We are seeking a good return on capital within a short timescale. If we cannot get that we must out. We may be a bank but we are also a business.'[2]

Lord Alexander's comments provoked a mixed reaction. He was praised by some for laying it on the line to the City slickers but was criticized by people with first-hand experience of investment banking. Alexander did much more for NatWest than he is given credit for and was right to impose a target on the equities business. At the time, I was head of research at NatWest Securities. I believe it would have been much better to have called in the senior management and told us the facts rather than dropping a bombshell in public. As it was, the staff were very rattled and, although a bloody-minded will to succeed was created, the encouragement given to NatWest's competitors made our task of winning clients and retaining staff more difficult. Matters were not helped by a meeting between Alexander and the equities directors which was supposed to rebuild goodwill. In the face of persistent criticism from a number of directors, Alexander finally rounded on one, J. J. McNeill, in a manner learned during a lifetime at the Bar. No more questions were forthcoming and NatWest's equities directors were in no doubt how the group chairman regarded them or their business. Alexander left the room to a deafening silence and I wondered whether he thought he had had a good or a bad meeting.

BZW AND NATWEST: THE END OF THE GLOBAL
EQUITIES EXPERIMENTS

Howard Coates at BZW and Tim Ferguson at NatWest had one last tilt at building global equities business until the parent banks demanded action to reduce the losses. Coates had been head of equities since 1987 and had done a good job in the UK building customer profile and integrating market making. He failed to get support for a US broking acquisition but the collapse of Drexel Burnham Lambert early in 1990 meant that one of Wall Street's leading equity teams was available and BZW hired half, the rest moving to NatWest.

It was bound to take some time for BZW's new UK team to build up revenues and 1990 was expected to be a loss-making year in New York. However, the parent's willingness to stand this was changed by losses of £30 million in Japanese warrants and Barclays demanded action. BZW had only just been given its seat on the Tokyo Stock Exchange and it was judged less embarrassing to cut back in New York than in Japan. The recently assembled team was laid off but Coates disagreed with the policy, was moved sideways into corporate broking and was replaced by Jonathan Davie.

At NatWest, Ferguson also faced continuing losses and declining support from the parent bank. A NatWest board meeting late in 1990 heard Ferguson describe the improving customer reputation of the equities business and his plan to supplement secondary broking with state-of-the-art proprietary trading. About a third of the board, including Derek Wanless, later on to be in charge of NatWest's investment bank, and Ian MacLaurin, chairman of Tesco and a non-executive director of NatWest, argued against the retention of a full-scale equity investment bank. The chairman was ambivalent according to one director:

Alexander chaired the meeting scrupulously drawing out everyone's opinion, but had not given his own view when he went round the table asking for votes. By the end it was clear that there was a majority in favour of staying in the business and he said 'that's it then, we stay in'. Someone said, 'But we haven't had your view.' Alexander's reply was very cautious, negative and we could see that he was instinctively against an equity based investment banking strategy.[3]

With the 'support' of the board established, the business continued to develop under Ferguson but the appointment of John Drury, a little-known Australian oil trader, to manage equities and corporate finance was controversial. Ferguson found life under Drury intolerable. He bore the brunt of Drury's outbursts and was forced into actions he disagreed with, such as the closure of the Asian equities business in July 1991. By August most of the management team were ready to give up. Jim O'Donnell, the head of European equities, and I took Ferguson out to a bench in Exchange Square one sunny afternoon to tell him that we had had enough and intended to leave. He told us that he had beaten us to it and had already resigned. O'Donnell and I felt that it would be too much for the business to stand if we all left and, reluctantly, decided to stay on. Ferguson's departure was announced to the trading floor on an emotional occasion and he received a huge ovation. It was widely recognized within NatWest's equities division that Ferguson had carried out the first of the heroic rescue jobs after Big Bang. He was the first and most effective of a new breed of securities manager, a group who were as comfortable with risk management as agency broking, who liked detail as well as 'the big picture' and who thought globally as well as domestically.

TIME TO FOCUS

With Coates and Ferguson gone, the new management on the equities sides of BZW and NatWest each pursued a policy of focus, beginning with the elimination of loss-making areas. BZW's global equities cost base had trebled from £50 to £60 million in 1986 to 1990 and was budgeted to be £200 million in 1991. Davie cut about 10 per cent from headcount in 1991 and concentrated on growing revenues in three areas: 'One, derivatives: we already had some capability here, but decided to invest into that, to broaden capabilities and knowledge – a light cavalry approach, making sure that they could work across the underlying equity products. Two, we would continue to build our

South East Asian capabilities. Three, we would turn the New York office into one able to sell our international products into the US institutional client base.'[4]

Whilst it improved profits, Davie's approach marked a watershed for BZW: 'All aspirations to be a global equities business disappeared. It was clear that BZW would not be present in all parts of the world and this was a turning-point for the BZW experiment. From then on I never felt that we would be important enough to Barclays for them to stick with us.'[5]

At NatWest's investment bank, management changes came thick and fast in 1991–2. Derek Wanless took over briefly before being promoted to be chief executive of the NatWest group and then Martin Owen was given the task of creating NatWest Markets out of the group's diverse investment banking businesses.

Owen was the group treasurer, was reputed to have made his fortune building and selling a financial services company and spent his spare time working for the Salvation Army. He is Welsh, an enthusiast, has good intuition about people and situations and is very well organized. Although he is not an investment banker and was never accepted within that charmed circle, he made vigorous attempts to make Nat-West Markets work and came close to succeeding before it all blew up in his face. In his first three years as chief executive he tried to create an investment bank by melding together and developing the constituent parts, later resorting to acquisition when the organic growth strategy caused strain in the profit and loss account.

Martin Owen appointed me to run global equities in 1992. I had been head of research since 1989 and had helped to build up the UK research department to fourth position in the Extel survey, laying the foundations for the surge to the top slot under Patrick Wellington's leadership in 1996. I was fortunate in 1992 to hit a bull market and to inherit a business that was beginning to show the fruits of Ferguson's work. There was a strong management team who were determined to succeed and strength in depth in the staff, but the business needed focusing.

I made four key changes. O'Donnell, the charismatic American recruited by Ferguson to run the European equities division, returned to New York to run US equities and equity capital markets. This became very successful, gaining a respectable market share in US equities and foreign shares and, under Joe Adams and Anne Kavanagh, building up a powerful niche in capital markets.

The second key change also involved a managerial switch. Ferguson's proprietary trading strategy was dusted off and refined and Philip Young was appointed finance director with a mandate to monitor the area. Young is meticulous with regard to detail and thinks carefully about the downside as well as the upside of situations; this makes him a good foil to brokers' natural instincts. He was a NatWest man and trusted by them and by me and this gave us the confidence to sanction an aggressive proprietary trading strategy.

My third move was to cut down market making in small companies in September 1992. The firm was losing money, providing liquidity in 300 small companies where it had no corporate connection or particular edge. This move had some benefit to the profit and loss account, but its principal advantage was to sharpen focus and give a message to the staff that profits mattered. Finally, continuing the process of focusing on successful, core areas and eliminating loss makers, the Tokyo equities business was closed in December 1992.

In 1994, a fifth important change was to bring the European and UK businesses together under the single management of Joe Lafferty. This was a controversial decision. Lafferty had done a good job rebuilding NatWest's presence in equities in Scotland and in turning round Continental Europe but he was a colourful, flamboyant figure and not universally popular. However, he proceeded to bring the businesses together both sensitively and successfully.

The results from equities improved but synergy with other parts of NatWest Markets was slow to happen. Despite immense personal enthusiasm and energy, Owen was neither able to overcome cultural differences nor to foster a united attitude amongst his high-level team. The introduction of a Medium Term Incentive Plan linked to NatWest Markets profits for all front-line staff was a brave attempt to draw everyone into the NatWest Markets vision. MTIPs never formed a big enough proportion of compensation to persuade staff to identify with the division's performance and the acronym was renamed by the cynics 'Martin Thinks It's Pretty Smart'.

In May 1993 a chance to integrate equities and corporate advisory was missed. Owen was aware that operational synergies were lacking in NatWest Markets and hoped that this could be addressed by putting equities and fixed income together under my management. I should not have taken this job, lacking the technical knowledge of the fixed income products, but at the time I believed that we could give a better service to clients by putting the businesses together. Closer analysis revealed that equities and fixed income spoke to different parts of the client base and a better fit would have been to link equities and corporate advisory. I could then have used my influence with the analysts to encourage a more cooperative attitude to working with corporate advisory and we could have begun to get leverage from our secondary market strengths. I regard this as a missed opportunity which would have given NatWest Markets a much greater chance of success.

HSBC AND UBS: DAMAGE LIMITATION

HSBC and UBS had two common characteristics in their approach to equities in these years: continuity and cost control. Bernard Asher, as chairman of HSBC Investment Bank, presided over James Capel throughout these years, and at UBS, Rudolf Mueller did the same for Phillips & Drew, backed up by Hector Sants.

Both firms put cost control above revenue generation. This was in contrast to every broker's instinct, caused constant frustration but explains why Capel and UBS Phillips & Drew survived for a lot longer than most of their competitors despite not having the highest profile in the market.

Mueller had taken over in 1988 and had won good marks for bringing the Phillips & Drew settlement mess under control. However, the task of creating an investment bank was complicated by structural barriers. Trading and sales and corporate finance, the key departments, each reported to a different main board member, and Mueller had no control over corporate finance. Furthermore, London and Switzerland 'were regional baronial operations and that is why UBS never made it as a functional business'.[6]

Sants' task at UBS Phillips & Drew (renamed UBS Limited in 1993) was initially confined to the London operations in this unwieldy structure. Modest steps to functional management were taken in 1991 when Sants was given Europe, Africa and the Middle East to run and in 1994 when a Global Equity Management Committee was set up but there was no global head of equities, the committee taking collective responsibility. The absence of a strong functional management unit meant that UBS's equities business never punched its weight globally or took full advantage of its regional strengths.

Sants decided at an early stage to build on the Swiss platform and to position the equities business as pan-European. UK and European research product was more integrated than was usual in the City at that time and distribution into Europe, Japan and the US was prioritized on the grounds that demand for European equities would grow faster in these areas than in the UK. Consequently the firm achieved a higher rating with overseas investors – often a top three position – than in the UK where it usually came in the middle of the top ten. Gradually the product range was broadened with the development of convertibles, futures and options, portfolio trading and quantitative research. Sants' efforts continued to be handicapped by structural difficulties and his derivatives business lacked an important element, over the counter equity derivatives, which were located in the fixed income division.

Sants regarded managing his relationships with UBS as a key part of his job: 'The Swiss style favours cost control above revenue enhancement and that's a great contrast with the style of the US investment banks who go for top line growth. UBS tended to focus on headcount, costs, the factors they understood. It was a constant battle to fill every position. This saved money in the short term but was not a winning strategy for the long term.'[7]

The final years of Capel's Big Bang generation brought more losses in 1989–90 and persuaded HSBC that they had to get more involved. Again the problem was on the risk taking side: 'We as a board were weak to have allowed this to happen. We got into a pickle again in 1989–90, the residual positions from programme trading had been allowed to hang around too long, there was a fall in the market, we lost a lot of money. HSBC got nasty. They couldn't understand how a so-called agency broker kept running up these losses.'[8]

HSBC ordered an enquiry, demanded measures to cut costs and removed Peter Quinnen. This single event symbolizes the passing of the Big Bang generation. Quinnen was the star of the broking industry in the 1980s and his achievement in building Capel's brand and business in this period was immense. But he was an agency broker used to running a small business and he did not adapt to the introduction of risk or to the constraints imposed by a large organization like HSBC.[9] Like many of his generation, he appears to have found it difficult to succeed in the new environment and there was friction with the bank's management. Quinnen's removal said very clearly to the City in general, and to Capel's staff in particular, that the Big Bang games were over: 'His going was a real shock to us. Suddenly it was clear that we had real problems. From that moment all pretence at domination was lost.'[10]

Bernard Asher, one of HSBC's five general managers and most senior men, was sent to London to sort things out. He landed in London from Hong Kong one Saturday armed with a letter from head office appointing him chairman of James Capel, with clear instructions that damage limitation was to replace the grand investment banking plans: 'We don't care about James Capel. Avoid embarrassment and don't let them disintegrate like Citicorp Scrimgeour Vickers,' he was told.[11] Asher agreed to follow this course but said in that case you must let me plead poverty and starve them of capital otherwise the staff will be unmanageable.

Asher had been a director of James Capel since 1986 but had attended only one board meeting which had been enough to convince him that the firm would never succeed. He reminds me of Sir Alec Guinness's George Smiley in appearance, manner and intellect. He has now retired but as chairman of James Capel and HSBC Investment Bank spent eight years working closely with the brokers and speaks of them as a parent might of an errant child, wearily but with affection:

When I arrived the business wasn't in great shape. It had expanded overseas with no controls or infrastructure. An example would be Paris where we, an institutional broker, had for some reason bought a private client broker which cost us £25 million one year in bad deals. Capel had expanded at the wrong moment with all the cost and none of the revenue. The cost of settling the business was very expensive; we had about 500 clerks on the payroll. There had been little investment in IT and standards were below those of our

Wardley Thomson business in the Far East. I forced them to put James Capel's Asian back office into Wardley, much to their disgust.[12]

Asher pursued a consistent and clever strategy. As a veteran of the bank, he knew that HSBC was usually slow to get a grip on its acquisitions and was a poor integrator. He was sceptical of the chances of building an integrated investment bank, especially since the merchant bank Samuel Montagu, that came as a result of HSBC's merger with Midland, was isolationist and not first division. One senior HSBC source told me: 'Montagu had delusions of grandeur. It was a collection of investment products loosely lashed together in the hope that it would become an investment bank. They adopted a policy of deliberate obfuscation as far as HSBC were concerned and just did things amongst themselves.'[13]

Asher embarked on a wearying course of saying no: 'In those early years I was very negative about everything they came up with.'[14] Through a policy of consistent pressure, he succeeded in persuading the senior management of James Capel that profits and return on capital were necessary if big bonuses were to be paid. This was no mean task, for the prevailing mood in broking was still to put strategic vision above short-term profits.

The structure of the cost base worried Asher:

If you looked at the American firms they would have base salaries of $150,000, no benefits and huge gearing through the bonus. At James Capel it was have any car you like, mortgage subsidy and a pension. I cut back on all that to give more flexibility in the bonus. Client entertaining was another extravagance. The first lunch I went to was served by waiters with a butler in attendance, about four courses, fine wines, port and cigars. I told them to change the caterers, serve a lighter cuisine and lower the cost. They brought in Roux Brothers. I was told that the butlers were necessary because, among their duties, they were very good at dealing sensitively with inebriated guests. There was a huge wine cellar. It was all sent to the sale room. Staff no longer had private access at cost to a splendid cellar.[15]

The difficulty with Asher's approach was that the vision and excitement that brokers thrive on was missing and the firm was regarded by staff as lacking in direction: 'We could see that costs were being got under control but there was a sense of foreboding that the glory days were over. The global imperialist ambition had been replaced by good husbandry but where was the strategy?'[16]

In the absence of such vision, the firm would have to pay up to retain staff, which Asher was unwilling to do:

I thought we had to manage within our resources. If we couldn't do that we had to ask ourselves whether we should be in the business at all. This did cause us to lose a few people and I was worried that we would slip below critical mass. But I had conflicting objectives: the need to hold position for corporate finance and the constraints imposed by Group Remuneration Committee. My colleagues at HSBC were supportive but they had trouble paying broking style packages to loss making businesses. Some of them thought £50,000 was a lot of money.[17]

Asher spent some years clearing up the mistakes of the old regime. Soon after he arrived in London, trouble emerged in New York: 'They had been trading illegally in New York. I had to bargain with the Fed to allow the company to remain open, having sacked the people responsible. The deputy head of legal affairs for the group had to run the New York office for a year or so.'[18] A new issue for an East European company, New European Hotels, flopped; investors queried Capel's due diligence procedures and had to be given restitution.

There was then a series of management changes until 1992, when Bob Benton took over as head of equities and held the position for over two years. He was an ex-salesman and is known as a straightforward, clean-cut man; a measure of stability returned to Capel under his leadership. But, under the tight financial disciplines imposed by Asher, there was a steady exodus of talent and the firm lost its leadership to Warburg in the Extel survey in 1991 and had dropped down to fourth position by 1994.

Despite the loss of client position, Asher emerges as an unlikely hero of this period. He is not much liked by James Capel executives. There was a culture clash, Asher's banking background clashing with their dashing approach: 'I loathed the corporate extravagance. There are men and women in broking who believe that it's a normal part of business life to take clients duck shooting in Kashmir. They act like merchant princes not businessmen. It's madness.'[19] There are many current and former Capel staff who believe that he caused the firm to lose its leading franchise but that had already gone before he took over. He is a loyal HSBC man who followed his instructions and avoided serious embarrassment for the bank from its broker. He and Mueller at UBS ran their brokers as businesses rather than trophy-winning machines and ensured that they survived: 'Some firms bought their way into the business but I didn't. I believed that you had to make profits to win loyalty and respect from staff and clients. I wanted people who were loyal, hard-working and knew that they had to service the capital in the business. What's wrong with that?'[20]

1994: NO NEARER A SOLUTION

At the end of 1993 the commercial banks must have believed that they were close to achieving the goals that they had in mind when they set out in 1986. They had all just turned in a profitable year from equities and were making some progress in primary markets. BZW's capital markets team had just developed one of the smartest products of the day, the innovative enhanced dividend scrip scheme, and UBS's capital markets team under Connor Killeen was eating up the competition in Europe. Owen was in his pomp at NatWest and Asher appeared to have James Capel under control.

However, the volatile markets of 1994 revealed just how fragile that progress was and the brokers returned to loss. This had a very damaging psychological effect on the parent companies at a crucial time, dulling their appetite for more strategic investment at a moment when the US investment banks were also in disarray. Nineteen ninety-four was the last possible moment for a European bank to have made a telling US acquisition at a reasonable price and so to have challenged Wall Street, but they all thought 'here we go again' and stepped back.

A good illustration of this is at BZW where Donald Brydon, recently appointed deputy chief executive, carried out a detailed review of opportunities in the USA: 'The US and New York form one of the largest market places in the world. We aim to be a European-based global investment bank and the US presence is important to that.'[21] Sir Peter Middleton, the chairman of BZW, put it even more succinctly, referring to 'a shortage of dollar products and we are determined to rectify that'.[22] But Barclays had seen enough of investment banking by this stage, chose to invest in asset management and a golden opportunity to buy a US investment bank was gone.

At NatWest it was becoming clear to me that patience was also wearing thin. The results for 1994 from equities were excellent given the problems being experienced by the rest of the industry but not good enough for the hawks at NatWest. Midway through the year I received a visitor from the office of the group chief executive, one of the strategy team. Owen told me that this was just a routine visit and that I should regard it as part of the process of educating NatWest in the equities business. I was deeply suspicious and wondered why NatWest still needed educating in equities nearly ten years after buying its first broker. The meeting showed that my visitor had done his homework and needed no educating in a business which he clearly disliked. After he had gone I noticed a piece of paper that he had left behind him on the table. I picked it up and read it: a note from Owen to Wanless telling him to 'ensure that Augar gets no inkling that the business is again under review as it would be destabilizing for him and his team'.

18

Merchant Banks

Following the withdrawal of Morgan Grenfell from securities and Hill Samuel's takeover by TSB, only Warburg and Kleinwort entered the nineties as merchant banks with serious equities ambitions, the remainder pursuing niche strategies. During the next four years, Warburg expanded apace leaving itself precariously poised by the end of 1994. Kleinwort was forced to focus its business after huge losses in 1990. Barings made the most money out of equities in this period but in a rather opportunistic way, with little evidence of strategic rationale. Schroders bought a presence in New York and Flemings developed a joint venture in Asia but they never followed an integrated securities plan with conviction. Despite a terrible year for Kleinwort in 1990, and regular ups and downs for all of them, only at the very end of the period, and then quite suddenly, was there any sense of a crisis.

Warburg pursued a full-blooded bond, equity and corporate finance strategy across the globe. Occasionally results from equities were poor, for example in 1990–91 and again in 1992–3, but it was the totality of what was attempted rather than the pure equity component that caused the group problems. These emerged in October 1994 when Warburg warned that profits would be between £55 and £65 million as against £149 million in the first half of the previous year, with 'minimal' profits from investment banking.[1] The market was stunned for the group's results the previous year had been excellent and it appeared to be mounting a credible challenge to the Americans.

Kleinwort had begun the 1990–94 period in the way that Warburg ended it, shocking the market with terrible results. In equities, £16 million of losses in Japan were accompanied by a loss of £34 million on the failed bought deal in Premier Consolidated Oilfields and contributed to losses of £95 million in investment banking. After this Kleinwort focused and profits recovered until 1994.

Amongst the niche merchant banks, the first signs of distress at Barings became evident. Having made £170 million in the previous six years, securities lost £10 million in 1991–2 but profits recovered to £62 million in 1993.[2] Schroders kept out of serious trouble and Flemings enjoyed some good years in European capital markets and Asian equities.

Table 10. Warburg and Kleinwort Investment
Banking Results, 1989–94, £ million[3]

	1989	1990	1991	1992	1993	1994
Warburg	128.4	78.8	101.2	65.9	187.5	(43.0)
Kleinwort	56.8	(95.4)	3.5	24.5	85.3	61.9

WARBURG: 'A EUROPEAN VERSION OF WHATEVER THEY ARE'

Throughout this period Warburg had a real go at building a world-class investment bank. Although it dominated equities, holding the leading position in the secondary broking markets in European equities and finishing top of the Extel survey every year between 1991 and 1996, the real action was in UK and European corporate finance. The annual report for 1992 accurately summed up the firm's position: Warburg was the leading adviser on European mergers and acquisitions and number one in all the significant surveys of brokers' services.

But from the inception of the integrated investment bank, Warburg's aspirations were not just European but global and in the early 1990s it tried to make these a reality. A Group International Committee was formed, 'accelerating this strategy'[4] and equity and bond operations were established in Europe, America and Asia.[5] The 1992–3 accounts showed just how far Warburg's reach now extended: investment banking in thirty-one locations and local securities exchange membership in twenty-two locations. It was the third ranked adviser on worldwide mergers and acquisitions in 1993; its 250 analysts were 'the largest and most international research resource of any investment bank'; and its equity and fixed interest derivatives team was active in Chicago, Frankfurt, Geneva, Hong Kong, London, New York, Osaka, Paris, Singapore and Tokyo.[6] The firm made markets in 2000 equity and equity derivatives and was a member of thirty-three securities exchanges.

Warburg stepped up the pace even more after Lord Cairns was appointed chief executive and deputy chairman late in 1991. Cairns had been with Warburg since 1979 and took over from David Scholey who continued as chairman. Cairns reinforced the ambition to be the leading European competitor to the American investment banks, 'a European version of whatever they are', and asked shareholders to accept lower returns during the building phase: 'Because of our perception that financial markets will be global, there is a willingness to accept lower returns for a while to establish ourselves in overseas markets.'[7]

Despite promises of 'tempering our drive with prudence and leavening keen pursuit of profit with a due sense of proportion', a very large operational risk was incurred in the form of a big cost base. Expenses escalated sharply in 1993–4, rising 32 per cent to £746.7 million and were 'budgeted to increase again in 1994–5, in full awareness that revenues must rise even faster if profits are to increase'. A chart showed compensation per employee to be at the top of the range for UK firms but low against US competitors; however, the more telling chart would have been revenue per employee for the US firms, which would have been much higher.[8] Principal trading and derivatives were expanded to try to close this gap.[9]

This development raised the question of whether Warburg possessed sufficient risk management skills. Shareholders were told: 'Senior management monitors risk closely; the group risk executive continually seeks to improve our systems and identify better ways to measure and control risks. While no system can ensure profitable trading under all conditions, we believe our risk controls are soundly based.'[10] A committee structure was put in place: 'The group risk control committee has overall responsibility for establishing and monitoring risk limits for market and credit risk and for ensuring that the group's aggregate risk remains within the guidelines approved by the group board. Risk incurred by operating units is monitored at least daily; risk limits are reviewed regularly to ensure suitability for prevailing market conditions.'[11]

By now Warburg had moved far beyond the old risk management unit centred around Akroyd's senior dealers and they moved on. In April 1992 it was announced that Peter Hardy, one of a three-man investment banking executive set up in 1991, would retire. Comments he made subsequently suggest that he was uncomfortable with the increase in costs. By 1994 Warburg had become a very complex animal. Not only was it spread across a number of geographies and products, but it had adopted a high-risk approach to developing its business. As events were to prove, it was not able to defend its cost base against volatile markets. Knowing the size of its risk positions was different from controlling them.

KLEINWORT: 'BEING FOCUSED IS
WHAT MATTERS TO CLIENTS'

Kleinwort's ambitions were shaped by the investment bank's losses of £95 million in 1990, forcing it to abandon its growth strategy and to concentrate on managing the business for survival. This worked well, and slowly and painstakingly the bank's profits and reputation were rehabilitated by 1994.

Equities suffered in the Japanese market downturn but it was a failed bought deal in Premier Oil that was the talking point in 1990. On 6 August, with the oil market rising following Iraq's invasion of Kuwait, a block of 139.9 million Premier Oil shares was bought at 99p. A placing was initially tried at 103p but, as word spread of Kleinwort's position, the price fell and the shares were finally placed at 78p on 17 October. The deal was turned into a *cause célèbre* by the press and Kleinwort's competitors who hoped to discredit the bank and to destabilize the staff: 'It was not just a deal that went wrong. What really rankled within Kleinwort was that it showed up our systems as badly wanting. Other firms might have done that deal after analysing the risk carefully; Kleinwort seemed to do it after a quick discussion.'[12] Charles Hue Williams, who had been appointed co-head of equities in October 1989, resigned from the board in October 1990 and the procedure for approving bought deals together with controls over UK equity market making was strengthened.[13]

However, quite a lot of this comment was little more than gratuitous advice after the event. Kleinwort was in a risk business, and, although it was unfortunate that Premier occurred in a year when several other things also went wrong, the deal was not in itself life threatening and was within the realms of Kleinwort's ordinary business. A competitor analysed the situation as follows: 'They had made money in oil bought deals before so this was not a complete flyer. The problem was that the size of the holding became known very quickly. Staff, competitors and the press made mark-to-market calculations and the very public nature of it made the deal more difficult and lowered the firm's reputation.'[14]

Not surprisingly at the beginning of 1991, as the full horrors of 1990 were being assimilated, there were reports of a split on the board over the future of equities. 'One faction backed by the founding banking families and led by chairman David Peake is pressing for closure of the troubled division and a return to KB's merchant banking origins. Peake, who is married to Suki Kleinwort, and his allies – the families hold nearly 20 per cent of Kleinwort Benson's equity – would like to see the axe fall after privatisation of the two electricity generators. The sale next month is led by KB.' Employees were sufficiently rattled for 'golden parachutes' to be given to a dozen senior corporate finance and equities staff to be used in the event of a closure.[15]

Clementi denies this split: 'There was no split on the board and there was no question of getting out of equities. It was a significant part of Kleinwort by then and was integrated with corporate finance. We would have preferred to sell the business and find an outside backer rather than get out of equities.'[16] Kleinwort opened preliminary discussions with BNP and Dresdner in 1991 but at that stage they did not want to take a majority stake.

The losses required a reduction in the cost base, involving redundancies and business closures and sales. The headcount dropped by 10 per cent in 1991, costs fell by £24 million and were kept under control through to 1995. The key was focus, a message reinforced when Lord

Rockley took over as chairman from Peake in 1993: 'we do not intend to attempt to be all things to all people'.[17]

By 1994, the business was performing well. The firm was mandated in 1994 as global coordinator or lead manager of twenty-two equity or equity-linked new issues raising $17 billion, topped the UK's league table of cross-border M&A deals and was ranked as one of the three leading houses for advising on cross-border M&A transactions worldwide. Privatisation continued to be an area of strength, the bank working on thirty-four privatisations in twenty countries. The equities division stayed in the top five of the Extel survey right up until the end. In 1994, its last year as an independent, Kleinwort's share increased in all the major markets where the equities division operated.

The 1994 reports and accounts were signed off on 15 March 1995 and were the picture of a group that had turned the corner after some lean times. The loss of confidence which had seen BNP taking a 5 per cent stake and discussions with Dresdner Bank seemed to be a long way behind the group. The view of leading sector analysts such as David Poutney was that 'Kleinwort looks to be enjoying something of a renaissance'.[18] But there was an ominous ring to Lord Rockley's closing comment that 'so far this year financial markets have been subdued and trading has been difficult'[19] and within three months of shareholders having received their accounts the board would have accepted an offer for the whole company from Dresdner Bank.

THE OTHER MERCHANT BANKS:
LIVING ON THEIR WITS

The early 1990s saw two developments at Barings: an increase in risk of the business as margins tightened in its original markets and a partial, belated integration of securities into the rest of the bank. Securities at Barings had been seen as an opportunistic profit centre rather than as part of an integrated corporate finance and equities strategy but there were some signs of change in 1991 when securities, although 1100-strong, was loss-making. Barings chose to pay $78 million for a 40 per cent stake in the US investment bank Dillon Read rather than pump more money into the existing securities business, much to the anger of Christopher Heath and his colleagues on the securities board.

The deteriorating results and requirement for capital persuaded the parent bank to appoint its own chief operating officer, Peter Norris. Norris carried out a swift review in the summer of 1992 and imposed 180 redundancies around the world with annual savings of £20 million. Under the existing formula the bonus pool would not be big enough to keep the staff happy so Barings provided £15 million in return for replacing the formula with discretionary bonuses under the bank's control.

The process of assimilation continued in 1993 when Heath was removed; Norris got to grips with improving the administration and Baring Brothers was combined with Baring Securities to form an investment bank. There were to be five divisions under Norris as chief executive, with Andrew Fraser in charge of equity broking and George Maclean in charge of banking, including derivatives, which was run by an Australian, Ron Baker, who had joined from Bankers Trust in 1992. Superficially at least it looked as though Barings was now exerting more control over its broker.

Flemings' strategy in securities achieved mixed results during the period. The joint venture with Jardine Fleming in Asia allowed the firm to build a strong position in corporate finance and broking throughout the region. However, one insider told me that 'JF was very independent. It was staffed by expats who kept Flemings at arm's length and with good local talent who didn't want much from London. They were quite good at IPOs for small local businesses but were missing the big international mandates at this time.'[20]

In the UK, where Flemings was one of the first merchant banks to build up a sales, trading and research team, success was harder to find. In June 1990, six years after having started up, it closed UK market making and became an agency broker in UK and European equities. The following year it pulled out of UK and European convertibles and warrants and was rumoured to be considering closure of the whole UK equities business.[21]

New life was breathed into corporate finance and securities by the recruitment of Bill Harrison from Lehmans in 1993 as chief executive of investment banking: 'We tried to make equities more integrated and work closely with corporate finance and to link with Asia.'[22] Tom Hughes-Hallett was recruited from Enskilda 'to build a European equity business of equal stature to the Asian business' but Flemings never became a serious force in European equities.[23]

Schroders also built up equities at this time without ever really getting behind the business. Its acquisition of Wertheim & Co. in the US brought in an equity broker with a mid-market corporate advisory business and a small capital markets presence. It became a member of the Tokyo Stock Exchange and developed a network of brokers across Asia without ever harnessing them into corporate finance and capital markets. In Europe, it went through phases of building up and then winding down equities.

The senior management and family shareholders were wary of securities and resisted too great an involvement. The corporate financiers dabbled with the notion of wanting distribution overseas but lacked the knowledge or commitment to build up a serious network. In the UK, the continuing availability of independent distribution through Cazenove and the maintenance of separate corporate broking at the other major firms meant that there was no pressure to build up domestic research and distribution.

Rothschild's involvement in equities was restricted to its stake in Smith New Court. Lazards also stuck to its guns, pursuing a policy of non-involvement in securities. It maintained a small trading team to enable it to make the most of niche opportunities that came along. Its approach had been explained by Nicholas Jones when he became a managing director of Lazard Brothers: 'There's a great emphasis on return on capital here. We prefer to be living on our wits than committing large amounts of capital. It's people who do the deal – capital is secondary.'[24]

CONCLUSION

Most of the merchant banks in the early nineties came to terms with a reduced role in world capital markets compared to the vision of the late eighties. If Kleinwort, Schroders or Flemings ever believed that they could be global leaders, Kleinwort's problems in managing its broking arm and its vulnerability to a bad year in investment banking would have shattered those illusions. Kleinwort's losses in 1990 showed the medium-sized merchant banks that they would need much improved risk controls and a much bigger base of complementary earnings if they were to be able to mount a global challenge. They all decided to get focused.

Two merchant banks, Warburg and Barings, persisted with their strategies. Barings continued to ride its luck, opportunistically seeking new niches as the old ones matured, but neglecting to build an infrastructure to control its overextended business lines and complex products. Warburg avoided serious losses for most of the period and stuck to its global vision. It believed it was expanding in a controlled way; it believed its risk controls were good. It performed well enough in the volatile markets of 1990–94 for its management, staff and shareholders to be confident that its vision was realistic.

But beneath the patina of success that these merchant banks habitually displayed all was not well. Senior management was having trouble controlling their businesses and, unbeknown to shareholders, the results were slipping. The first external signs of trouble came from Warburg with the October 1994 profit warning; then, at 11 a.m. on 8 December, Warburg and Morgan Stanley announced that they were in merger discussions. It did not take a moment's thought to decide which would be the dominant partner. Warburg, the flagship of the UK merchant banking sector, was in trouble and the farewells to gentlemanly capitalism could begin.

19

The Independents

The years 1990–94 were successful ones for Smith New Court and Cazenove as they improved their market position and proved that independent brokers could survive without the backing of a bank's balance sheet. In fact, the evidence of these years suggests that brokers had a better chance of being profitable if they were entirely responsible for their own destiny. The knowledge that there was no one to bale them out if losses became too large produced focused, simple strategies that were easier to operate and more fun to work in than the grand investment banking plans of the giants. By the middle of 1993, Smith claimed to have lost money in only three or four of the previous sixty-five months.[1] Cazenove says that it never had a loss-making quarter in the period.

Both firms had their moments of crisis but their survival was not in doubt. Cazenove stuck to its plan of agency broking in support of its corporate clients and continued to dominate corporate broking in the UK. Smith transformed itself in the period from a market maker with a small agency broker tacked on into a fully integrated research, trading and sales operation. It was, with Warburg, the dominant force in institutional equities in this period. However, by 1994, it had reached a size where it faced some strategic decisions: grow or shrink to niche, and if grow, how to achieve that off the restricted capital base?

SMITH NEW COURT

The year to April 1990 was an important one for Smith. Credibility had not been seriously damaged by the losses of 1988–9, which were regarded by the press and the market as excusable given the carnage amongst other brokers in London, but another loss-making year would have eroded share capital and reserves and led to questions about the firm's durability.

The year got off to a very bad start when a bought deal in Ferranti went wrong, costing the firm £10 million. Despite this, profits for the year recovered to £15 million, an excellent turnaround from the loss of £12.5 million in the previous year. Pre-tax profits dipped again in 1990–91 to £7.5 million (Gulf War, East Europe and recession) but then rose steadily to £95.2 million in 1993–4, a 48 per cent return on capital after a £48 million rights issue. These results were achieved in benign market conditions but were hugely impressive coming only four years after heavy losses and left the firm acknowledged as an industry leader. What was the secret?

The profits driver was trading and during this period Smith joined BZW and Warburg as the leading market maker in UK equities, closing the gap which had existed before Big Bang. The agency business with institutional clients was developed, with agency market share approaching 10 per cent in 1994, not far behind the leaders, Warburg, and over a percentage point clear of a pack of chasing firms led by NatWest. Under Mike Unsworth as head of research, a good reputation was won for research, the firm usually holding an Extel ranking of between six and eight.

On a stand-alone basis the profits from the agency business were small and it was not until 1992–3 that it moved out of loss. However, it enabled the trading side to see a good flow of business and gave it more control over its own positions. Active management of the cash positions was an important part of Smith's risk control and access to in-house distribution meant that positions could be flattened or built up more quickly than if the market makers had to go through intermediary brokers or the network of inter dealer brokers.

Smith was primarily a risk-taking firm, and a very good one at that.

At least prior to the Barings collapse, which caused most firms to formalize their risk management, Smith's approach was instinctive:

We had a very astute trading side. Risk management came from gut feel and very rigid control of the money. Book positions were reported to the trading management every hour and in volatile times every half-hour. Positions that were being held too long were cut by senior management. It was the aggregate trading position that mattered: if the total of the bull positions was too long, we were not in a position to quote for business and that was no good. Very occasionally big positions were put on a back book and God help you if you got it wrong. Mainly we kept very tight position control and this helped to provide liquidity even on days like Black Tuesday.[2]

The chairman's remarks after the collapse of Barings, a time when most firms were rushing round trying to create a paper trail that would stand up to scrutiny in the event of an accident, spoke volumes for Smith's confidence and capability in this area: 'Having traded equities for seventy years, we have always been aware of the specific risks which can arise in the securities industry.'[3]

Smith's prowess as a risk firm enabled it to dominate the wave of bought deals that occurred in London in the early 1990s.[4] An excess of capital in broking and a determination by many firms to build a high profile meant that competition was strong in this area. A senior Smith's employee recounts the bought deal process:

This was most exhilarating. When one of these things came along there was a small bought deal committee, quite informal. Michael Marks, Tony Abrahams, Ken Taylor, Paul Roy and Geoff Lewis were usually involved and one or two more of us if it was a stock we knew about. The five of them would take input from relevant parties and sit and talk about the trade. How quickly could we distribute it, what should the price be. Firms that took the view 'we like the stock so the client will like it' always lost money. The key is price, it had to be a discount to the prevailing price, that was Kleinwort's mistake on Premier, they tried it at the wrong price. We would look at the average daily volume, the list of recent dealers in the stock, get lots of input from the broking side and perhaps a bit of discreet pre-marketing. We only ever lost money on two bought deals, and one of those was Ferranti.[5]

There is an interesting contrast between Smith's experience with Ferranti and Kleinwort's with Premier. Kleinwort's description of its internal process for deciding on Premier is not significantly different to Smith's bought deal process. Both deals failed due to two unexpected extraneous events – Kuwait's invasion by Iraq; and the emergence of fraud at a Ferranti subsidiary. Neither deal posed a threat to the company's survival. Both deals came at a time of other trading problems (in banking and Japan for Kleinwort and following on from the UK market making war for Smith). What is different is the reaction in the market and the press to the two losses. Kleinwort was vilified and was on the run, under pressure from competitors and clients. Smith sailed serenely through, not because of any public relations exercise but because the firm was known as a market maker, as a trader and it was recognized that that sort of thing happened in a risk business. Kleinwort, on the other hand, was still educating the market about its move into broking and was still known mainly as a corporate finance house. It was therefore vulnerable to criticism in this new venture and was much more damaged by Premier than Smith was by Ferranti.

A key element in Smith's profit growth in the early 1990s was the development of a significant business overseas. In addition to building a strong business in New York through the purchase of Carl Marks, it acquired and started up broking firms overseas dealing in their domestic equities. A strong network across South East Asia was rolled out; a 49 per cent stake was taken in a South African broker, Davis Borkum Hare; a Japanese branch office was upgraded when full membership of the Tokyo and Osaka exchanges was bought. Early in 1995, it was announced that Smith would take control of a leading broker in Karachi. In Europe, the approach taken was to do sales, research and trading out of London although 'the case for opening local offices in the major European financial centres' was kept under review.[6] The success of the international development strategy was such that, by 1994–5, 58 per cent of revenues came from international sources.

The diversification away from market making was also pursued through corporate broking and there were 120 brokerships by April 1993. Although the firm managed to avoid serious damage from its involvement with Robert Maxwell, it was not able to mount a serious challenge to the leading firms in UK corporate broking.

Smith's growth in the period represents the working of a strategy followed with a mixture of well-assessed risk taking and caution. The discipline imposed by a small capital base is very evident from an early stage, for example when Michael Marks explained the strategy: 'We stick to what we know, we don't pay large amounts of money for goodwill and we don't get involved in businesses we don't understand.'[7] Employee involvement was increased by the introduction of plans to pay bonuses in part in shares and to encourage savings related share options. By June 1994, employees had an interest in 9.9 per cent of the equity.

Smith's new-found scale raised some issues: was it big enough to compete on the global stage? The firm's achievements were put into perspective after the grand opening of its new offices in Farringdon in the company of the Prime Minister and the Governor of the Bank of England, 'adding to the perception that SNC is one of Britain's great success stories. Perhaps it is in City terms. But for a company with a market capitalization of under £40 million and an annual staff bill more than twice the combined pre-tax losses of the last five years, such pageantry seems over-blown.'[8]

The issue of scale was acknowledged in the 1995 chairman's statement:

The year under review has also seen much discussion about the future shape of the securities industry worldwide and the possibility that larger groupings will emerge as a response to the competitive pressures placed upon every firm. Whilst we take careful note of all of these discussions and keep our strategy under careful review, we believe that the mix of skills that we have at Smith New Court in research, sales and market making will continue to ensure that we are in the best possible position to meet the needs of our clients. We intend to pursue our expansion plans, described in the chief executive's report, by adding to those product areas, particularly internationally, where we can see the best returns on capital employed. We see nothing to deflect us from this course.[9]

However, these remarks did not reveal the whole story, since consultants had already been appointed to help review the company's future viability.

CAZENOVE

Whilst many of the integrated brokers in London were enduring the vicissitudes of volatile markets through their trading books in the early 1990s, Cazenove was able to use its agency status to its advantage. Its income was less volatile, its mission more simple and so it was able to present a consistent front to its clients. Cazenove's consistency stood out from the turmoil at many of the other brokers and this gave it a strong competitive edge with staff and clients.

UK corporate broking remained pre-eminent. Although the American firms began to appear alongside the established merchant banks and brokers in deals, Cazenove scarcely lost a client to a new competitor and it remained comfortably at the head of Crawford's league table of corporate stockbrokers. The fact that there was no question about the firm's survival prospects or risk of Cazenove's partners or senior executives rushing off to join a new firm gave the senior management of corporate clients much confidence.

It was characteristically Cazenove that its conservative image was accompanied by progressive business practices. Bought deals, where brokers bought lines of stock from clients and went on risk as they tried to place the shares, seemed to be a more natural business for the American investment banks than for UK brokers. The Americans were experienced, well-capitalized and skilled at hedging the risk. They were also desperate to do the deals as a way of breaking in to the UK market. In practice, as bought deals emerged as a market phenomenon of the early 1990s, Cazenove was there, usually in partnership with another broker.

A landmark event in this area was ICI's sale to Warburg Securities and Cazenove of its 24.9 per cent stake in Enterprise Oil for £680 million, a huge deal by the standards of the day, and over the winter of 1990–91 a series of such deals occurred as stakes built up in the bull market were unwound. Often Cazenove worked with Smith New Court, a powerful combination of the two independents focusing totally on the need to price correctly and distribute quickly. Cazenove preferred to avoid market risk but its market judgement was sound and it had to participate in bought deals if its position at the centre of UK corporate and institutional broking was to be preserved.

A Cazenove partner told me:

This was both a natural business for us and an unnatural one. We had experience of pricing in rights issues so our view was probably as good or better than anyone's. We knew how institutions would react to propositions because we had seen it before and we knew the top decision-makers on a different basis to the average secondary broker. We usually only got involved with companies where we were corporate broker with a clear knowledge of the individual shareholders and their attitudes to the company. It was unnatural for us in the sense that a single wrong decision could be life threatening. It wasn't done by committee, but the senior partners were made aware of what was planned.

Another said:

David Mayhew, I think, took most of the decisions consulting with sales; it wasn't very scientific at all. The crux of it was an assessment of the quality of demand for that company's shares. We were theoretically on risk but the deals were always priced to go. It was clear that a shared deal was a better deal and quite often we worked with Smith New Court because their market making skills fitted quite well with our broking experience.[10]

Cazenove's success in bought deals was down to its corporate relationships, distribution skills and instinctive nose for risk. Clients trusted Cazenove to offer a fair price and to place the stock with quality buyers. The personal liability of the partners helped ensure total focus on the business in hand since a failed bought deal could have been fatal.

The rapid globalization of the equities business at this time also posed a challenge to Cazenove: it lacked the resources and probably the desire to match the ambitious overseas development plans that were being rolled out by many brokers yet it could not remain a purely domestic firm if it was to stay competitive. The solution was to open representative offices in key centres, concentrating on distributing UK equities to local investors – for example, in New York and Tokyo – and to do research and sales, but not trading, in the emerging markets of Asia – for example, Japan, Malaysia (Kuala Lumpur was opened in 1990) and Singapore (opened in 1991). Full Stock Exchange membership was comparatively rare, an exception being Australia from 1987, which helped the firm to carry out an underwriting business there. Cazenove had had a long involvement in South Africa and, as the political situation improved, the broking business became more viable. The essence of Cazenove's overseas activities was careful expansion to secure an involvement without overextending managerial or capital resources.

CONCLUSION

Cazenove's stability and Smith's exciting surge were the most positive developments in institutional equity broking in London in the early 1990s. The important themes were teamwork, continuity and focus, all stemming from ownership. A high degree of staff participation, whether as partners, employees with a profit-related bonus or share-holders, bred a commonality of purpose. Cazenove partners and staff and Smith New Court employees, especially in trading, stuck together, helped each other and put client service above internal politics. There was a shared culture in each firm that helped people work together.

Neither firm had a rich parent to bale it out of a mess. They could not waste money on loss-making new businesses and costs had to be tightly controlled. Their clients could identify with what they were trying to do and a groundswell of support for Smith and Cazenove developed. This support clustered around the core products: corporate broking for Cazenove and trading for Smith. The continuity at Smith and Cazenove contrasted with the frequent changes in policy and personnel at the big investment banks. The consistency of the independents and comparatively low rate of staff turnover, relative to the big banks, reinforced their position.

The virtues of teamwork and focus born out of independence left both firms very well placed in 1994. Cazenove was happy with its lot and looked forward to a profitable future despite the rapid changes in the industry. However, unbeknown to its staff, clients and many of its directors, the top management of Smith had already settled on a more ambitious role in the world than could be achieved under independent ownership.

20

The Foreign Banks

Anyone who believes that it does not matter if British brokers are owned by foreign banks should look at 1990–94. In these years the commitment shown by the Americans and Japanese to London as a financial centre and to the people who worked there waxed and waned with their fortunes in New York and Tokyo. If Wall Street or Japan was booming, London was a priority; if there were losses at home, there were redundancies, pay cuts or disappointing bonus pools in the UK. The London operations did not help themselves by reporting generally poor results over this period.

After a poor year in 1990, when investment banks made a return on equity of 5 per cent and 1600 jobs were cut, 1991–3 were very good years on Wall Street. Return on equity was around 25 per cent every year and employment picked up. With resources to spare, the leading firms invested and expanded in London until the market volatility of 1994 dragged the US banks into loss. Their London operations were then scaled down as part of a global retrenchment.

This period also saw the retreat of SecPac from equity broking in London following the departures of two other American commercial banks, Citicorp and Chase Manhattan. These commercial banks combined the disadvantages of working a long way from home with the challenge of learning a new industry and their departure, while no surprise, did serve to reinforce the City's scepticism about foreign firms.

The Japanese market slumped in 1990 and the leading brokers got into serious profit difficulties. Initially they trimmed their London businesses but, once it became clear that broking in Japan was in a prolonged bear phase, London came in for radical surgery.

SECPAC: WHAT WENT WRONG?

Security Pacific had been the first outside bank to link up with a broker when it took its stake in Hoare Govett but it had been revising and reducing its strategy ever since Big Bang. After negotiations lasting a year or so, terms were announced in September 1990 for a management buy-in. Two entities were established, Hoare Govett UK/Europe and Hoare Govett Pacific, each of which was to be 51 per cent owned by the employees. SecPac was to be the principal lender to the employees and looked to share its own 49 per cent stake with strategic investors. Once a signal had been given that it was no longer committed to securities, the rest of SecPac's investment banking operations appeared anomalous and within weeks were gone.[1] Hoare Govett's management tried to make the best of things: 'Securities businesses do not work well when 100 per cent owned.'[2]

However, in the summer of 1991 BankAmerica and SecPac merged and SecPac pulled out of the proposed management buy-in, telling the management to find an alternative backer. Hoare Govett cast around and in January 1992 made sixty of its 440 staff redundant, refocused research and cut back on market making. It intended to develop a strategy around corporate broking which had remained a strong area for the firm, with the market judgement and excellent client relations of Peter Meinertzhagen the key factor. Despite the uncertainty and an indifferent performance on the secondary side, the blue chip client list remained loyal. Later in 1992 ABN Amro, the seventh largest European commercial bank, stepped forward as Hoare Govett's buyer and it suddenly seemed more possible for securities businesses to work well when 100 per cent owned.

Although Hoare Govett continues in existence under Dutch ownership – indeed, parts of the business have flourished – the sale to ABN marked the end of Hoare's Big Bang experience. How could what was arguably the City's leading equities firm in 1986 have got it so wrong?

The answer lies in the choice of partner back in 1983. An employee of Hoare Govett in 1983 takes up the story:

Richard Westmacott, the senior partner, nearly got it right. We knew we weren't big enough, we knew it would be a big boy's game and that we would need capital. So we broke the mould by getting outside capital but we went to the wrong place. Traditional American bankers knew nothing about risk, volatility or underwriting. But we went too soon with SecPac and too soon with market making and it took years to recover. SecPac had problems of their own on the banking side and the relationship was doomed. We wanted their capital but not their interference. We should have gone to Goldman Sachs or Merrill Lynch.[3]

THE AMERICAN INVESTMENT BANKS

The efforts of the US investment banks to establish themselves in London in the early 1990s were marked by continuity in corporate finance but regular advances and retreats in the supporting equities business. None of the Americans was exempt from this but Salomon was the least consistent, Morgan Stanley the steadiest and Goldman somewhere in between. Merrill Lynch was low profile in this period.

Salomon's commitment to London was constrained by its struggle in New York to re-orient itself from an old-style bond trader of 1989 into a modern investment bank. In the 1980s 'Europe was always regarded as a sort of ugly stepchild. For years head office never took it seriously. London was a nice reward posting for those near the end of their careers.'[4] In 1990, as the high yield market crashed, undoing Drexel Burnham Lambert and others, Salomon avoided the worst of the trouble and stayed committed to London: 'It's a very tough market out there but London is still a good place to be. We are not here for a short stay. We take a global view from London.'[5]

Having been one of the first London brokers to see European equities as a growth area in the late 1980s, when Peter Clark and Nick Bedford put together an idea-based sales and research team backed up by lots of trading capital, the firm had an interesting and differentiated product by 1990. However, in the summer of 1991 it emerged that some of the firm's New York traders had rigged US Treasury bond market auctions and the firm ran into serious trouble with the regulators, clients and staff. In the UK it was replaced by Goldman

Sachs as US lead manager in the BT privatisation of that year.[6] From New York, the new management regime of Warren Buffett in the chair and Deryck Maughan put a different structure in place and waged war on costs.[7] Jim Massie was installed in London and ran a dour regime, making it clear that there were no funds for bonuses and showing no enthusiasm for equities. Most of the analysts and salesmen left, Massie returned to New York and there was virtually nothing left in European equities. Massie was succeeded as head of European investment banking by Stephen Posford and Denis Keegan, two senior proprietary traders from New York, and as one insider recalls, 'for two years Europe was abandoned and was not a priority. European equities became not much more than a proprietary trading desk.'

Goldman started from a more rounded position in investment banking than Salomon and it was easier for the firm to extend its business into Europe. It sent some of its best investment bankers to London from the mid 1980s onwards and made it a priority. In the middle of 1991 the *Financial Times* assessed Goldman's position:

In terms of its presence in London, Goldman also figures prominently. Goldman has just moved into a gleaming new colossus of an office block. Goldman has made its name in London through cross-border mergers and acquisitions and privatisation work. Its appointment to advise ICI, following Hanson's appearance on its share register, has confirmed that standing. Two things are likely to determine whether Goldman still stands at or near the top of the heap by the end of the decade. First it needs to establish a stronger presence on the Continent. The second challenge is the extent to which Goldman can bring Europeans into senior management positions.[8]

The internationalization of Goldman personnel was successfully achieved. In London, the firm continued to be able to recruit the best of the next generation as well as some of the leading corporate financiers and securities staff of the day. These were supplemented with a leavening of top-quality US management. By the end of 1992, in the global business more than 30 per cent of the employees and 10 per cent of the partners were non-US citizens. In London and Europe the firm had successfully inserted itself into the investment banking community and was accepted into the establishment by clients and competitors.

However, it then went through a more difficult phase when the Maxwell affair broke. Robert Maxwell's business empire had become overextended and in the recession cash flow could not cover debt service charges. The share price of Maxwell Communications Corporation came under pressure and 'Maxwell, it was subsequently revealed, resorted to a share support operation using money looted from the *Daily Mirror*'s own pension fund'.[9] Goldman had advised and acted for Maxwell and there was a Securities and Exchange Commission investigation in 1993, a law case brought against Goldman and one of its partners, Eric Sheinberg, by the Maxwell pension trustees in 1994, and finally in 1995, whilst continuing to deny liability, Goldman paid $253 million to settle the case. The Maxwell affair shook the foundations of the City. Pension fund investment was the source of much of the liquidity that drove financial markets and any challenge to its sanctity jeopardized the whole system. Maxwell himself had long been a controversial figure and many banks and brokers would not deal with him. Goldman's involvement damaged its reputation and cast doubts over its judgement, especially in London. In 1993, at the peak of the scandal, the British Treasury ensured that Goldman was left out of the syndicate being formed to privatise the third tranche of BT shares, a punishment similar to that meted out to Salomon Brothers at the time of the T-bond scandal.

Just as Goldman was recovering from this, the bond market collapse of 1994 caused further disruption in London. During the 1990s Goldman evolved from a business where trading had been largely a flow business for clients to a firm where its own capital was risked in proprietary trading. This introduced volatility and in 1994 profits fell by $2 billion to little over $500 million and in the fourth quarter the firm actually lost $42 million. This caused considerable internal tensions and over twenty partners resigned in the closing months of 1994. In December 1994 a memo was sent to all staff from Jon Corzine and Henry Paulson, the bank's senior partners, stating that 'the firm is examining all aspects of its cost structure. Our goal is to cut costs quickly and retain our high level of client service.' Following 300 job losses in the fourth quarter of 1994, a further 900 across all parts of the firm were planned.

London took its full share and this resulted in some deterioration in the firm's reputation on the equity side in the UK and Europe. Institutional clients had finally been persuaded that Goldman was fully committed to the domestic equities business and the retreat from research in several important sectors led to a widespread view that Goldman was just another American firm coming and going in line with profitability on Wall Street. However, corporate relationships were not damaged and relationships with the institutions were soon repaired so that the firm's placing power on corporate deals survived. The willingness of the institutions to forgive and forget confirmed Goldman in its view that the secondary business was just that – secondary – a means towards an end rather than a leading business in its own right.

Morgan Stanley followed a similar policy to Goldman, prioritizing corporate finance above equities but staffing equities with quality people organized along pan-European lines. Like Goldman, Morgan Stanley sent some of its best people overseas and in 1992 moved four managing directors from New York to London and Tokyo and the global equity business was run for a while out of London by Bob Metzler.

Goldman and Morgan Stanley regularly appeared at around number ten position in the Extel survey of analysts rankings, a position which they considered good enough for them to impress corporates. By contrast to this mediocre secondary position, both firms were regularly in the top five of the corporate finance league tables, and often in the top three.

THE JAPANESE BROKERS

The Japanese firms had their efforts to build investment banks sabotaged by problems at home. The push into London continued in the early 1990s and Nomura realized that London had to be strengthened and given more autonomy if it was to succeed. In 1990, centralized functions such as accounting and personnel were delegated to London for Europe and the capital of its London operations was increased by £50 million to £100 million. More capital was given to Europe, a limited market making operation was started in European stocks and UK market making was strengthened.[10]

The firm avoided serious damage in the Japanese market crash of 1990, helped by its low profile in proprietary trading, but Nomura was stopped in its tracks when, in June and July 1991, evidence emerged of loss compensation payments to select investors and dealings with gangsters. Its former president and chairman resigned and many of its branches were banned from dealing in equities through to 26 November. By 1992 the slump in the Japanese Stock Market required action in London. Several of the Japanese firms trimmed costs in June 1992 and, in October, Nomura made a more radical move. Forty-nine jobs were cut as market making in European stocks and research coverage of some sectors were dropped.[11] The other Japanese firms gradually trimmed their ambitions in London. Nomura made another push in 1994 with a slightly different strategy in emerging markets and a full prime brokerage service including stock lending and custody to hedge funds but they did not make a serious impact on corporate finance or institutional clients in equities during the whole period after Big Bang.

CONCLUSION

By the end of 1994, Morgan Stanley and Goldman had become established parts of the corporate finance scene in the UK and Europe. They had sent their smartest bankers over to London and won corporate clients through good ideas and hard work on relationship building. They had made less progress on the secondary side of the business, however, having been tarred with the brush of inconsistency that was more fairly applied to the US commercial banks, Salomon and the Japanese.

When looking back on the period, it is surprising how little adverse comment was made on the foreign banks' lack of loyalty to their UK operations. There was very little coverage in the press, the regulators appeared indifferent and the British staff accepted that the risk of summary dismissal was one of the reasons that the foreign banks paid them a premium. The loudest protests came from the clients, particularly in 1994 when, after three years of consistent progress, Goldman suddenly pulled back. Even then, the clients were quick to forgive and forget.

There were three probable reasons for such indifference. Firstly, investment banking was known to be a volatile industry and all participants expected to be treated harshly if business got tough. Secondly, the UK firms were also prone to periods of retreat and, apart from Cazenove and Smith, it was impossible for clients and staff to find a consistent approach. Finally, the Americans in particular had a product that the clients wanted with global ideas, global distribution and lots of capital.

Even so, there was nothing in 1994 that would have suggested that the Americans were about to sweep the board in broking. After nearly a decade of trying they had no serious institutional broker and Morgan Stanley and Goldman Sachs were ranked only ninth and tenth in the Extel survey for calendar year 1994. That other US start up, Merrill Lynch, occupied eighteenth place in the same survey and had largely disappeared from the institutional radar screen. This might have been a good moment for the UK merchant and investment banks to try to squeeze out the competition; instead they were getting ready to throw in the towel.

PART FIVE

THE END GAME?
1995–2000

21

Barings

The years after 1994 were the most dramatic in the City's history and were to change the face of British banking. An enormous bull market, beginning on Wall Street, enriched the US investment banks. This enabled them to set the agenda of globalization and scale for the business world. They took full advantage of the new opportunities that the e-comm revolution created. Despite the mood change in the UK which swept New Labour to power and challenged many traditional beliefs, the British banks failed to keep up. They retreated from investment banking and their position of leadership in global financial services looked increasingly insecure.

The first I heard of Barings' collapse was on Saturday 25 February 1995. I was sitting round the family breakfast table, the phone rang, unusually early for a Saturday, and my wife told me it was Martin Owen, the chief executive of NatWest Markets. He was a great respecter of family time and would not have rung except on a matter of emergency. The only other time he had disturbed me at home was after the Bishopsgate bomb had damaged our offices and I knew the call was important. I moved into another room, not knowing whether to expect news of a terrorist attack, a senior resignation, a takeover bid by or for NatWest or whether he had found out about my negotiations for a move to Schroders which were underway by then.

Martin spoke first and he sounded shocked, subdued and not his normal, upbeat self: 'Phil, we need you in the office on Sunday. I can't tell you any more but arrange for a car and be at Lothbury at 5 p.m. Don't go far from the phone, we might need you before then. I am sorry to be so mysterious but there's nothing more I am allowed to say.' I swallowed my irritation at his habit of calling me 'Phil', a name used only by my parents and a few old friends from the sixties, and began to work out what was going on. He wanted me at Lothbury, the group head office, so whatever it was concerned the whole group and not just NatWest Markets which seemed to rule out a resignation, either mine or anyone else's. I did not want to let him go without getting a few more clues and managed to glean that a bank was in trouble, that it wasn't ours, but that it might have serious implications for us. A bit more ringing round over the weekend and a look at the Sunday papers meant that, by the time I arrived at Lothbury on Sunday evening, I knew that it was Barings.

A number of other senior executives and directors of the bank were waiting in the group chief executive's office. After quite a long wait, Derek Wanless appeared from a meeting across the road at the Bank of England, thanked everyone for coming but said there was nothing left to decide, Barings could not be saved and what we now had to do was work out our counterparty exposure and assess the commercial significance. We debated the immediate threats and opportunities to our own business and the meeting broke up at 10 p.m. I went out into Lothbury, which should have been deserted at that time on a Sunday night but was packed with cars waiting to take bankers home. We turned on the news and heard that the full story was breaking. What really happened?

BARINGS: BACKGROUND

One of the great ironies of the period is that Barings was brought down by its equities business, having decided before Big Bang not to have one. It drifted into equities in order to protect its Japanese convertible new issue business but that was forgotten as the profits generated by Baring Securities in Far Eastern markets became a major part of the group earnings. While profits were good the securities staff demanded and were allowed operational independence. No one could have been surprised if a major profit accident had occurred at this time since head office were not fully aware of how the money was being made and exercised no real control over the business.

However, when the profit stream dried up as markets matured,

Barings did impose some structure on the business through the creation of Baring Investment Bank in 1992, the removal of Christopher Heath, the founder and head of Baring Securities, in March 1993 and the simultaneous introduction of a formal structure and reporting lines. On paper Barings' investment banking operations were better managed in 1995 than they had been at any time in the previous ten years but events of the first quarter showed that there were still huge weaknesses.

The collapse of Barings has been covered intensively through investigative journalism, several books, television programmes, a film and, most thoroughly, in the Board of Banking Supervision report *Inquiry into the Circumstances of the Collapse of Barings*.[1] There is no need for another detailed account but a brief summary of the key events of 1995 is necessary background to an understanding of why it happened.

Quite often in financial markets rumours start about particular firms. Such gossip is rarely totally right but usually contains a grain of truth and, if the story affects your firm and you are responsible for that firm, the correct starting-point must be that there is no smoke without fire. In January 1995 market rumours reached Barings management in London that Barings had a customer on the Osaka Securities Exchange who could not meet a margin call; that is, did not have the funds to pay for the futures positions they had dealt in. At the end of the month the rumours resurfaced in different form, to the effect that Barings itself had margin losses in the futures contract on the Nikkei and could not meet its margin call. Depending on the circumstances, this could have left Barings exposed in a highly geared way to market movements but Barings' management ruled out such risk because it believed that its Nikkei positions on the Osaka Stock Exchange (OSE) were matched by equal and opposite positions on the Singapore International Monetary Exchange (SIMEX). It therefore discussed the rumours, made some inquiries, concluded that it was not at risk and dismissed the stories.

On 26 January Baring Asset and Liabilities Committee (ALCO), which had only been formed the previous November as part of the tightening-up process, instructed that Nick Leeson, the head of Baring Futures in Singapore, be told not to increase the size of the positions on the OSE and SIMEX, these having been rising in January. In typical

Barings fashion, this request was not followed through and no action was taken when the positions continued to increase. A few days later ALCO discussed a letter from SIMEX reminding it of its responsibilities to ensure that it had sufficient funds to fulfil its financial obligations to them. The many warning signals that were flashing around Baring Futures in January 1995 should have put management on red alert and they should then have started a full investigation.

The amber lights continued to flash into February. On or around 1 February 1995, Barings auditors, Coopers & Lybrand, informed Barings group finance director of an amount of £50 million in Baring Futures Singapore balance sheet as at 31 December 1994 apparently due from Spear, Leeds & Kellogg, a New York specialist securities trader. This transaction later turned out to be a fiction of Leeson's but not enough action was taken to follow up the auditors' letter, despite the market rumours.

Belatedly management in the region began to call for action. On 3 February James Bax, the regional manager for South Asia at Baring Investment Bank, sent a memorandum to Peter Norris, the chief executive of BIB, and to others, referring to 'the current operational weaknesses of our SIMEX business and an urgent need for a new approach.'[2] A few days later, Tony Hawes, group treasurer BIB and Tony Railton, futures and options settlements senior clerk, went to Singapore to review the significance of the SIMEX letters and the £50 million year-end debtor. Hawes was reassured when he was told that the debtor had subsequently repaid the funds. In the following week, as he analysed the transactions and netted off opposite deals, Railton realized that 'If you close out all the positions there is absolutely no way on God's earth that you could actually return all the yen' which he estimated at Y14 billion ($140 million).[3] By 17 February Railton was really worried but still believed at this stage that the missing money might be explained by his lack of understanding of the complex BFS margining system. He knew that only Leeson could help him understand this but Leeson did not appear for meetings with him on 20 and 21 February and it was only on Wednesday 22 and Thursday 23 February that the two met. Leeson agreed that there appeared to be a problem but characteristically carried on trading during the first meeting and left the second after thirty minutes.

Leeson disappeared from that point, faxing his resignation to Barings on Friday 24 February from Kuala Lumpur and reappearing in Frankfurt on Wednesday 1 March, at which point he was arrested. Early on the morning of Friday 24 February Singapore time (the evening of Thursday 23 February London time), Hawes and Railton 'started trying to reconcile the cash position and Hawes concluded that the apparent settlement of the SLK year-end receivable had been manufactured'. They were joined by Bax and Jones. Hawes started looking at a computer printout and noticed 'an account called an error account with goodness knows how many transactions on it, all of them seemingly standing at enormous losses'. This was the account 88888 which was used to conceal losses from London.[4]

On the morning of Friday 24 February, Peter Baring met the Deputy Governor of the Bank of England 'and informed him that he considered that Barings had been the victim of massive fraud . . . vigorous attempts were made to save Barings over the weekend, but, owing in part to the uncertain cost of closing the open positions when the markets reopened on Monday morning and the related difficulty in establishing the facts about Barings' financial state, these efforts were unsuccessful'. Administrators were appointed in London on the evening of Sunday February 26 1995, and judicial managers in Singapore the following day, when BFS failed to pay a margin call. Just over a week later the majority of the assets and liabilities of the Barings group were purchased by ING, the large Dutch banking and insurance group.[5]

HOW DID IT HAPPEN?

Most of the analysis of the collapse of Barings has focused on the character of Leeson (which will not be re-examined here), and the culture at Barings which allowed him to go unchallenged. There is, however, an important area which has not previously been given enough prominence and that is the failure on the part of the regulators to supervise Barings adequately. As we shall see, the Board of Banking Supervision tried very hard not to blame the regulators, minimizing direct criticism in its report, but could not help but reveal deficiencies at the Bank of England, the Securities and Futures Authority and in the way they worked together.

The cultural problems began with Christopher Heath and the haphazard way in which Barings developed its broking business. Because securities was not an adjunct to corporate finance or any other part of the group, it lacked a senior sponsor within Barings. Although the senior directors of Barings were happy to pick up their bonuses on the back of securities' results, none of them identified closely with the business. In practice it was the staff of Baring Securities who managed it with minimal supervision from group management.

This was encouraged by Heath who believed that 'banks bugger up brokers'[6] and who ran the unit as a stand-alone operation. His personal style – informal, verbal rather than written, unstructured chats rather than formal meetings, doing rather than debating – established an all-pervasive culture that survived his departure. Such a culture might have suited the small agency business that existed at the beginning but, by the time it involved trading, hundreds of employees, and three continents, the organization needed structure.

Peter Baring and Andrew Tuckey had recognized this by 1993 and sought to bring the independent minded securities firm under tighter control by establishing a single investment bank. Tuckey told the Board of Banking Supervision: 'this concept was developed because of a difficult relationship with the wholly owned subsidiary BSL in 1992 when we had basically a management disagreement between the centre of Barings and the people who were running Baring Securities'. Peter Norris, who had been made chief executive of Baring Securities in March 1993 after Heath's removal, describes the old attitudes at Baring Securities: 'The ethos was, really, that the last thing you need in a stockbroking outfit is management in a formal bureaucratic sense.' Tuckey elaborated on the different cultures operating at Baring Brothers and Baring Securities: 'Brokers are generally different from corporate financiers anywhere you find them in any organization. I saw that difference in timescale. Everything in the broker's world is today and tomorrow – whereas when you talk to a corporate finance person he is interested in what his clients are going to be doing next year.'[7]

The new structure was established in the second half of 1993 and was known as the Investment Banking Group and later Baring Investment Bank. A weakness in the new structure was the lack of an independent risk management unit, Group Treasury and Market Risk being asked to supervise it. But they were not dedicated, specialized or demonstrably impartial and should not have been given the job. The operating units (Equity Broking and Trading, Banking, Corporate Finance and Emerging Markets Corporate Finance)[8] were linked by a matrix reporting structure. This meant that management with global responsibility for the product led on front office matters and that management in the local geographical entity dealt with operational items such as systems, controls, accounting, settlements and administration.

The use of matrix reporting combining functional and geographic management was widespread in investment banking by the mid 1990s but management needed to work at it to make it real. A starting-point was to write it down but 'no clear or complete organization chart of IBG/BIB was prepared and disseminated at the time the organizational structure was being formulated. Nor had one been prepared by the time of the collapse.' As a consequence Barings was full of ambiguities and no one knew exactly who was responsible for what: 'It appears from our interviews that reporting lines and responsibilities were not fully understood by a number of individuals, especially concerning FPG, headed by Ron Baker, and BFS of which Leeson was general manager.'[9]

The direct result of this was that, when the warning signs appeared in 1995, no one took responsibility for following them up.

Failure to make the matrix work was at the heart of Barings' collapse. With a clearer structure and documented lines of responsibility, people would have known what they had to do and what they were accountable for. As it was, 'One of the consequences of the ambiguities in the IBG/BIB organizational structure was that some members of management believed that responsibility for certain activities (e.g. equity derivatives, Baring Futures) rested with other managers who deny they had such responsibility. This resulted in confusion and a pervasive lack of management control over these activities.'[10]

A failure to follow things through was a characteristic of Barings management style. The events of January 1995 gave so many clues that something was wrong, all pointing in the same direction, that

Singapore should have become management's top priority. The most critical structural weakness, that Leeson was in charge of the front and the back office in Singapore, was pointed out to management in an internal audit of 1994 but nothing was done to rectify it. On 3 February 1995 it was highlighted again, this time by Bax, yet again nothing was done about it. As the Board of Banking Supervision pointed out, 'Clear segregation of duties is a fundamental principle of internal control in all businesses and has long been recognized as the first line of protection against the risk of fraudulent or unauthorized activities.'[11] It is one of the most basic principles of securities management, was known by Barings management to have been breached in Singapore, yet no mechanism existed to make things happen, no individual took responsibility for closing these most obvious loopholes.

There was very little synchronization between the different parts of Barings. For example, London failed to establish the reason for very large payments being made to Singapore. It assumed that they were for clients but even then failed to run client credit checks of the kind that were routinely carried out in other areas of the bank.[12] The fact that huge payments could be made from London to Singapore without serious questions being asked is further proof that there was no culture of challenge within Barings and minimal cooperation between departments.

There was also a gap between the aims of the business and the skills and experience of those charged with implementing it. For example, Ron Baker had joined Barings in April 1992 from Bankers Trust, from the debt trading side. Late in 1993 he was asked to take over the equity derivatives business. Although he had knowledge of using derivatives on a proprietary basis, these were debt derivatives and over the counter (OTC) rather than exchange traded equity derivatives. Baker told the Board of Banking Supervision: 'There is no doubt in my mind that if I had had ten years' experience in exchange traded equity derivatives, this would not have happened.'[13] But the problems went further than Baker:

Barings' experience shows it to be absolutely essential that top management understand the broad nature of all the material activities of the institution for which they are responsible and that product management have a detailed understanding of all aspects of the activities they manage. This detailed understanding must include a thorough and continuing analysis of the risk and potential return of each product, how they relate to one another, and the type of control systems required to reduce the risk of error or fraud to a level acceptable to the institution. Management must demonstrate in their everyday actions their belief in, and insistence on, the operation of strong and relevant controls throughout the institution. This is particularly important in high volume, volatile products where the associated risks are correspondingly higher.[14]

ROLE OF BARINGS' REGULATORS

The regulators would have done well to have heeded their own advice to financial institutions such as Barings: 'There must be no gaps and no room for any confusion so that the situation of one manager believing another manager has responsibility for an issue, and vice versa, is avoided.'[15] Such criticism levelled by the regulators at Barings' management applies equally well to themselves. This starts with the Bank of England which was 'at all relevant times the consolidated supervisor of the Barings Group'.[16] There is no doubt that the Bank took too relaxed a view of Barings' management based on the old values of the gentlemanly capitalist: 'The Bank regarded the controls in Barings as informal but effective. It had confidence in Barings' senior management, many of whom were longstanding Barings' employees. Accordingly it placed greater reliance on statements made to it by management than it would have done had this degree of confidence not existed'.[17]

The Bank of England's views of the risks being run by Barings seem to have been out of date. It should have been obvious that a securities business, especially one with operations in some exotic markets and instruments needed extra close attention. Instead, 'With regard to Barings' overseas subsidiaries the Bank undertook no reviews. In that respect, it placed reliance on what it was told by Barings and its auditors and reporting accountants (C&L) . . . and (in accordance with recognized supervisory practice) on the supervision performed by the relevant overseas regulators.'[18] The Board of Banking Supervision considered that the Bank 'reasonably placed reliance on local regulators' and that it was 'entitled to place reliance on the explanations given by management'.[19] This view seems inconsistent with the Bank's duties as lead regulator and with the board's own views.

These views emerge much more clearly further on in the report:

Had the Bank a greater understanding of Barings' Far Eastern operations and a greater awareness of the degree of control of these operations exercised by Barings in London it would have been better placed to supervise the consolidated group. There does not appear to have been any guideline or system in place within the Bank for determining whether the situation with regard to a member of a banking group for which the Bank was responsible for consolidated supervision was material such that it could affect the wellbeing of the bank.[20]

The SFA displayed a similar lack of vigour in taking its duties to their logical conclusion:

The SFA did not regard itself as required to consider the activities or financial position of the subsidiaries of BSL and considered that its responsibilities with regard to subsidiaries were limited to the express notification requirements relating to subsidiaries set out in its rules. However, we consider that the SFA's responsibility for monitoring a member firm's obligation to maintain adequate financial resources to meet its investment business commitments and to withstand the risks to which its business is subject requires it to have regard to the activities and financial soundness of a member firm's subsidiaries insofar as they are capable of materially affecting the financial integrity of the member firm.[21]

This was later softened by the view that 'it would not be right to criticize the SFA' on the basis of the information it was given.[22] This is all very well and gentlemanly, and no doubt the SFA laboured under severe resource limitations, but if the SFA or the Bank of England had been more proactive in test sampling the overseas subsidiaries of Barings instead of relying on local regulators who were pursuing a different, local agenda the failures on the part of Barings' central and

Asian management would have been more likely to have been detected. The Board of Banking Supervision report does the best it can to couch criticism of the regulators in the nicest terms it can but it is an honest piece of work and the truth is there for all who care to look.

NO ONE CARED

Barings was undone by a combination of a rogue trader, a lax regulatory regime and weak management. Nine warning signs missed by management and listed by the Board of Banking Supervision should have been spotted: lack of segregation identified by the internal auditors in July and August 1994; the high level of funding required by BFS; unreconciled balances; suspiciously high profits; apparent funding of clients; letters from SIMEX in January 1995 identifying the 88888 account and its large funding requirements; questions raised by regulators; high level of switching/arbitrage business; market rumours in January and February 1995.[23] The failure to act on these can be attributed to lack of management expertise; structural weaknesses; and possibly a fear of disturbing or alienating the source of profits that made the group's results and funded the bonus pool. Barings' regulators lacked the resources, the resolve and the coordination to pick up the deficiencies of management. This situation was exploited by Nick Leeson, an individual who had been overpromoted and who found himself swimming well out of his depth.

In the final analysis, there was no one at Barings who spotted the problem and that was because there was no emotional owner of Baring Securities once Heath had gone. No one felt sufficiently proud of Baring Securities to impose best management practice, no one saw it as his main task to manage it. No one felt sufficiently threatened by the risk of failure there to persist with inquiries, to ask about detail or to correct obvious deficiencies. It was the same with the regulators. No single body except the Bank of England was responsible for the totality of Barings' business and the Bank relied on the SFA and the local regulators. The Bank failed to appreciate the risk being run in Barings in a way that would have been inconceivable if it had been able to rely on a tough, independent-minded regulator like the SEC in the US. The consequence was that Britain lost a bank, the City lost one of its own and the viability of the other merchant banks was seriously undermined.

22

Warburg: The Final Year

If you had to choose a day that was the beginning of the end for Warburg it would be 24 February 1994 when the board decided to expand the group's bond interests. The decision to seek a bigger position in bonds to support its aspirations to the bulge bracket was reportedly driven by the chief executive, Lord Cairns, and the chairman, Sir David Scholey, and Peter Bass and Peter Twachtmann, the co-heads of the bond and treasury division, also attended the board meeting.[1] The timing was unfortunate for, during the board meeting, European bond markets dropped sharply in response to the first increases in US interest rates since 1989 and ushered in a year when even the best-established bond houses lost money.

Warburg pressed on with its plan to recruit more traders and salespeople and to increase the amount of capital that was to be traded in fixed income securities. Losses mounted during the summer as costs rose with the recruitment programme whilst revenue suffered in the volatile markets: 'Cairns thought of pulling back but hesitated. "We were saying, cool it, by July but if we had retrenched we would have lost our best people" says an executive.'[2] Instead, the decision to pull back was not taken until September 1994 by when a further few weeks of trading losses and cost build-up had occurred.[3] It later emerged that, in the six months to the end of September 1994, dealing profits dropped by £100 million from the comparable period in 1993 and investment banking profits were a paltry £5 million.

BETTING THE BANK ON MORGAN STANLEY

It was against this background of Warburg's deteriorating results, which Cairns knew but Morgan Stanley did not, that John Mack, president of the US bulge bracket firm Morgan Stanley, came to lunch with Cairns in late September. The agenda was a plan of Mack's, which he was discussing with several competitors, for investment banks to save money by pooling aspects of their support structures. The conversation moved to a blue sky discussion about joint ventures in emerging markets but Cairns told Mack that cooperation would only work on a grand scale: a merger.

The two banks agreed to talk seriously about this idea in early October but by this time Warburg was on the back foot. On 3 October 1994 it was forced to issue the first of its three profit warnings in the next seven months which created widespread debate in the City about the achievability of Warburg's goals. A dinner between Mack and his chairman, Richard Fisher, and Cairns and Scholey at Claridges Hotel in London 'marked the start of serious merger talks. At first only a few senior executives knew of these talks – dubbed "Project Sparkling", with Morgan Stanley known in internal documents as "Highland" and Warburg as "Spring", after the mineral water consumed at Cairns' and Mack's lunch.'[4]

Discussions continued amongst a very small group until the end of November when the circle was broadened to include the top 100 executives in the two firms. There were three principal issues that needed resolution: the name of the new entity; the balance of rationalization between the overlapping businesses in London; and the position of Mercury Asset Management (MAM).

The name of the proposed new entity was problematical, involving legal issues as well as pride. Morgan Stanley had been born out of J. P. Morgan in 1935 when the latter sold off its broking business to help comply with Glass–Steagall. At the time, Morgan Stanley agreed not to drop the Stanley part of its name and this agreement was still in force. This meant that the obvious name, Morgan Warburg, could not be chosen and that issues of balance between the two parties' representation in the new title came into play. Warburg believed that

Morgan Stanley Warburg tilted too much to the American firm and Morgan Stanley had a similar objection to Warburg Morgan Stanley.

Rationalization was an issue in London where Morgan Stanley had a staff of 2000 of its own. This was always a bone of contention when investment banks merged. The conventional wisdom was that people choices needed to be made by reference to some overall scorecard as well as to business logic. In reality it is doubtful whether such a balanced approach was the best policy and later mergers were effected through more brutal 'best person for the job' criteria. In the case of Morgan Stanley and Warburg the debate was made more difficult by a leak which was reported in the press on 8 December, eleven days ahead of planned impact day. The two parties were faced with an instant decision, confirm the talks or call them off; they elected to confirm. The frenzied debate this engendered in the City, on Wall Street and in the press did not make it easy to reach a considered conclusion. In particular, newspapers began to speculate about where the inevitable job cuts would fall, and Morgan Stanley's London operations were rapidly identified in the press, in bars and in trading rooms as being the most vulnerable. This caused problems with Morgan Stanley's staff and began to affect management behaviour in two respects. Firstly, pacifying the staff became a distraction from the strategic planning which was required at this time and this helped to destroy the momentum which the deal had had. Secondly, it became increasingly important not to be seen as the loser if the deal failed and Morgan Stanley appear to have planned for this better.

The third problem area, MAM, was what finally caused the deal to crumble. Warburg owned 75 per cent of MAM, the remaining 25 per cent being listed on the Stock Exchange and held by a mixture of institutional and private shareholders and staff. The business was performing well, forming one of the Big Four pension fund managers in the UK along with Schroders, Phillips & Drew and Gartmore. It also contributed over a third of group profits even in the golden year for investment banking, 1993–4, and it contributed about two thirds of the entire group's Stock Market capitalization.

MAM was brought into the Morgan Stanley discussions late and meetings between the senior management of the two firms did not go particularly well. MAM was about twice the size of Morgan Stanley

Asset Management and expected to dominate in a merger and to continue its existing ways. At a meeting at MAM's offices in King William Street on Tuesday 13 December, Richard Fisher, Barton Biggs and Jim Allwin, the chairman and president of MSAM, were told by MAM's directors that they wished to remain independent and that they wanted a protocol ensuring their continued independence of name and operation in the event of the merger going through.

The following day MAM's advisers indicated to Fisher the size of the premium they wanted to buy out MAM's minority shareholders. This was well above what Fisher had in mind and, coming on top of the difficulties of integrating MAM, Morgan Stanley's operating committee decided to call off the talks at some time very late in the evening London time.

What happened next illustrates Warburg's naïvety, or Morgan Stanley's ruthlessness, or the problems of global communication, or the consequences of misunderstanding – or perhaps all four. Rather than telling Warburg that night, Fisher and Mack briefed their senior executives at 7.30 a.m. and then called Cairns with the decision and faxed him a draft announcement: 'When the fax arrived it was in Morgan Stanley's name alone. It was vital for Warburg that the ending of talks was seen as a joint decision. Cairns rang back and said that Warburg wanted to soften the tone and make it a joint statement. Mack agreed to change part of the phrasing but said they did not have enough time to make it a joint statement.'[5] The text was on screens around the world within minutes. Stephen Waters, co-head of Morgan Stanley in Europe, told the *FT* 'MAM was the reason for us to do this deal' which kept Warburg on the defensive. It had exposed the weakness of its investment banking strategy and now the world was being told that Morgan Stanley had viewed Warburg's investment bank as a make weight in the deal.

AFTER MORGAN STANLEY: PICKING UP THE PIECES

Warburg faced the consequences of the ignominious collapse of talks with all of the stakeholders in its business: MAM, the staff, clients, and shareholders. Warburg went into retrieval mode, reassuring them of its commitment to and ability to deliver the global vision. It also needed to address the problems that were draining Warburg's financial and spiritual resources and on 19 December Cairns replaced Bass and Twachtmann as heads of fixed income and treasury. January 9 1995 saw 'the closure of substantially all of the group's international bond activities' with sterling fixed income and global equities businesses being merged into a single securities division.[6] This radical step might have saved the group had it been implemented six months earlier but it now came too late to rescue the results and further damaged credibility.

In straightforward business terms closure seemed a sensible decision. Warburg's non-sterling bond operations lost £20 million in the half-year to end September 1994, suggesting that revenues were minimal on an annual cost base of £25 million. In theory Warburg's withdrawal need not have affected its position as a top-quality global corporate advisory and equity issuing house. Eurobond issues were considered to be a commodity item and not an integral part of the broad relationship between a corporate and its investment bank. However, competitors and commentators would not allow Warburg to get away with this. Many journalists commented on the irony of Warburg pulling out of a business area it had invented: 'S. G. Warburg, the UK investment bank, yesterday announced it was pulling out of the Eurobond market created thirty years ago by its founder Sir Siegmund Warburg, after the collapse of merger talks with Morgan Stanley' was how the *Financial Times* began its coverage of the story.[7] Competitors contrasted Warburg's ambitions to join the Wall Street bulge bracket with its retreat from a major capital market and tried to sow seeds of doubt in clients' minds. David Band, the chief executive of BZW, argued that withdrawing from bonds would hinder Warburg's ability to win equity mandates from corporates and Governments: 'If you are not doing day-to-day things for clients, it makes it harder to get in at the top table.'[8]

The withdrawal from international bonds accelerated the realization amongst the staff that Warburg's vision was changing. According to one Warburg executive, 'It was the right thing to do but a lot of people found it difficult. We tried to move them from taking a step-change towards being global at the start of 1994 to saying "whoops" in 1995.

It was too many degrees in too short a time.'[9] Staff retention became a problem as competitors realized that, for the first time since Big Bang, Warburg's best staff might be amenable to a move.

In February two of Warburg's brightest stars, the co-heads of equity capital markets, Maurice Thomson and Michael Cohrs, resigned to join Morgan Grenfell's latest initiative in investment banking. Warburg spent two days trying to turn them round but to no avail. Thomson and Cohrs were interpreted as having voted with their feet in regard to the bank's prospects. Not only were they known within the bank to be world-class operators, they were in a position in which they had had a lot of exposure to institutional and corporate clients and their defection could not have been more high profile or more damaging. They were soon followed by other senior staff in equities and capital markets.

After the Morgan Stanley affair, Cairns faced a desperate fight to re-establish leadership. He slimmed down management to an eight-man committee but the group did not function well and his own position was weak. The style of the gentlemanly capitalist, no matter how good, no longer fitted the needs of the time. A Warburg executive summed it up: 'Simon prized effortless achievement and the gifted amateur. A crisis demands a determined professional who is seen to be doing something.'[10] Within a few days Cairns resigned as chief executive, telling the chairman that the ground had been cut from under his feet by the collapse of the Morgan Stanley talks. His departure was described by Scholey in terms of which the gentlemanly capitalists would have been proud: 'I did not say to him "You have got it wrong." He is a big enough man to decide these things for himself.'[11]

Scholey, who had been due to retire shortly as chairman, returned as chief executive to try to hold things together. He appointed an executive committee of younger directors to run the business. Michael Sargent for securities, Mark Nicholls for corporate finance, Edward Chandler for the Nordic region and Colin Buchan for UK equities joined Scholey to try to rally the firm. This appeared to bypass the heads of broking and banking, Nick Verey and Derek Higgs, who had reported direct to Cairns and who were associated with the failed strategy. Scholey's team took over amidst much talk of needing to 'regain our old habits of rigorous quality and cost control'.

However, Warburg still appeared accident-prone with the staff rather than management running the firm. It was announced that John Holmes had been hired from Credit Lyonnais to be in charge of the UK equity sales team but, as Holmes explains, the troops would have none of it: 'There was a palace revolution by the salesmen. Warburg withdrew the offer after three months of interviews. The place was in a state of anarchy at the time.'[12]

FALLING DOWNSTAIRS: THE DEAL WITH SBC

Scholey knew that there were even more fundamental issues than unrest in equities and in February 1995 he appointed the US investment bank, J. P. Morgan, to advise Warburg on its strategic options. But the most pressing problem was MAM. When Morgan Stanley claimed that MAM, rather than the investment bank, was the reason for its interest in Warburg, the balance of power within the Warburg group shifted and it became inevitable that MAM would soon need to be independent. This was reinforced when MAM found itself on the defensive about its parent's performance at meetings with its own clients.[13] At a meeting with MAM directors in February 1995 Scholey was told that, in MAM's view, Warburg needed to seek a merger with a stronger partner, a view which was reinforced by the collapse of Barings on 26 February which led to an open debate in the City and the press about the viability of the traditional British merchant bank.

It became increasingly apparent that, whilst Warburg's European corporate advisory and equity capital markets aspirations were attainable as an independent firm, it would need access to a stronger balance sheet and an alternative stream of revenue as a cushion against volatility if it was to pursue its global aspirations. In March Georges Blum and Marcel Ospel, respectively the chief executive and head of the international and finance division of Swiss Bank Corporation, visited Scholey and approached the question of a merger. Scholey had received other approaches from, amongst others, NatWest and Smith Barney, but SBC was a more interesting proposition. Although it lacked the presence in Wall Street that Smith Barney might have offered, it had an entrepreneurial spirit. It already had a strong fund management arm in the form of Brinson Partners so it did not need MAM. It had built up its investment banking operations in Europe with an impressive trading approach which it had used to lever its way into primary business but it did not have a full-scale corporate advisory business that would overlap with Warburg. The chemistry between the two sides was good and, although disclosure of talks was forced slightly early by a leak naming Warburg's alternative suitor, Smith Barney, the boards of MAM and Warburg ratified the deal on 9 May.

The agreed price valued the Warburg group at £850 million with Warburg shareholders getting £3.65 cash and 0.538 MAM shares for every Warburg share held. There is no doubt that, as a distressed seller, Warburg went very cheaply. SBC paid 8 per cent above book value for Warburg, the UK's premier investment banking name. By the end of the year Merrill Lynch were happy to pay 2.4 times book value for Smith New Court and Dresdner Bank two times book value for Kleinwort.

WHY DID IT HAPPEN?

Warburg's collapse boils down to four basic reasons: costs ran out of control; revenue collapsed; ambition exceeded resources; and the firm's culture was diluted.

The cost build up in the financial year to end March 1994 was startling. Group expenses rose 32 per cent to £747 million with staff costs up 40 per cent to £470 million. This was explained away at the time as being 'principally caused by higher performance related payments',[14] which was understandable given the record results that year. But in 1994–5, when profits collapsed, staff costs fell only 5 per cent to £444 million, casting doubt over the previous year's explanation. In reality it was the increase in headcount as much as the need to pay high bonuses that caused the problems. The average number of employees in investment banking in 1994–5 was 4353, up from 3835 the previous year, and it is a fair bet that most of these 500 new people were on guaranteed bonuses, some for two years. Once this expansion had occurred, and given the need to keep other staff happy in a competitive market, Warburg had little control over bonuses and found itself locked into an inflated cost base.

Table 11. Segmental Analysis,
Investment Banking, Warburg,
1994–5, £ million[15]

	Fees & commissions	Dealing
1995	451.1	38.8
1994	527.6	207.2

The increase in costs became a serious problem when revenues collapsed from £735 million in investment banking in 1993–4 to £490 million in 1994–5. It was this decline of £245 million, together with a low variable element in the cost base that obliterated investment banking profits.

It is generally believed that all of Warburg's problems lay in bonds and in America. In fact, as the table above shows, fees and commissions, which were almost all derived from equities and corporate finance, also performed badly with a drop of nearly £80 million in 1994–5 and this in itself would have been enough to damage the group's reputation. Warburg's general malaise was also evident from the firm's published regional analysis which shows that the main problems lay in the UK. North America and Asia Pacific actually improved in 1994–5, Continental Europe slipped by £12 million but the big hole was a drop of £146 million in the UK.

The mismatch of ambition and resources was both a tactical and a strategic issue. Tactically it caused the firm to miss an opportunity to retrench in the summer of 1994. Had the bank frozen the development strategy and concentrated on refocusing the business, it is possible that

Table 12. Geographical Analysis, Dealing Profits, Warburg, 1994–5, £ million[16]

	UK	Other Europe	N. America	Asia Pacific	Discounted operations
1995	41.2	5.4	11.6	12.9	(32.3)
1994	187.3	17.9	(0.1)	(1.2)	3.3

it might have survived. But Warburg's global ambition was a sincerely held belief as well as a business goal. It had been iterated from the early days of Big Bang. Warburg's senior management were as concerned about the message that would be given to staff by a retreat as they were about clients. An investment bank's staff are stakeholders in the enterprise. Without them the bank has no business and, once the staff had been sold a global vision, it was judged impossible to sell them an alternative.

The strategic problem with Warburg's global vision was that the target was so exalted that the bank was drawn into a range of activities that stretched its managerial and financial resources. This had always been known to be a risk: 'It's quite clear that the British Government would love to see one British firm genuinely compete on a global basis. S. G. Warburg is the only merchant bank in the United Kingdom that has a global aspiration to compete on that scale although there are some who can compete in boutique structures in various markets. I won't suggest Warburgs can't do it but it will be very, very difficult for them.'[17]

Charles McVeigh's caution proved justified and his analysis after the collapse was equally astute:

Quite simply they didn't have the capital base or earnings power to meet their aspirations globally. We went through a period in the late 1980s and early nineties of incredibly favourable markets – lower interest rates, an enormous amount of equity underwriting, significant fees being paid for M&A advisory business. It was difficult to envision a more favourable period for the industry as a whole. The question was always, what happens when the music stops and the economic environment is a lot less favourable? That really happened in 1994 for a lot of us . . . The great challenge for Warburg was the huge cost of trying to compete in America, Japan, in Hong Kong, in the emerging markets, in Europe and in maintaining what had generically been a very profitable UK business. It became increasingly obvious that this geographic platform could not be maintained.[18]

There were errors of judgement along the way, and Cairns took responsibility for the failure of the bond and Morgan Stanley strategies.[19] Although Cairns must take some of the blame, the global strategy preceded him and the problem was that from the beginning it was at the outer edge of the bank's managerial and financial capabilities. Once the threshold of competitiveness for global investment banks increased beyond a certain scale with the US mergers of 1994, Warburg was operating beyond that limit. In the words of one competitor: 'Warburgs tried to go too fast, too far and fell downstairs.'[20]

A consequence of the dash for growth was that Warburg lost its unique culture and became just like any other firm. This has been clearly explained by Warburg insider, Peter Stormonth Darling, who reports a view that the problems began with addition of the Rowe & Pitman and Akroyd securities businesses, which were domestic and diluted the firm's unique European flavour. Further expansion then watered down ownership, leaving only 1 per cent of group equity in staff hands with little to encourage the employees to share objectives with the shareholders.

During the growth of the firm after Big Bang too little regard was paid to cultural issues and Siegmund Warburg's philosophy was lost: 'There were rules relating to personal behaviour. We should acknowledge the predominant influence of people and of our clients. We were taught the essential virtue of self-criticism and the necessity of carrying out our activities with a measured rhythm or tempo.'[21] While it was a small firm with a strong personality at the helm this culture was maintained. As the firm grew and management changed this was weakened. Many believed that the cult of the individual had been given too free a rein, commenting on Thomson and Cohrs that 'All they do is a lot of shouting down telephones and they were allowed to generate a mystique that shouldn't have been permitted. Someone should have told them to come off it.'[22] No one ever told them or anyone else to come off it and Warburg appeared to become like many other firms, a collection of hired hands working for themselves first and the company second. The tragedy is that Warburg could have been different if its culture had been nurtured and its strong position in the early 1990s developed a little more slowly. Instead Warburg completed one of the swiftest falls from grace ever seen: from hero in June 1994, with the record results, to villain in December, with a botched merger and a profit warning to its name. The best of the Big Bang experiments was over.

23

Kleinwort and Smith

The Warburg–Morgan Stanley affair put Schroders and Kleinwort in the spotlight. They were substantial, quoted merchant banks that might not be able to complete the transition into investment banks. The family controlled 48 per cent of the voting shares at Schroders and they made it clear that they were 'rock solid' which deflected most of the speculation on to Kleinwort, where the family influenced under a third of votes and to the independent brokers.

KLEINWORT BENSON

Before Barings went under, most commentators did not believe that a bid for Kleinwort was likely:

Both Kleinwort Benson and S. G. Warburg might fit well within a larger investment banking group. Neither will be able to fulfil its global ambitions by remaining independent. But it is hard to see the logic of a continental European bank such as Dresdner buying Kleinwort, the rumour that sent its share price yo-yoing last week. What the continental banks lack most is what Kleinwort and Warburg also lack most – a strong presence in the US. If poor commercial logic were not enough of a barrier to such deals, banks' need to fulfil stringent capital adequacy limits set up by their regulators places another obstacle. To acquire Kleinwort or Warburg would involve paying roughly twice net assets.[1]

Speculation intensified after the fall of Barings, a few clients moved their deposits away from the smaller merchant banks to bigger counterparties and, until sentiment stabilized, it was difficult to assess the situation. There was widespread speculation in the press that the days of the independent quoted English merchant bank were numbered and panic might have set in.[2] A massive programme of reassurance by the directors and senior executives of the merchant banks ensured that clients and staff were settled down in the weeks after Barings.

However, privately Kleinwort had been reviewing its position for some time. The inner circle, known as the 'chairman's group', had discussed the need for an outside partner at their planning meeting in the summer of 1994 and had recognized that it might not be possible to remain independent. Early in 1995, the chairman, Lord Rockley, told the full board that no option could be ruled out. The management was now in a difficult position: deliberating whether independence was viable; being questioned regularly and in public about the issue; yet needing to maintain an unyielding determination to carry on in order to reassure staff and clients and to discourage competitors. Therefore, they played down the need for a partner: 'With real knowledge and commitment you can go up against the giants.'[3]

The collapse of Warburg gave rise to another bout of press speculation and gave management more work to do in reassuring staff and clients. They distanced themselves from Warburg's failed bond strategy, pointing out that the capital-intensive approach tried by Warburg and in which the US investment banks were involved was not relevant to Kleinwort's corporate advisory and equity capital markets plan.[4]

Kleinwort's credibility was helped by its progress in corporate finance,[5] which helped protect the results for 1994. These were released in February 1995 and showed a dip in investment banking profits largely balanced by improved profits in investment management; inevitably, Rockley was asked about merger speculation: 'I am not going to make any public statement. We have got a strategy – we focus on what we are good at and deliver. It is succeeding and we are going to carry it on in the future. We are not looking for anything else.'[6]

However, behind the scenes doubts persisted amongst the senior directors and these were confirmed by the sale of Warburg to SBC. They were therefore receptive to an approach made in the spring by Jürgen Sarrazin, chairman of the board of managing directors of

Dresdner Bank, to Rockley. After a long debate the group decided to respond to Dresdner's initiative. For two months discussions were held between Kleinwort (code name 'Carat') and Dresdner (code name 'Diamond'). Simon Robertson, Sir Nicholas Redmayne and either Robert Jeens, the finance director, or Clementi represented Kleinwort in the discussions and Hansgeorg Hofmann and Horst Müller or Gerhardt Eberstadt represented Dresdner. These teams briefed the respective chairmen who dealt directly with each other. Much of the debate centred around culture and autonomy and Robertson was later quoted as saying that it is 'very important for our people that we can keep our own culture'. Kleinwort's semi-official biographer reminded readers why this was such a major issue: 'It is not so long ago that teams of unhappy people moved elsewhere at the height of Big Bang. It was therefore not until Dresdner could satisfy KB that it recognized and wished to uphold these cultural differences that the negotiations could move forward.'[7] A formal offer was announced on 26 June and the acquisition was completed for £1 billion on 7 August 1995. The accompanying statement showed that Kleinwort had negotiated successfully a degree of autonomy: 'corporate advisory, mergers and acquisitions and the non-German equities business of Dresdner Bank and the group will be managed by the group as Dresdner Bank's investment banking arms outside Germany. The group will operate as an autonomous entity within overall Dresdner Bank Group strategy and business policy.'[8]

Dresdner was accused of being more concerned to keep up with Deutsche Bank's latest aggressive investment banking strategy than being genuinely interested in the business but was generally regarded as being a good home for Kleinwort. It offered capital, a reasonable position in European fixed income in which Kleinwort was weak and no overlap in equities:

Dresdner looks a good match. Though the culture clash could be massive, there will be little overlap and little blood letting. Dresdner also seems likely to use Kleinwort as the heart of its investment banking strategy – ramming home just how poor are Frankfurt's prospects for challenging London as Europe's leading financial centre. The putative £1 billion price tag is fair but not outstanding. If Kleinwort's investment management operations are valued at 2.5 per cent of funds under management, the investment banking business comes in at a 20 per cent premium to net assets. That is more than SBC paid for Warburg, but then again Kleinwort is not falling apart in the way Warburg was.[9]

GETTING OUT OF THE PUBLIC EYE

Kleinwort had made an excellent recovery from its mistakes of the late 1980s and early 1990s. It ranked fifth in the 1995 Extel survey, seventh in the *Acquisitions Monthly* table by value of merger and acquisition deals and fourth by number in 1995. Profits for 1994 were down but not disastrously so. Yet from the middle of 1994 onwards the senior management was prevaricating about the viability of its strategy. A poor start to 1995,[10] together with events at Barings and Warburg, seems to have shaken the resolve.

Monthly income was volatile. Unlike Schroders, Kleinwort had no big stream of cash flow from asset management. Management felt that if the price was right, and the firm could be the centrepiece of a bigger platform in equities and corporate finance, they should do a deal. Management wanted to be out of the public eye for, as a quoted business, they were being watched all the time. Kleinwort saw its competition as the major firms in equities and UK corporate finance and felt that it needed a partner with muscle and no overlapping corporate finance business.[11]

The decision appears to have been welcomed by the family share-holders. There had been moments of triumph but also near disaster in the previous ten years. The major shareholders had been very support-ive during the difficult times, encouraging management to stick at it. But in the end they were relieved to get out at a price which compared well with the £850 million Warburg went for.[12]

Kleinwort could have carried on for longer on its own. It had developed a focused equities and corporate finance strategy, building out from the UK into Europe, staying within its means in Asia and Japan and keeping clear of North America. Its staff and its clients knew what they were getting, there was no bravado about competing with the Americans or Warburg-like hype about the global vision, it would be a solid international investment bank not a global leader.

But investment banks can only survive if all three stakeholders – management, staff and shareholders – want them to and, in the case of Kleinwort, none of these groups felt strongly enough about survival. The principal shareholders were understandably nervous about their investment and were glad to get their cash. The staff as a group were no better and no worse than other City people and their considerations were mercenary and short-term. By 1995 Kleinwort's senior management were entitled to feel exhausted by their great recovery from the back office disasters of Big Bang, the losses of Premier and the market making war. They had held their own in the staff wars of the period, surviving the emotional drain experienced when close colleagues defect, and had enjoyed the elation of deals well done. But as a member of the dwindling band of independent merchant banks and a quoted company to boot, Kleinwort's every move was avidly discussed by the press and analysts. Management began to feel that it would be better out of the public eye. With the precedent of Barings and Warburg together with intensifying competition from the global investment banks, they concluded that Kleinwort's future lay as part of a larger group.

SMITH NEW COURT – STUNNED SILENCE

Good traders buy on the fall and sell into the rally and that had always been Smith's approach to developing its business. It had not been deterred by the industry's problems in the late 1980s from expansion and it was not fooled by its sensationally good results in 1993–4, when profits had jumped by 146 per cent to £95 million: '1993 had been a very good year for the securities industry but by the year end we were worried about the business. We had grown from a couple of hundred people to a couple of thousand people all round the world. We feared we were in the dangerous middle ground, not big enough to keep up with the Goldmans of this world but too big to shrink.'[13]

Phoenix Securities, the firm of corporate advisers with a special expertise in investment banking, were appointed early in 1994 to write a strategy paper and in the summer delivered their view that, over the medium term, there would be no room for Smith. Phoenix believed that Smith would need to do a deal with a bigger partner at some point in the next two years.

Although the Smith New Court chairman's statement for 1994–5 signed off on an optimistically independent note, the firm's executive committee had begun to think seriously about selling the firm in the closing months of 1994. Capital and credit were the key issues, according to a Smith New Court director:

For the first time, we began to feel balance sheet constraint. This was not in terms of our ability to trade or to take on bought deals etc, but more from the credit committee type pressure that was building up from the clients in the US. Although we thought that we had done a pretty good job in the US, more and more we began to find that we could not get onto commission lists because our credit standing was considered too much of a risk. In the UK also, and in spite of the very large market share that we had built, a number of friendly clients told us that it was becoming increasingly difficult to give us more business, for the same reason. There was little or no prospect of a large balance sheet injection from NMR, and certainly not at a price we would find acceptable, so this was something we would have to solve ourselves.[14]

A further factor was the escalating pay rates in London at this time. Smith foresaw that the Americans would step up their efforts and bid up for the best staff. The firm's management did not believe that it would be able to withstand such pressure from its own resources.

Marks describes the events of 1995:

We were approached by a handful of firms and narrowed the choice down to two, Commerzbank and Merrill Lynch. Commerzbank had no equities business in London and not much elsewhere and would have wanted to retain our management and our name. They were very nice people with lots of old world courtesy and it was the deal of the heart if we just wanted to roll along. We would have got cash for the shareholders and bags of autonomy. But for the staff and clients we would still have been struggling to build a business, facing the same problems as before of trying to break into America and to build up corporate finance. Merrill was the deal of the head. Smith's UK presence and Merrill's awesome distribution in the US would be good news for our clients and that would mean that our individuals would also prosper.[15]

Merrill Lynch had a well-established business in Europe by the summer of 1995, employing 2200 people and profitable since the early nineties. This had been built by organic growth and, although Merrill had looked hard at buying parts of Barings in February 1995, it decided to stick with its existing five-year growth plan for Europe encompassing fixed income, private banking, fund management, equities and corporate finance. This plan was approved by the New York management committee but the spate of acquisitions of London's investment banks, together with Merrill's increased confidence and determination to become a global leader, prompted it to accelerate the European strategy.

Terms were agreed between Smith New Court and Merrill Lynch in June 1995 and initially the takeover was not well received by all the Smith staff. A stunned silence followed the announcement at a Smith New Court directors' meeting that Merrill Lynch would be the new owner: 'We couldn't think of anything more ridiculous. The Thundering Herd, the biggest broking firm in the world, interested in us? It just seemed far fetched.'[16] Although Marks believed that the merger would benefit the staff in the long term, several directors disagreed with the decision and the process and the principal shareholder, Rothschilds, who owned 26 per cent of the equity, was not initially in favour. A main board director told me: 'I don't think we needed the capital. We were doing extremely well in the markets where we operated. All we needed was a partner to improve the corporate finance deal flow. We did not need to sell the firm.'[17]

Another objected to the process: 'The main board was kept in the dark. They started talking to Merrill very early and the board was not told, nor of other approaches. It was very unsatisfactory.'[18] Initially N. M. Rothschild voted against the deal but Merrill would only proceed on a unanimous basis and Rothschilds was persuaded to change its mind. My source was very critical of Marks' tactics: 'He kept the board in the dark, kept Rothschilds guessing until the last moment, squared off the market makers on the board and pushed it through. It might have been clever politics but it was no way to run a public company.'[19]

In fact, it would have been difficult to widen the circle of those in the know too early. There were thirty-eight executive directors, which was too many to have a full debate on issues without running the risk of a security leak, and the business was run in practice by the executive committee of seven. However, several Smith directors believe that they should have had the chance to debate the matter at some stage and they believe that a large number of staff agreed with them: 'The first we knew of it was when we were shown this enormous offer from Merrill. But we were not short of capital, we had a group of very bright senior and middle managers and a very good staff. In whose interests was the company being sold? Not Rothschilds, who did not want it to happen, nor the staff nor the directors. Within a year many of the staff and main board had left.' I asked my source why they all went along with it: 'We were left in no doubt that the stakes were pretty high, that the Smith show was over and that it was just a question of whether we went gracefully. It was the same for Rothschilds. It would have been brave or foolish for them to have stood up to the executive committee with all the risk of people walking out and the business unravelling.'[20]

The early days of integration were quite traumatic as the independent minded Smith New Court staff had to come to terms with the more bureaucratic approach of the larger firm and with the more rigorous standards in risk management and compliance required by US regulators. In the first six months some 300 staff were reported as having gone, although Marks described only 10 per cent of these as representing a real loss of talent.[21] Many of these were the disaffected independence party but many others stayed on, worked through the integration pains and achieved the fulfilment Marks had predicted. In the 1997 Extel survey, the firm climbed from sixth to third place and in the same year secured a top five position in the major corporate finance league tables.

SUCCESS OR FAILURE?

Smith surrendered its independence from a position of strength and secured nearly two and a half times book value for its shareholders. It had moved from being a middle ranking market maker in the middle of the 1980s into being a leading integrated broker by the middle

1990s. Assessments of its performance need to consider the reasons for its success as well as its failure to survive.

Its success stemmed from ownership. The firm had to stand on its own; there was no deep pocketed parent company in the background ready to bale it out if things went wrong. This instilled in management a responsible attitude to business development. Unlike many firms pursuing a grand strategy on behalf of a financial services conglomerate, Smith did not invest in new enterprises until previous developments had begun to pay off because it simply could not afford to have too many loss-making operations. Smith, in fact, was managed like a real business for profit, not like a football club running up huge losses in pursuit of a rich owner's desire for trophies.

The staff at Smith were loyal to each other and to the company. The old market making side held together and the agency business was successfully grafted on to it. It helped that the broking acquisition was small since this avoided major cultural issues that would have arisen if too many large egos had been introduced at any one time. The fact that Scott Goff was a team of equals meant that its staff were easier to get along with and did not have an inflated view of their own importance. Team spirit was helped by the knowledge that the firm was an outsider trying to break in, an underdog, as Ken Taylor puts it: 'The whole ethos of the firm stemmed from our inferiority complex. That was the reason for our success. We were a bunch of street fighters who aimed to win. We had to fight to stay alive. Money was a secondary consideration. It was team spirit that did it.'[22]

It also had the required skills. Trading ability was essential for the post-Big Bang integrated brokers and Smith's market makers and risk management ensured that business won was executed properly and profitably. Salesmen were able to focus on selling and management were able to think strategically as a result. Protracted problems in market making sapped morale at many firms and Smith's team spirit was able to flourish in an anxiety-free environment.

Management was at the heart both of Smith's success and its ultimate sale. There was a small cadre of management at Smith running from Tony Lewis, the chairman at the time of Big Bang, through Michael Marks and Paul Roy, that ran the business with common sense and great instinct. Senior market makers such as Tony Abrahams, Geoff Lewis and the Lederman brothers were on hand to give a real life view of the business. Nothing was allowed to run away with itself: positions, egos, ambition were all regularly reined in.

But in the end Smith was confronted with two obstacles it believed to be insurmountable. It had never built a corporate finance business and without one would not be able to justify the escalating salaries that were required to retain and hire top analysts and salespeople. It might have been possible to develop the relationship with Rothschilds but that firm was also a small player in global terms and would not have helped Smith solve the second problem: America. Smith believed that it was not viable without a significant presence in the US and that it could not build or buy one there. With its limited resources, it is true that it could not attempt what BZW, NatWest and Warburg had done in organic growth in the US. However, it could have remained independent as a leading European broker with a profitable business in Japan and Asia if it had wished but, as with Kleinwort, the senior management preferred to tackle a bigger problem as a small part of a bigger firm.

THE CLASS OF '95: FINAL REPORT

Conventional wisdom held that it would be a bear market that weakened the resolve of the Big Bang players and the sale of Barings, Warburg, Smith and Kleinwort did indeed originate in the difficult market of 1994 and the early months of 1995. Inside the banks and brokers, 1994's markets exposed the newly inflated cost bases to volatile income. Anxious managements became aware of the risks in the organizations they had just created and debated how to respond. Warburg's profit warning and the discussions with Morgan Stanley brought this issue out into the open but it was the collapse of Barings that really changed the landscape because it provided a worked example of what happens to investment banks when things go wrong. It suddenly became very clear to the senior directors of Warburg, Smith and Kleinwort that failure was not a hypothetical thing that happened to other people in other countries in other banks. It had just happened here, in London, to one of their own, and it could happen to them. Individual managers saw how senior figures in the City like the Barings and Andrew Tuckey were pilloried in the press and held accountable by the regulators and we all looked much more closely at how we discharged our duties. After Barings, the debate that most banks and brokers were holding internally about their future took on added urgency, in some cases turned to panic and, by the end of 1995, Warburg, Kleinwort and Smith were also gone.

The position of the merchant banks was not helped by trends in the industry towards scale. This first became an issue in 1993 when, on the back of booming markets, the US investment banks unleashed a global initiative. Although this subsided in 1994 during the bond market crisis, UK firms had seen enough of how a global landscape might look to question their role within it. Thus Warburg resolved to gear up and Smith and Kleinwort began to question their future.

The volatile markets of 1994–5 exposed another problem for two of the banks – mismanagement. Warburg made errors of judgement in timing its expansion, failing to draw back early in 1994 when the problems of the bond markets should have been apparent and forgetting the basic disciplines of prudent business development. Barings' management did not follow through so that detail was not chased down properly. This allowed ambiguities to persist in the reporting structures, ill-discipline to flourish in trading and loss of focus on financial flows.

The fate of all four firms shows the importance of management in the investment banking industry. Failure of control at Barings stemmed from the highest levels in the firm. At Warburg, a couple of poor decisions in 1994 blew the firm away. At Kleinwort and Smith, the judgement of a handful of senior directors saw them give up their independence.

Underlying the immediate failure of three of the firms was the inability of several generations of management to build a cohesive culture after Big Bang. Only Smith was successful in building a spirit across the firm that was bigger than the self-interest of the individual employees. Warburg had it in the days of Siegmund Warburg but lost it, and Kleinwort and Barings never had it. The consequence was that these businesses were collections of individuals loosely bound together by a few men at the top. The year 1994–5 exposed the frailty of the organizations and they did not survive.

24

Shareholders Rule OK

With the merchant banks in disarray, the two years after 1995 should have been the period when the European commercial banks exerted their power on London's investment banking industry. The collapse of Barings reinforced the advantages of a strong balance sheet and the process driven approach of the clearing banks. For a few months at least, bureaucracy and conservatism became strengths not weaknesses: 'It has made the advantage of the balance sheet obvious to everybody. Perception is everything in these things. Before, although we had that advantage, people didn't realize how important it was.'[1]

However, a bull market of gigantic scale brought as many problems as the bear of 1994. Buoyant conditions in US equity and corporate finance markets were echoed in Europe. Merger and acquisition activity soared as did stock market turnover and indices. The average level of M&A activity in 1995, 1996 and 1997 was six times what it had been in 1994. Stock market indices ended 1997 60 per cent higher than they had ended 1994.

The problem for the City was that the boom on Wall Street was even bigger than the boom in Europe. After the negative return on equity posted by the large American investment banks in 1994, their returns recovered to 11 per cent in 1995 and in the next two years jumped to 26 per cent in 1996 and 23 per cent in 1997. Nineteen ninety-six was Wall Street's best year since 1986, and returns looked very attractive when compared with the low interest rates and falling inflation of the time. Employment on Wall Street fell in 1995 reflecting the downsizing carried out in 1994, but hiring resumed in 1996 and, by the end of 1998, 42,964 people worked in the large investment banks, an increase of nearly 7000 from 1995's low.

The profitability of the US banks was such that they were able to cross-subsidize their European operations by paying staff more than they were generating. While conditions on Wall Street were so good, losses in Europe could be tolerated. The US banks believed that long-term strategic benefits would emerge from building a position in Europe and that it was worth bidding up for the best staff even if there was a short-term cost. For the Europeans, who had to match these remuneration levels without the same earnings base, this caused serious strain in the profit and loss account and by early 1998 NatWest Markets had vacated investment banking and UBS was sold. Superficially it was the shareholders who called the shots and, in the case of UBS, the bank's loss of independence had very little to do with investment banking. But at NatWest and BZW it was the failure to carry the shareholders with the investment banking strategy that caused the retreat. That failure to convince was due in part to the short termism of the shareholders and in part to the lack of conviction of the senior managers themselves.

BZW: DRAWING ITS TEETH AND CLAWS

Martin Taylor joined BZW as chief executive at the beginning of 1994. Initially, BZW was the least of his worries: '1993 had been a good year superficially for BZW but in reality the profits had only been made by using the balance sheet to play the money markets. Everyone was full of the investment bank, the board were very proud of it and the BZW people had every reason to talk themselves up.'[2]

BZW performed relatively well in 1994, avoiding serious damage in the difficult markets of that year, but 1995 was disappointing: 'The industry recovered and BZW didn't. BZW fooled itself that its time was coming. There were enormous problems with the bonus pool. Costs were rising more than income. We were hiring, paying a premium to get them in and then they under-produced when they arrived because our platform was weaker than they expected.'[3]

By the autumn of 1995 Martin Taylor's view of BZW had begun to harden and he was not impressed:

It was full of cultural tensions, people from tribes with different strategic persuasions. Some of the traders were good quality, corporate broking was B+, corporate finance was the old Barclays Merchant Bank (which was not highly regarded) plus a few new hires like David Band and Graham Pimlott. It was the Barclays Bank treasury department which actually made all the money. The IT infrastructure was a mess and they were in several buildings. This jumble was never really sorted out; the business was held together through a series of unilateral relationships.[4]

Late in 1995, Taylor told Band that he wanted to bring in a new chief executive for BZW and they jointly embarked on a search. Their choice was Bill Harrison, the head of investment banking at Robert Fleming. Harrison recalls that Taylor first phoned him 'one wet Sunday afternoon in February 1996' telling him that Barclays' top management had decided to give BZW real impetus, that they had decided to build rather than buy and that he had been identified as the man for the job.[5] Negotiations were complicated by Band's death in the spring which caused an internal succession war between Donald Brydon, Jonathan Davie and Pimlott. By the time Harrison had accepted the job and served notice at Flemings, it was September 1996 before he started work. Martin Taylor takes up the story: 'During that period the industry's profits had soared, BZW's had fallen, costs were rising and we were not breaking through. By October or November it was clear to me that BZW would not make it. Yes, it was embarrassing.'[6]

Bill Harrison enjoyed his first four months:

Martin was genuinely supportive at first and I enjoyed getting my teeth into it. Equities was a good business and we encouraged the analysts to work closely with the industry teams in corporate finance. We tightened up between corporate finance and corporate broking, nominating one person and one person only to be in charge of each relationship. We pitched capital markets pretty aggressively under Amir Eilon and started hiring in corporate finance, especially in the industry teams. There was a lot of talent to work with; it was a big job but definitely achievable.[7]

Taylor, however, was beginning to believe that the problems were beyond even Harrison: 'Bill came in like a whirlwind. He gripped the

IT problem straight away and started hiring. Together we brought in Bob Diamond who professionalized fixed income and Bill threw his energies into M&A and corporate finance. On the surface it looked OK but it was pretty clear that the numbers would not stack up.'[8]

In January 1997, Taylor called up Harrison with some startling news. He said that he had written a paper for the main board on investment banking and told him, 'I think it's beyond us. The competitive gradient has steepened too much. The US investment banking mergers have raised the entry barrier beyond our reach.'[9]

Taylor's paper to the Barclays plc board in January 1997 was a broad review of the bank's position. The principal point was that it faced the risk of being sub-scale in all of its industries, retail and wholesale. Taylor wanted to invest in retail banking to prepare it for the e-comm revolution and to get out of investment banking. Harrison delivered his response: 'Bill made his speech on the beach in favour of BZW. Everyone was impressed with his passion and the board were concerned about the embarrassment of changing direction so soon after appointing him.'[10] Taylor had to accept the board's decision to stick with investment banking but later regretted 'not going to the wire at the time especially as the next day the problems of being sub-scale were brought home when Morgan Stanley bought Dean Witter'.[11]

When Barclays reported its profits for 1996, it revealed below expectation results from BZW, £204 million down from £289 million. This represented a return on capital of only 8 per cent and a second half operating profit of only £42 million.[12] Recruiting in 1996 added £120 million to costs and at the AGM in April BZW's poor results attracted shareholder criticism. What Barclays had to pay Harrison, superficially for four months' work but in fact representing the buy out of his deferred compensation from Flemings, was singled out.[13]

The prospect of embarking on an even more expensive programme of organic growth in the US was adding to Taylor's doubts. At the round of post-results meetings with institutional shareholders, he came under increasing pressure to follow the role model of Lloyd's which had no investment bank: 'Within two or three months it was very clear that we had to do something. The investors were baying for blood. BZW was tying up more and more capital, making lower returns and compensation was taking a higher proportion of revenue. I was encouraged that the investors saw things the same way as me. I was having to calm down the institutions, reassure the staff and the board was stopping me from taking the action I wanted.'[14]

Meanwhile Harrison faced constant rumours about the sale of BZW which, together with the prospect of an unpopular move from the City down to Canary Wharf in Docklands, made the staff very uneasy. Harrison sought a reaffirmation of the board's support in the face of Taylor's increasing scepticism. He gave the board an analysis of the resources needed to stay with the global competition. The amount of further investment required persuaded the board that it could not keep up and this time a decision was taken to sell the business. Options such as a joint venture with a strong US partner were advocated by Harrison but Taylor was adamant that he was under pressure from shareholders to find a permanent solution.[15]

That pressure had mounted after NatWest's decision to review its investment banking operations in June 1997 following its losses in derivatives. There was a huge amount of press speculation concerning the future of NatWest Markets and BZW. The popular cry for closure became very powerful and the impression was created of a tide of discontent about the clearers' involvement in investment banking. In October Barclays announced that it was selling the equities and corporate finance parts of BZW. Harrison decided that he should not preside over the disposal, which he saw as being a Barclays process, and resigned immediately. Barclays' claim that it was selling only two sevenths of the revenue earned in the first six months of the year did not fool commentators: 'Yet those two sevenths are the teeth and claws of the beast – not to mention half the staff – and no investment bank is worthy of the title without equity and corporate finance divisions.'[16]

The decision to sell equities and corporate finance was very much Taylor's and, although he was supported by the Barclays board the second time round, once Taylor left Barclays criticism began to surface. The Barclays chairman, Sir Peter Middleton, chooses his words carefully:

I was chairman of BZW for a long time. It was a model that could have worked. We had already spent a lot of money on fixed income and Bill Harrison wanted to do the same on equities and corporate finance. Martin lost confidence in our ability to deliver and was concerned at the high salaries and bonuses we were having to guarantee. It wasn't a problem for me; you just have to pay the market rate even if it's high as it is in investment banking or IT. The problems of BZW weren't that acute. Martin faced a lot of pressure from shareholders. But they play games with you. At these meetings they all want you to sell the least profitable bits and keep the best but they don't understand that the maths don't work like that.[17]

Although Harrison and Taylor maintain a good relationship, some believe that the scale of Harrison's ambition frightened Taylor. Harrison is a stocky, dynamic Midlander with the nickname 'Attila the Brum' and a reputation for vigour as a manager equal to his reputation for excellence as a corporate financier. A former senior Barclays man believes that 'Bill was such a contrast to David Band's balanced, consensual style. He shook them up a bit with his wish list and wanted to get on with it very quickly. He's a better client man than manager.'[18] Taylor had originally intended to pair Harrison and Band, which he saw as a complementary team, but he believed that 'even if Bill had come in March and if David had survived, we would have come to the decision to sell eventually'.[19]

A Barclays' director has no doubt that, by the time Taylor took over, 'BZW was a rich man's toy, an expensive distraction. Equities never really made money. It showed a profit because they bullied Band into taking lots of the costs centrally. They massaged their numbers all the time.'[20]

Martin Taylor agrees that BZW did not level with itself:

Early in 1996 Band held an away day at some hotel in Essex. I wanted to be supportive so went down for dinner and made a speech. The first question was about bonuses. I said that we had to balance market forces with the fact that you have missed your budget by £150 million. There was silence. I realized I'd put my foot in it. I asked them to raise their hands if they knew they had missed budget. Two out of fifty put their hands up and one of those worked in planning. David was furious but I was astonished that the fifty top people in the business could not be told honestly how they were doing.[21]

The obituary in the Lex column was brutal:

The tragedy of BZW is not so much that its equity and corporate finance arm is now being sold but that its weaknesses were not tackled earlier. Faced with a choice between pouring perhaps billions of dollars into BZW to take it into the top division or cutting loose, Barclays' board had a fairly easy decision. BZW's only really strong non-debt business is UK equity trading and research. In mergers, equity capital markets and the rest of Europe, BZW is middling; in the US it has no significant presence apart from selling non-US equities. These weaknesses, though, have been apparent for a decade. That ought to have been long enough to put them right.[22]

I am not convinced that BZW was so far from success. It is lamentable that the cultural issues Taylor and others describe were allowed to fester for so long but the product range was not far short of critical mass. Its principal weaknesses were the two identified by Lex – the US and corporate advisory work. These were not insurmountable obstacles. Corporate advisory relationships take a long time to build but in Harrison BZW had someone who could have accelerated that process. Alternatively, Barclays could have bought a merchant bank. Barings, Warburg, Kleinwort and Schroders have all changed hands at prices Barclays could have afforded and, soon after Taylor took over, Hambro Magan suggested such a plan to him. The hole in the US was common to many aspiring investment banks and BZW had the resources to buy its way in. The acquisition of Wells Fargo Nikko Investment Advisors for $440 million could easily have been matched by a comparable acquisition of a mid-sized US investment bank and several such firms changed hands around the time of BZW's exit from the industry.

In the final analysis there were three factors that brought about the sale of BZW's equity and corporate finance businesses to Credit Suisse. The legacy of mismanagement left BZW with problems in culture and product range. Shareholder support had evaporated. The group chief executive believed in a different, debt-based model. The consequence was that the BZW experiment failed but it is hard to disagree with Lex that ten years ought to have been long enough to get it right.

NATWEST: A BLACK HOLE

Before falling apart in 1997, NatWest Markets had appeared to be making many of the right moves in the two previous years. In 1995 and 1996, Martin Owen switched tack from organic growth to acquisition and filled in the key gaps in the bank's product range. At the end of 1996 NatWest had good claims to be the leading UK investment bank. Its broking firm was top of the Extel rankings, it was on the fringes of the top ten in corporate advisory and corporate broking and it was the leading foreign firm in US equities and investment banking, with a position in the top twenty. Weaknesses in fixed income and asset management had been addressed through acquisition and, while it was not yet a fully fledged investment bank, most of the building blocks were in place.

However, there was still work to be done on the underlying fundamental problems of control, integration and culture which had dogged NatWest Markets and its predecessor, County NatWest. It was not enough to assemble the components of an investment bank: the people had to be controlled and persuaded to work together. These weaknesses were to bring NatWest Markets down.

I was surprised by the progress that Martin Owen made in 1995 and 1996. I resigned from NatWest in March 1995 after an incident which convinced me that NatWest was not close to being a successful investment bank. It was December 1994 and time to review the bonus proposals for the firm. The bonus round in an investment bank is the crucial time of the year: get it wrong and the firm unravels, pay too much and profitability is shot to ribbons. We went through an endless round of bottom up proposals from the line managers, knocking back their opening shots until, in my judgement, their howls of protest showed that we had gone too far with the cuts; we added a bit back in to keep them happy and submitted the proposals for 2000 people to Owen.

After a few days I was summoned to a meeting in Owen's large meeting room. There was a long table with a dozen chairs round it; Owen sat at one end and asked me to sit down at the other end, about fifteen feet away. The remaining chairs were filled by senior men from the bank and NatWest Markets. Owen kicked off by saying that the bonus proposals were unacceptable, that the bank was concerned about its cost:income ratio and that too much of profits were being paid away to the staff. I explained that 1994 had been a difficult year in the world's securities markets, that we were unusual to be making profits at all, that we had got ourselves into a strong competitive position and that the bonus proposals on the table were the minimum necessary to retain the staff.

At this point the attack started. Owen lost control of the meeting and looked embarrassed by what occurred. From all round the table I heard wave after wave of criticism about the bonus proposals. The attack varied from the general – 'bonuses are less than 10 per cent of salary in the retail bank, why are yours 50 per cent' – to the specific – 'he's a crook and should be fired', 'he's been critical of the bank and shouldn't get a bonus at all', 'she's only thirty-two and she's earning more than the group chief executive', and so on, for an hour or two. I stayed calm, defended the individual proposals on the basis of perform-ance and market rate, name-by-name, and at the end of the meeting Owen waved them through. But the hostility evident from my senior colleagues (some of whom were themselves supposedly investment bankers) shook me badly. Martin Owen was excellent and stood out from them as a person with vision and courage but he was clearly under enormous pressure from the bank to produce an investment bank on the cheap and was surrounded by bankers who just did not understand. From that day I never believed in NatWest's desire to make it and it would have been dishonest for me to stay and continue to motivate staff and persuade people to join or not leave the bank when I myself had lost faith.

When I made my resignation to Owen he asked me if there had been a turning-point and I recounted this episode. He smiled and said he had sensed it and asked me to see Derek Wanless, then the group chief executive. Wanless is a man with a real ability to do strategic analysis and he is very honest. I went across to his office; he took one big leather sofa, I took the other and coffee was poured. 'What's this all about then?' he asked. I told him that I didn't think NatWest was committed to investment banking, that the shareholders would force him to close it and that I could not remain under those circumstances. He replied,

'Of course we're committed, strategically it's very important to us. You know that.' I told him that I disagreed and that NatWest did not have the right corporate culture for such a volatile business and that, unless the culture could be changed and the shareholders re-educated, it should concentrate on the treasury and debt aspects of corporate and commercial banking. A look crossed Wanless' face that I can only describe as that of a man who has just heard the ring of truth. He smiled, said 'I think I'm wasting your time', we shook hands and I left, our coffee untouched on the table and still hot.

My resignation prompted Owen to review the policy of combining equities and bonds. He determined that it had not been a success and the two streams were separated out again with bonds reporting to Philip Wise, a NatWest insider and previously chief operating officer of NatWest Markets, and equities reporting to Tom Whelan, who was then between jobs after a career at Morgan Stanley.

NatWest Market's principal faults in 1995 were a weak position in bond markets globally and a weakness in corporate advisory business. The latter meant that synergies were being missed since the equities business now had a strong position in Europe, especially the UK; in the US, where Jim O'Donnell had a built a top twenty ranked firm; and in Australia. These positions had enabled NatWest to build a capital markets business in all three regions but advisory mandates remained elusive. Advisory work was important as a revenue source but also as a badge announcing the arrival of a fully-fledged investment bank.

What NatWest lacked in corporate advisory was high profile rain-makers, senior corporate financiers who had the ear of chief executive officers of large companies in the UK, Europe and the US. Such individuals proved to be unhirable, at least for NatWest. There were many reasons for this. NatWest was not a good marking name with corporates and corporate financiers feared that they would not be able to persuade their clients to move over with them. The culture of NatWest Markets was still patchy, and only some bits of it felt like an investment bank. Senior recruitment always required the involvement of senior management, many of whom were commercial bankers by background, and they put off many candidates. Others were plainly mediocre and had a similar effect on potential recruits. The effect of all this was that NatWest was not able to recruit top-quality corporate financiers. It recruited some very good people, many of whom performed well at NatWest, but at the senior level it could never quite pull in the very best.

Organic growth required some very high packages to be paid and these were charged directly to the profit and loss account. This had the effect of worsening the cost to income ratio, the key number by which analysts were measuring NatWest at that time. NatWest's cost to income ratio compared poorly with that of the other clearers and there was not enough support for the investment banking strategy amongst shareholders and analysts for an expensive organic growth strategy to be tolerated. Martin Owen regularly got a tough time from the group on this matter. The 1994 budget process was particularly difficult with NatWest's chief financial officer, Richard Goeltz, pinning Owen down with clinical questions about the cost base and revenue projections and Owen desperately trying to explain why costs needed to grow again in 1995 when revenues for 1994 were below budget.

Acquisitions could be written off through the balance sheet, were likely to be profit-enhancing in year one, and were less consuming of management time than a gradual build by recruitment. They also offered the prospect of immediate market place impact, which all of NatWest's managers felt under pressure to deliver, and in 1995 Owen secured backing from the board to change tack from organic growth to acquisitions.

During 1995 he made approaches to a number of firms which would have solved many of NatWest's corporate finance problems. Banks such as Schroders and Rothschilds politely replied that they were not for sale. NatWest did not dare to take on Barings' unknown liabilities during the weekend when it was desperate for a new owner. Discussions were held with the senior managers of S. G. Warburg but the chemistry between the clearing bank-trained men from NatWest and the Warburg investment bankers was so poor that the Warburg men told their advisers 'not at any price'.

The failure of these discussions was a turning-point in the histories of Warburg, NatWest and the UK investment banking industry. Wanless recalls: 'We tried hard to buy it; it was a serious effort. Warburg were panicking. Scholey told me afterwards that the problem was Owen but he never went to Alexander, chairman to chairman, to say that and so Warburg sold itself too cheaply and lost shareholder value. We made two offers and it would have been a transformational deal. I am sure we could have made it work.'[23]

The result of this failure was that Warburg was sold too cheaply, NatWest was left searching for critical mass, and a chance to build a British investment bank of scale was missed. I can understand the poor rapport between Owen and the Warburg men. Owen is not a merchant banker; he is not of that ilk. He has a regional accent, he mixes in different circles and he did not attend Oxbridge or a major public school. The Warburg people were classic gentlemanly capitalists and would not have been able to stomach reporting to him. At a crucial moment for investment banking in the UK, class got in the way. The gentlemanly capitalists turned to the Swiss and Owen looked for smaller fry.

With the prospect of a substantial acquisition in corporate finance receding, Owen's next plan was to make some smaller, but still significant, infill acquisitions. These included the US merger and acquisitions boutique of Gleacher and partners, headed by Eric Gleacher, who had been involved in many of the major deals of the late 1980s and early 1990s. Gleacher was a high profile rainmaker of exactly the kind that NatWest lacked. His price for joining NatWest was high – $135 million for the business and a large degree of independence for himself and his group – but Owen had put in place another important building block.

In the UK, where the mismatch between the equities position and corporate finance was even greater, a similar move was made when the corporate finance boutique business of Hambro Magan was purchased. George Magan had been one of the principal members of the Morgan Grenfell corporate finance department in its heydays of the mid 1980s and he remained an effective deal-doer during the period after he formed Hambro Magan. With Gleacher and Hambro Magan, NatWest now possessed quality equity research and distribution and corporate finance skills in both the UK and the USA.

In 1996 Owen moved to fill the remaining big gaps in his business, fixed income and asset management. Gartmore, one of the UK's top four pension fund managers, was purchased to take over NatWest's own ailing fund management unit. On the fixed income side, $590 million was paid in July 1996 to buy Greenwich Capital, a leading US Treasury bond broker, from the Long Term Credit Bank of Japan. Although this did not fill the obvious gap in corporate bonds, the acquisition brought scale and risk management skills which had been previously lacking in NatWest's US fixed income operations. The deal also brought an interesting cultural mix since Greenwich had an informal style and profit-sharing partnership with LTCB. The partnership was dissolved but the style, including dressing down, was imported to NatWest Markets and was extended across the firm.

Further developments were under way in equities where Citicorp's defunct Japanese business was bought in order to regain a seat on the Tokyo Stock Exchange. In Asia, which NatWest had been re-entering in reversal of the policy implemented in 1991, the joint venture partner, Wheelock, was bought out in November 1996 and the business was integrated into NatWest Securities. By this stage the global equities business employed around 2000 staff. Of these, 1200 were in European equities; 250 in Asia; 100 in Australia; and the remainder in the United States. It was bigger than BZW's equities division which totalled 1250 at the time.

NatWest Markets entered 1997 in perhaps the strongest shape it had ever been with most of the serious product deficiencies addressed by acquisition. Two things were now required for the bank to make a major push into the big league: integration and time. Integration would not happen on its own. The senior managers of the business units forming NatWest Markets had been brought up in an environment which mistrusted the skills and motives of colleagues in other departments and very few shared Owen's belief in the future of NatWest Markets. They preferred to protect their own positions by guarding their own client bases rather than sharing them with colleagues and unlearning this kind of behaviour would not come naturally. What was now required was a period of bedding down with a strong focus on integration of the disparate parts and the development of a solid infrastructure to support the business.

By the beginning of 1997, Owen had won the support of the board: 'In February 1997 there was a board discussion about Owen's plan to expand derivatives and everyone got very excited. Even hardened cynics like John Melbourn, the main board director responsible for risk, and Sir John Banham, were very supportive and gung ho for an expansion and big commitment to this area. Sir Michael Angus told the board "we are in serious danger of having a success on our hands".[24]

Before the derivatives plan could be implemented, the bank discovered a loss of £77 million in interest rate derivatives just after the 1996 results were published. This discovery holed NatWest Markets, not 'above the line' as Owen claimed at the time, but below the line, costing him his job and the investment bank its future. The incident itself involved mismarking one of the interest rate options books by a derivatives trader. The amount involved was large but not in itself serious enough to have provoked the furore which followed. However, the mismarking had gone undetected for nearly three years and this was very damaging. NatWest's response was to commission external reviews from independent lawyers and accountants, to suspend the people directly involved and for Owen to forgo £200,000 of his half-million pound bonus for the year. A further response came in June 1997 when news of an internal review of NatWest Markets' strategy was followed by Owen's resignation.

In August, the bank revealed the results of the review. The real engine of NatWest Markets' profits – treasury, foreign exchange, money markets, interest rate trading and currency options – were to form a separate division, global financial markets, under the leadership of Stefan Harris who had been running treasury for several years. The rest of the old NatWest Markets business retained the name and, after a perfunctory search for an outside candidate to run it, Chip Kruger, who had previously been running Greenwich, was put in charge. Alton Irby was head of advisory, mainly the former Gleacher and Hambro Magan businesses; Whelan headed up equities; and Gary Holloway ran fixed income bonds.

Although there was talk of the advantages of promoting from within and of the teamwork between the four Americans – Kruger, Irby, Whelan and Holloway – the reasons for the early abandonment of the search for an outsider soon became apparent. In November 1997, after two weeks of informal discussions and two weeks of formal negotiations, NatWest rejected Deutsche Morgan Grenfell's bid for the global equities business, ostensibly on grounds of price, although strong pressure from staff who feared that job overlaps with Deutsche's existing equities business, together with another commercial bank culture, would make for an uncomfortable working environment.

A month later agreement was reached with Bankers Trust which paid £129 million for the European equities division. US and Asian derivatives were sold to Deutsche Morgan Grenfell for £50 million and the Australian equities business was sold soon after to Salomon Smith Barney. Asian and American equities and UK equity derivatives were closed.

The options problem had produced a strong reaction from the board: 'From having been gung ho about derivatives two weeks before, the board got a dose of "what sort of infrastructure do we have here and how much capital is derivatives going to absorb". The board swung from wanting to expand derivatives in February to wanting to get out of the business altogether in March.'[25]

Why did the options black hole cause the board to retreat from an investment banking strategy that was much closer to working than has generally been realized? The fundamental issue was one of control. It was damaging that the mismarking had carried on for three years undetected but that could have been corrected by a massive injection of resource into the infrastructure. It was also damaging that the losses only emerged after the final results. Had they emerged in time for them to be absorbed into the results, the outcry would have been loud but not fatal. Owen's response to the options problem had annoyed the board: 'He seemed fairly unconcerned by it, said that he would sort it out and did not seem to recognize the deep-seated infrastructure problems that existed. This was why he had to go.'[26]

In the end, the factors that brought an end to NatWest Markets were very similar to those that had done for BZW. BZW and NatWest Markets each underestimated the time it would take for new recruits and new businesses to build up to full revenue generation. The cost investment Owen had made was not paying off in the short term. News at the AGM that the rest of NatWest Markets was experiencing a downturn was not much commented on at the time but caused the board to question the whole of Owen's strategy, not just the risk controls. Poor results on an increased cost base were a factor in the group's decision to change strategy.

This must be seen in the context of divided opinion going back a long way. The investment banking strategy had never carried the whole board or senior managers just below board level. This meant that, once a slip had been made, the balance of opinion was easily swayed. A similar position existed amongst the institutional investors, who were reluctant to give the management any more time to make the strategy work. Just like Taylor at Barclays, Wanless and Alexander faced intense institutional pressure to make a change.

Derek Wanless recalls: 'The shareholders were starting to complain about our capital requirements and make unfavourable comparisons with Lloyds. NatWest Markets became an issue at every meeting; it was a real pain in the neck. They said, even when it's going well, even if you do succeed, we won't value it so why bother to go through all this pain? If you fail, you've had it, and if you succeed we won't value it.'[27]

Barclays and NatWest shared another common characteristic: the chief executive did not believe in the investment banking strategy. I asked Wanless why, if he had been sceptical about investment banking in 1992 when he voted to close equities at a board meeting, he had kept it going for so long:

The progress Natwest Markets was making persuaded me for a while that we could succeed. In any case I saw it as my job to implement the board's policy and the board felt very strongly that we should be in investment banking. The board would not have appointed me if I had said that investment banking was not the right strategy and it would have been dishonest to have cynically accepted the job with the intention of recommending a different policy.[28]

UBS: NOT MUCH HELP

UBS managed to keep out of high-profile problems in investment banking for most of the 1990s through a combination of good judgement and by virtue of its foreign ownership which kept the UK press and institutional shareholders off its back. It was involved with NatWest in the Blue Arrow affair but managed to escape the vilification suffered by NatWest in the British press. It encountered its own problems in derivatives, enduring heavy losses in convertibles in 1994 and a black hole in 1997, but the focus was on the retail banking side and press and shareholder criticism was mild. The end of the London-based investment banking strategy that had begun with the purchase of Phillips & Drew came early in 1998, when UBS merged with another large Swiss bank, SBC, a move that was driven by the retail side of the business.

For once investment banking was not the culprit but UBS never made the leap from its strengths in equities and capital markets into an all-round firm. After the losses of 1994, the European operations finished their life as an independent firm on a profitable run in 1995, 1996 and 1997, helped by a strong contribution from capital markets. Results were also helped by the inclusion of the Swiss retail broking business and by 1997 the equities division was contributing towards £100 million to UBS. Global headcount was 1700 and per capita revenue generation was high, about 50 per cent above the Warburg equivalent, it emerged at the time of the merger.

However, there was very little support from other parts of the investment bank which had not been developed to the same degree:

The flaw was UBS as an owner. The board was out of its depth in investment banking, there was never a convincing strategy for investment banking, a global culture was never embraced, it was always management by committee and very bureaucratic. The culture was too Swiss, there was virtually no international representation at board level. It was too retail and the import-ance of individuals to a successful investment bank was not recognized. The equities people did their best but clients want research in a global context and you can't do that without a big US business. UBS should have stuck to fund management, private banking and maybe bonds, where it is possible to succeed by leveraging the balance sheet.[29]

Another former employee from the equities side who was there for most of the period after Big Bang sums up: 'We did genuinely take an old-fashioned UK agency broker with no corporate finance and with no acquisitions, grew into a pan-European investment bank making good profits with no help from head office. The company balance sheet got us through 1988 and 1989 and the Blue Arrow compensation but even this created a no-win situation with them. They baled us out but couldn't sustain us in the long term.'[30]

MISSED OPPORTUNITIES

By 1997 it was clear that there was no point in having brokers without an all-round investment banking product. The cost of building this up was considerable and there were no worked examples of success in their peer group for the banks to see. The senior management of the banks did not believe that such a task was achievable, their shareholders were sceptical and it seemed easier to pull out. UBS, for all the excellence of its European broking and capital markets business, never got close to developing a full investment banking presence but BZW and NatWest Markets were much closer to success than their chief executives and shareholders believed.

BZW had a stronger corporate advisory and capital markets position than NatWest but it was weaker in America. One acquisition of the size that it made on the asset management side of the business in 1995 would have plugged that gap and it would then have been well positioned to develop into a leading investment bank. NatWest had actually made all the right steps by the end of 1996 and had all the right building blocks. What was then required was an improvement in risk management, expertise which it already owned thanks to the Greenwich acquisition, and a thorough programme of cultural integration across the business.

By this stage there was reasonable support for BZW and NatWest Markets from the boards. The Barclays main board of January 1997 rejected their chief executive's proposal to drop BZW. The NatWest main board of February 1997 showed strong enthusiasm for investment banking, and 'encouraged NatWest Markets to persist, arguing that the board not the shareholders ran the bank'.[31]

However, the chief executives of Barclays and NatWest did not buy into the strategy. Without this self-belief they were not able to convince shareholders to give them the time for their strategies to work. The discovery of NatWest's black hole took the issue of the clearers' investment banking strategy out from private meetings with share-holders into the public domain and it became easier for Taylor and Wanless to give up than to continue.

Nineteen ninety-five was the crucial year. BZW was in a strong position through the default of the merchant banks: 'In terms of its own objectives and of the global industry, it was now unquestionably the British investment banking leader.'[32] The decision to buy in asset management rather than investment banking in America represents an opportunity lost to consolidate that position. NatWest's missed opportunity came when it failed to impress Warburg's senior manage-ment: 'NatWest was not favoured by some Warburg's directors, who did not like the idea of working for a clearing bank . . . NatWest and Warburg would have been a strong British combination with synergy to be gained in several business areas.'[33] Again one has to ask: where was the Government? There was no central guidance to Warburg's directors because neither the Government nor the Bank of England believed it to be their job to encourage the emergence of a strong British standard bearer in global investment banking.

25

Schroders (and Flemings)

Early in 1995 I moved from NatWest to Schroders as group managing director, securities. In the last week of November 1999 I was invited to a dinner by Win Bischoff, Schroders' chairman. The year had been difficult, with a few high-profile staff departures leading to speculation about our ability to remain independent. No doubt Bischoff wished to discuss these matters. The dinner was held in a private dining room at Brown's Hotel in London and was also attended by Peter Sedgwick, the deputy chairman, Nick MacAndrew, the finance director, and David Challen, Schroders' most senior corporate financier. The mood was a touch conspiratorial but deadly serious. After the food was served the waiters were told not to re-enter the room unless they were called and conversation began in earnest.

MOVING OUT OF DENIAL

Bischoff began by explaining that a number of approaches had been received to buy all or part of the group and that we needed to look at them. The directors were concerned about the future of the investment banking division, a board meeting was to be held the next week to discuss the issue and the views of Challen and me would be helpful in reaching a decision. Challen is one of a handful of corporate financiers most trusted by the chief executives of British companies. His sound judgement under pressure and ability to deliver balanced, objective advice had won and retained many clients for Schroders over the years. But, increasingly, Schroders had been losing ground to the US investment banks, giving him first-hand experience of the competitive pressures we were under. He was the first to give his view: corporate clients required their investment banks to offer a global platform, Schroders' New York business was not strong enough for us to do that and we had shown ourselves unable to fix it. It was therefore inevitable that our market position would continue to decline. The responsible advice to the board, Challen reluctantly concluded, was that shareholder value could best be served by selling the investment bank to a suitable new owner. Delay would lead to a further weakening in our position and a reduction in the value of the investment bank.

I took a slightly different line. There were clearly problems with the New York business but these were not insoluble. They could be corrected by redefining our market position and, provided that New York and Europe worked closely together, Schroders could represent itself to clients as being a global firm in the products it offered. We might need to accept a less rarefied position in the league tables than we currently occupied in the UK but we could still offer a service that would be valued by clients and was commercially viable. I raised one further issue. In bull markets such as the one we were experiencing at present, the bigger banks could afford to bid up for our staff and we would not be able to compete with the packages on offer if cash was our only weapon. We would need to give the employees significant ownership in the business and this would mean persuading the shareholders to release some of their equity to the staff. With 48 per cent of the votes in the hands of the Schroder family, this proposal could be tested easily.

The debate carried on until 10.30 p.m. and finally a consensus was reached. Bischoff would tell the board that, whilst a successful independent future for the investment bank could be envisaged, it would require substantial investment and near perfect implementation. There was no room for error, no guarantee of success, and, with our chances at less than 50:50, it would be prudent for the board to examine other options. We could then take a long, cool look at the alternatives available to us. As we filed out into the night, I noticed that the dinner had been held in the Graham Bell Room, location of the world's first international telephone call and Schroders' last cry.

The board meeting of the first week in December 1999 was held as usual on the top floor of Schroders' headquarters at 120 Cheapside.

Portraits of Schroder family ancestors looked down as Bruno Schroder, his brother-in-law G. W. Mallinckrodt, and the other directors gathered round the green baize table to discuss the bank's future. 120 Cheapside was a no smoking building but this rule was not enforced on the eighth floor and the air thickened with cigar smoke as the debate unfolded. Three options were considered: sale of the entire Schroder group; sale of the investment bank leaving asset management as the group's only business; perseverance with an acquisition in North America to fill the gap in investment banking.

As head of the family which controlled half of the shares, Bruno Schroder had always regarded it as his duty to hand on the business to the next generation in better shape than he had inherited it. His nephew, Philip Mallinckrodt, worked in the business and could reasonably expect to run it at some future date. Bruno did not believe that disposal was the answer but a majority on the board, led by the non-executives, believed that Schroders lacked the scale to compete in the modern world.

There was no real interest in selling the whole group but, to enable a balanced decision to be reached, the board asked the executive directors to explore all three alternatives. This meant opening discussions with some of the parties who had registered their interest over the previous months. This in itself was a significant event. Other banks regularly cast a fly over Schroders and were always told firmly that the shareholders and management were committed to an independent future. In deciding to examine these opportunities, we moved out of a state of denial and into the real world.

WHO'S HUNGRY?

Following the December board meeting, Bischoff sounded out the interested parties. For confidentiality reasons, their identity cannot be revealed and at the time of going to press only the name of Citigroup is in the public domain. We identified them as one of the strongest runners together with one other organization, which I shall call 'York', to whom we wanted to talk seriously. In the second and third weeks of December we met senior executives from Citigroup and York.

Schroders was represented by Bischoff, MacAndrew, Will Samuel, Andrew Sykes and me. We met York first and the meeting did not go well.

The location was an apartment York owned in Manhattan, inevitably furnished in the style of an English country house. We shook hands in an anteroom, moved into the dining room and lined up on opposite sides of the huge table. Their chairman made some opening remarks, acknowledging that they understood how painful this must be for us and proposing that each side describe their business. We presented first and undersold ourselves. It was clear from York's questions that we were being too frank about our weaknesses, not bullish enough about our strengths and were altogether too reserved and too English for our hosts. After we had completed our presentation, York's chairman looked across the table: 'That's all very well but what I want to know is, are you hungry?' Bischoff started to explain that, despite our understated style, we were determined to succeed. York interrupted: 'No, I mean are you really hungry?' We looked at each other wondering how best to convince him that we were desperate for success USA-style but he put us out of our misery: 'Look, who wants to eat lunch?'

The York delegates left after lunch, leaving us to use their apartment. Our adviser was Geoff Boisi, to whom we had got close during discussions to buy his corporate finance boutique in the summer. Boisi told us that we had not been positive enough, and that we would need to do a better job with Citigroup. We were all very flat. None of us was enjoying hawking our business around; we all found it difficult to accept that we, proud Schroders, had to think of selling ourselves to a bunch of Americans. There was a brief debate in the York apartment about whether we really had to go through with this before reality set back in.

The next week we were back in New York and met early in the morning in Bischoff's apartment on Central Park South. Boisi made it clear that this time we had to portray the glass as being half full not half empty. We divided into three groups in case we were spotted and made our way past Schroders' New York headquarters, through the rain and the crowds of Manhattan Christmas shoppers, to Citigroup's executive suite on Park Avenue. This was a much better meeting. The layout was less formal, big comfy armchairs arranged into a circle, and Citigroup were clearly as interested in us as we were in them.

Citigroup fielded most of their top investment banking team. Deryck Maughan, who had been chief executive of Salomon before Citigroup bought them, and who had often made clear to Bischoff his interest in buying Schroders, made some introductory remarks and handed over to us. Our presentation was more polished and more confident this time but, as we worked through the story, I noticed that MacAndrew's next slide still had York's name on it. I passed across a note, he turned deathly white and just managed to stop the technician from displaying it on the screen. We finished our pitch, there were a few questions and then Michael Carpenter, the head of investment banking at Citigroup, gave a full exposition of their business. It was obvious to everyone that, in Europe at least, we were complementary to each other and that a deal could make sense. The meeting broke up at 3.30 p.m. and we knew that we had at least one serious and credible organization interested in our business and that we would shortly be called upon to make a hard choice.

We reassembled in London and worked up the other options that the board had asked us to look at, going it alone or selling the whole group. Bischoff met some of those who had expressed an interest in buying the whole group but no one favoured wholesale sell out and this option was not explored very seriously.

During December, Bischoff and MacAndrew sounded me out about becoming chief executive myself in the event of us carrying on. I told them that it was something I was not keen on, even on a part-time basis, but I was less sure in my own mind than I sounded to them. On Christmas Eve Samuel phoned me and pressed me to define the conditions under which I would do the job and I read out a list I had scrawled that afternoon on the back of a petrol receipt while I was in the car wash.

Over Christmas and New Year I wrestled with my conscience. I really wanted Schroders to stay in investment banking, I believed that we could find a profitable niche, I felt that I could help make it happen but the fit with my personal interests was terrible. Finally I resolved that, if there was any sign of support from the senior executives and directors for remaining independent, I would step up but that I would not show my hand yet. I was looking for some evidence of their conviction in the business, not just faith in me. I did not want to be the last roll of the dice; there needed to be a real determination and self-belief from the board.

In fact I need not have lost any sleep on this matter. I subsequently learned that serious concerns had been voiced at a board meeting in the summer, that the die had been cast since late November, that I was little more than a contingency if all else failed and that influential figures on the board were convinced that the investment bank did not have an independent future. By the time I stepped forward in January it was much too late and a board meeting in early January endorsed the sale of the investment bank over the other options.

By this stage preliminary discussions were being held with the senior managers of Salomon Smith Barney (SSB), Citigroup's investment bank. For me this meant working again with Jim O'Donnell who was now in charge of SSB's London-based equity operations. O'Donnell had told me good things about SSB during the previous months and, during Schroders' internal deliberations, this information helped us decide that our staff would not be put off by the chequered reputation Salomon had in London. We sketched out how the combined business might look during the second week of January and on the weekend of 15–16 January began to widen the circle of those in the know. I had to brief Richard Wyatt, Schroders' head of European equities, and we met at the Angel Hotel, Bury St Edmunds, halfway between our houses, at 10 a.m. on the Saturday morning.

It was a beautiful winter's morning. I fought with the Saturday shoppers for a parking spot and joined Wyatt, who had already ordered tea and biscuits, in the lounge. He was visibly shocked and saddened when I told him the news but he is resilient and pragmatic and, as I briefed him on the outline of the new structure, he became excited about the potential of the new business. We talked for about an hour and then went home to prepare for a dinner that night back in London with the senior management of SSB and Schroders. The conversation was about to move into locking in the key people and the millions of dollars that would be required to do so. I paid the bill at the Angel for our tea and biscuits: it was £4. Later that night Challen told me that he had had a similar meeting with a corporate finance colleague at the

Berkeley Hotel in London and their bill had been £34. '"David," I said, "that's the difference between our world and yours."' How had we got into this position?

THE 1995 STRATEGY REVIEW

I joined Schroders in 1995 knowing that the group faced some major challenges. Win Bischoff had taken over from George Mallinckrodt as chairman at the end of 1994 and, within weeks, both were at the Bank of England advising on the rescue of Barings. Soon Schroders was advising Warburg and then Kleinwort on the sale of their companies. These events gave added importance to a long-planned strategy review of Schroders which was carried out with the help of management consultants in the summer and autumn of 1995.

The review did not really get off the ground. The consultants never succeeded in fully engaging with management. Many of the issues that were avoided persisted right through to the end in investment banking. As a result, in 1995 Schroders started out on a newly agreed strategy but with the wrong management structure and competing cultures between London and New York. These unresolved problems were always bubbling away near the surface and finally boiled over in 1999.

The 1995 review encompassed all parts of the group but Schroder Investment Management's strategy appeared to be clear and the bigger issue was investment banking. At that time the instincts of the senior executives and the family shareholders were to remain independent but the question was the one faced by all of the merchant banks ever since Big Bang: whether to pursue a capital markets or an advisory only strategy.

A capital markets strategy would try to win mandates to place shares and raise new equity for corporations and would require broking distribution. An advisory only strategy would give advice on market transactions but would use other brokers for distribution of equity if that was required. The former offered more revenue potential but carried more operational risk, the latter was low risk, was Schroders' traditional business but was thought to be vulnerable to competitors who offered the whole advisory and distribution package.

Schroders had wrestled with this issue since 1983 and had made a number of unconvincing attempts to build a securities business. During my interviews with Schroders over the winter of 1994–5, Bischoff told me with refreshing candour that they did not know which way to turn on securities, that they needed in-house advice to help resolve it and that, if it was decided to retrench into an advisory only position, I would either be paid off or re-employed in another part of the business. I had rarely encountered such openness in the City and from that moment decided that I wanted to work for Schroders.

However, soon after I started in April 1995, I realized that Schroders had already started down the road to a capital markets and equities strategy and it would have been difficult to turn back. The acquisition of Wertheim, a US securities firm with a small middle market corporate finance practice; capital markets progress in emerging Europe and Italy; expansion in securities in Asia and Japan; and the expectations raised by my appointment as group managing director for securities had created a strong momentum towards the capital markets approach.

The real drive for this came from Europe, where Richard Broadbent had been appointed head of corporate finance in 1994. Broadbent had shaken up successfully the old-fashioned management structure and practices in UK corporate finance, which was Schroders' biggest profit earner. With the help of Panfilo Tarantelli, who had built a strong investment bank for Schroders in Italy, teams of corporate financiers were recruited in the other Continental countries. Pan-European teams of specialists in industry sectors were formed, ready to link with their counterparts in the US and Asia and our securities analysts around the world.

By the time of the strategy review it was too late to turn back and the predictable outcome, which was endorsed by the plc board at the turn of 1995, was to proceed with the capital markets initiative. We would try to develop a strong transatlantic business with a differentiated niche business in Asia. The consultants correctly highlighted the management stretch this implied, especially in Asia, but missed the most glaring problem: the dysfunctionality between Europe and the US.[1]

In Europe, the plan to integrate securities and corporate finance into an investment bank was working well. In securities existing strengths in the emerging markets and Italy were rounded out by the development of other countries, sectors, sales and sales trading. The head of research, Michael Crawshaw, developed a creative research product and European securities revenues, which had been under £10 million in 1995, increased ten-fold by 1999. Schroders' corporate finance reputation and the leadership of Tarantelli helped bring a good flow of capital markets business in Continental Europe.

A key decision for Schroders was whether or not to build broking in UK equities. Corporate finance was concerned that the increasing dominance of American investment banks would break down the traditional British practice of using separate firms for advice and corporate broking and it was decided to go ahead. A UK sales and research team was built up and began UK broking on 2 January 1997, quickly winning a market share of 2 per cent. Progress in UK capital markets was disappointing, in contrast to the successes achieved in Continental Europe. In part this was due to the survival of the traditional bank–broker structure in the UK which was reinforced by a Monopolies Commission report on underwriting in 1999,[2] but also to the difficulty that Schroders' traditional UK corporate financiers had in adapting to the bank's changed product mix.

PROBLEMS IN NEW YORK

Schroders' New York operations were run by Steven Kotler, a former Wertheim partner who combined an ability to focus on the bottom line with a good understanding of the need to get equities and corporate finance to work together. However, he believed that Schroders' market position in the US was so different to that in Europe that there was little synergy to be achieved from integrating the two areas and, as a result, ran the firm as a semi-independent entity from the rest of the Schroder group.

The equities business was solid but old-fashioned. The salesmen were paid on a commission sharing basis and this fostered an 'eat what you kill' attitude that spread throughout the firm and made integration difficult. The head of research, Barry Tarasoff, had instilled a good research culture and was particularly good at spotting and developing young talent. Corporate finance had a few large clients but its main strengths were with middle market companies. This was a fundamental mismatch with European corporate finance whose clients were much larger.

A golden opportunity to re-orient New York was missed when Schroders' management – and I was a part of this – failed to spot the growth of the new economy. If we had been smart enough to have identified and backed this trend early, we could have developed an additional revenue stream. Instead we remained committed to the old economy. One of the highlights of Schroder & Co.'s year was a conference for investors in industrial manufacturing companies. The conference motto was: 'In rust we trust.' The cynics said that Schroder & Co.'s management had trusted in rust a bit too long, leaving them with a dated, decaying product range.

It was equally damaging that Schroders had allowed its US arm to operate as an independent subsidiary. The consequence was that the place felt like it was still Wertheim and many of the staff still acted as though they worked for Wertheim. Five years after the partnership had been dissolved, invitations were still going out to senior managers to 'The Partners' Christmas Party', many staff still answered the phones by saying 'Wertheim', and clients still called the firm 'Wertheim'. The name was not dropped until late in the 1990s, having moved cautiously through an evolution from Wertheim Schroder to Schroder Wertheim to Schroder & Co. Inc.

Business practices matched these superficial signs. In the equities division the US salesmen were too busy calculating their personal commission to cooperate with colleagues from Europe or Asia. The corporate financiers were more concerned as to where the credit for a deal would lie if we won it than in putting all of the firm's resources together to win the deal. The firm was New York-centric and inward looking and was not in tune with Schroders' requirements.

Not all of this was New York's fault. Schroders had left a vacuum in New York, allowing old habits to become engrained. The senior management in New York did not in their hearts understand or believe in the merits of integration. They found that their product was becoming increasingly old-fashioned. The rest of the world was exploring the new economy, Schroder & Co. were stuck in the rust belt. Competitors were flying industry experts round the world to present global analysis to clients, Schroder & Co. were still arguing about the fee split. The dysfunctionality of Schroders' American and European businesses was never gripped so the firm had no chance to show what it could do.

However, the growing importance of scale in the US economy and financial markets would have presented Schroders with a stiff challenge even if both sides of the Atlantic had been working in perfect harmony. The Wall Street bull market meant that the biggest investment banks got bigger, offering their clients more balance sheet and more resources. All medium-sized US investment banks, not just Schroder & Co., faced this squeeze and many sold themselves to much bigger firms than Schroders. For example, Alex Brown, Montgomery Securities, Hambrecht & Quist and Robertson Stephens all moved from being medium-sized independent competitors of Schroder & Co. into the arms of very large banks. Schroder & Co. clearly faced an enormous challenge if it was to resist this trend.

The excellent progress that was being made in corporate finance, capital markets and securities in Europe widened the gap with New York. Tarantelli and Broadbent had built a team that combined discipline and flair and were winning senior positions in the biggest deals on the Continent. They upped their objectives, believing that Schroders was capable of commanding a top five position amongst the investment banks competing in Europe. They began to pressure me to accelerate the growth of European securities. I believed that they were aiming too high in going head-to-head with the leading American banks, a position I doubted that we could sustain. I never felt comfortable with this pace so Broadbent manoeuvred Tarantelli into position as head of European securities, jointly reporting to me. As they built up resources in corporate finance and securities, the type of business we were pitching for required us to present a global team and Broadbent grew increasingly frustrated by our inability to do so due to the misalignment with New York.

In desperation, Broadbent agreed to go to New York to take charge of US corporate finance in 1998. He carried out a thorough review of the business, interviewing all of the staff and talking to clients and competitors to help him build a full picture of the firm's position. His analysis was that root and branch surgery was necessary if Schroder & Co. was to have a chance of surviving. The firm needed shaking up from top to bottom and required such radical change that, in his view, it could only be done with a new chief executive. He pressed for the removal of Kotler, doubting that modernization and attitudinal change could be achieved with him there, and wanted to take over as chief executive himself.

This was too much for Bischoff and Peter Sedgwick, Schroders' deputy chairman, who had been spending half of his time in New York overseeing the business. They did not believe that Broadbent was qualified to lead the entire US business at that stage. He was inexperienced in many of Schroder & Co.'s products such as equities, clearing and high yield, activities that accounted for the vast majority of capital employed, headcount and profits. Furthermore, he was thought to be fully occupied with some of his existing reporting lines and Bischoff and Sedgwick wanted more evidence of this working well before trusting him with such a job. Instead, in January 1999, Broadbent was offered a carte blanche to clean up US corporate finance, including a large budget to spend on recruiting and acquisitions. Kotler would remain as chief executive of Schroder & Co.

At first Broadbent appeared to go along with this. In January 1999 he swept out a number of executives he believed to be below the required standard and held a firm-wide meeting in New York to announce his expansionary plan. He spoke eloquently and passionately about the challenges ahead but within days he had a change of heart, collected his bonus, took a week's holiday and resigned. New York was in uproar and many of the European corporate financiers who had admired Broadbent's work in London were seriously disquieted. Bischoff and Sedgwick were accused of supporting Kotler over Broadbent and faced a credibility problem with the staff. The eighth floor at 120 Cheapside had always been spoken of with great respect at Schroders but was now felt to be out of touch and outdated.

Samuel, Sykes, Tarantelli and I felt that something had to be done; we could see our senior staff spinning out of control, easy meat for competitors seeking to recruit them. We met Bischoff for dinner at the Grosvenor House in late February and told him that Kotler would have to retire as chief executive within a reasonable time or there was a serious risk of the investment bank blowing up. A few weeks later it was announced that he would be stepping down as chief executive at the end of June.

This announcement bought some time but the failure to come up with answers to the US issue contributed to a number of senior staff resignations during the summer. Bischoff took over Sedgwick's role as minder of the US business and, with Samuel, conducted a thorough search for a new chief executive for New York or for an acquisition. They settled on the Beacon Group, a corporate finance boutique started by Geoffrey Boisi who had been one of the leading partners at Goldman Sachs. The fit looked ideal. It would bring a handful of top quality corporate financiers to seed Schroders' US investment bank and Boisi himself, who had a good track record in management and was a possible successor to Bischoff. A price was agreed, board support was lined up but at the last minute Schroders backed down.

Three things occurred to change Schroders' view. A leak in the *Financial Times* specifying a high price to be paid for Beacon created fears that the Beacon partners would be so wealthy as a result of the deal that they would be unmanageable. I had met the Beacon people and have seen enough of Boisi at work to know that this was nonsense. Secondly, as Schroders got to know more about the Beacon business, they feared that it was not big enough in the right areas to make a difference. Thirdly, some of Beacon's activities overlapped with other parts of the Schroder Group, for example Schroder Ventures, and it became clear that major turf issues would occur if the deal proceeded. Several of us were horrified by the turn of events, including Bruno Schroder who offered to buy Beacon and give it to Schroders, so desperate was he for a solution to the New York problem.

Schroders faced problems in the autumn of 1999 following the breakdown of the Beacon deal. Bischoff and Samuel continued to interview candidates for New York and looked at other corporate finance boutiques to buy but none fitted. The US staff became very disquieted at the lack of progress and many of them made plans to leave the company after bonuses were paid in February 2000. Staff in Europe, especially in corporate finance, expressed concern at Schroders' inability to provide them with a strong US partner. 'Schroders' US problem' was frequently written about in the press and exploited by competitors trying to win clients and staff from Schroders. The senior management looked under pressure and the winning feel began to slip. Predators scented blood, made their interest known, and, in November 1999, Bischoff issued his invitations to Brown's Hotel.

TOO BIG TO BE SMALL, TOO SMALL TO BE BIG?

Press comment on the sale of the investment bank was unanimous about one thing: the inevitability of it all given the global trends to scale in the industry. The *Financial News* summed up the views of nearly all the papers on 24 January 2000 with the headline: 'Victory for inevitability in Schroders' sale.'

The bank's president, G. W. Mallinckrodt, commented that 'we were too small to be big, too big to be small'. I have hardly ever dared to disagree with him but on this occasion I wonder whether he was right.

If the only acceptable benchmark was a position in the bulge bracket, then Schroders' demise was indeed inevitable. The bank lacked the product range or capital base to go head-to-head with the industry leaders. The bigger banks have a balance sheet to finance deals and open up new relationships. They have lots of products with which to impress clients and to outgun the likes of Schroders. Their global revenue base is so large that they can afford to take chances with expansion without running the risk of a Warburg-type collapse. However, going head-to-head with the bulge bracket was not the only model available to Schroders.

It is debatable whether Schroders needed to follow a capital markets strategy at all. It had a very good list of advisory clients although this would inevitably have come under pressure from integrated investment banks offering a broad range of services. But Schroders might have been able to retain a better position with its clients by offering them a different service to that offered by the big banks. By trying to compete directly with the bulge bracket, Schroders was bound to appear inferior.

It is not clear whether the capital markets question was properly debated before 1995 (by which time it was too late) or whether

Schroders just drifted into it. Events such as the acquisition of Wertheim, essentially a securities firm, in stages from 1986; half hearted attempts to build an equities business after Big Bang; and the expansion of securities outside the US in the early nineties were opportunistic rather than strategic moves. A chance to reassess was missed in 1995 at the time of my appointment and the strategy review.

Once we were committed to a capital markets strategy after 1995, implementation needed to be very careful given the risks in the business and our size. But there were two areas – European securities and US corporate finance – where we overreached ourselves. In European securities after 1997 cautious, slow build-up gave way to the more aggressive pursuit of league table rankings and we tried to hire in stars rather than grow our own talent. This reduced profits and confused the culture. In the US, from 1998 onwards, an attempt was made to change the corporate finance department into a miniature bulge bracket firm. A senior executive in New York told me: 'We had a model that was surviving, dodging between the giants, making money, good money. We went wrong when we tried to take on the giants instead of stepping around them. What brought down Schroders was the $25 million of losses in New York corporate finance incurred once management of that department was handed over to London. They neglected our existing clients, could not attract new ones and lost control of the cost base.'

I believe that it would have been possible to have followed a capital markets strategy without taking on the giants. We would have needed to promote the brand more than our people, encouraging teamwork and putting home-grown talent above imported stars. We needed a differentiated message for clients, building on the bank's reputation for quality, objectivity and trustworthiness. Independent, trusted advice and top-quality execution is valued by many clients as an alternative to the service provided by the transaction-oriented investment banks. It might not have brought a position at the top of the league tables but the business could have been profitable, viable and fun.

For this model to be fully effective, Schroders needed a US presence. That presence did not need to be large-scale but it had to be integrated with the rest of the group and management must take responsibility for not achieving that in over a decade of ownership. Even so, in the summer of 1999 we were a stroke of the pen away from achieving the required position in the form of the Beacon group. Boisi and his partners had agreed terms only for Schroders to back off at the last minute. We lost access to good management, a quality team of corporate financiers, blew our credibility with those who favoured Beacon and were on the run from then onwards.

Would the model I have described have earned enough to compensate and retain the best staff? Only if equity participation could be offered and in the closing weeks of 1999 Bischoff had performed miracles in making that possible. By the time the investment bank was sold, subject to trustee and regulatory approval, he had got agreement to plans which would have given the employees ownership or options to nearly 25 per cent of the company over a five-year period. This would have given the potential for the creation of an alternative investment bank in which ownership would have been an attractive counter to playing on the big stage with other people's money.

In reviewing the final years of Schroders' investment bank, we as management must admit our mistakes. We missed the growth of the new economy, remaining value not growth investors. We challenged the bulge bracket in Europe and New York, a task that was within reach when we started but was taken beyond range by the ever-increasing resources poured into investment banking by our bigger competitors. We wandered into a capital markets business almost by chance and failed to examine properly whether an advisory only strategy was viable.

Despite all this, the investment bank was sold to a good new owner at a premium to book value. We sold from a position of strength on the back of record profits. The management had steered a way through a very demanding course, survived as a profitable independent firm for longer than virtually all the peer group and delivered good rewards to staff and shareholders. In my opinion, the sale of Schroders' investment bank was unnecessary but was certainly no disgrace.

FLEMINGS' POSTSCRIPT

Shortly after Schroders sold its investment bank, Flemings' share-holders (including the Fleming family which spoke for a third of the equity) accepted an offer for the group from Chase Manhattan Bank. The press assumed that this was a direct response to the news from Schroders but in fact Flemings' directors and major shareholders had been considering their options for some time, especially in the later months of 1999. Although Schroders made it slightly easier for Flemings to announce their decision, they were already close to reaching their own conclusions when the news broke from Cheapside.

Flemings had pursued an integrated corporate advisory and capital markets strategy since Big Bang and had been most successful in Asia Pacific through its joint venture, Jardine Fleming. It recovered well from the Asian crisis of 1998, ending its life as an independent bank by reporting record profits in 1999–2000. In Europe, although it won a number of high-profile capital markets mandates, it did not become a major force on a sustained basis, perhaps lacking the breadth and depth of advisory relationships from which to gain capital markets leverage. In the end it reached the same conclusion as Schroders about the viability of a medium-sized investment bank in the twenty-first century.

26

The Survivors

By the end of the year 2000, only five of the firms that we started following in 1983 were still operating independent, equities-based investment banks. These were Cazenove, Goldman, Merrill, Morgan Stanley and HSBC. Lazards and N. M. Rothschild continued to be advisory-led banks. The survivors embarked on their journeys at different times and with wide-ranging objectives from global domination to domestic niche. How did they do it?

HSBC: SURVIVING IN SPITE OF ITSELF

By the end of Bernard Asher's period in charge in 1998, the broker had been cowed into subservience and it had no spirit left to make a strategic breakthrough. Capel was just about profitable in the late 1990s but its overall market position declined. Research had lost its top slot in the Extel survey to Warburg in 1991 and by 1994 it had slipped to fourth. Although the research ranking was rebuilt to second in 1996 under Quintin Price's leadership, research was no longer the power it was and fell away again. Where once Capel had dominated institutional business in London its market share in UK equities of 10 per cent in the glory days slipped to 6 per cent in 1996 and to 3.5 per cent in 1997.

The company's top management felt that its agency status was a factor in the loss of market share and in July 1995 Capel announced that it was to move into mainstream UK market making.

The timing of Capel's move was determined by concern that Smith New Court under Merrill Lynch's ownership would be less accommodating to agency brokers than it had been as an independent house. Capel relied on Smith New Court for up to a third of its execution and it was considered too risky to rely on the new and unknown owners of Smith to remain obliging. Douglas Baker, NatWest's head of market making, transferred to Capel and was soon followed by some of NatWest's leading sales traders and market makers. But the required culture change in the switch from agency broking caused difficulties and losses in the first year or two were large. In an effort to keep the losses down, capital was controlled very closely, it became harder for the salesmen and sales traders to execute for clients and morale and market share were further weakened.

In other parts of the world Capel had pockets of strength but could not count itself as being among the leading global brokers. Good business was done in Continental European equities but this too was hit by staff departures from 1996 onwards. Despite HSBC's strong presence in Asia as a commercial and retail bank, the broking and investment banking sides there were never as strong. A good equity trading business in the US was briefly developed in 1996–7 but it did not last and, like the rest of HSBC's brokers, was never integrated with other parts of the business.

Peter Letley, the deputy chairman of HSBC Investment Banking, took charge of the broker after Benton left in 1995. He was an administrator rather than a front line leader and was too similar to Asher to form an ideal management team with him. Letley remained at the helm of Capel until he retired in 1998 but underneath him there was a kaleidoscope of management in the equities business.

In research, a former star of the oils sector, David Gray, was not happy as head of research and there was a mighty power play involving three of Capel's senior analysts. Price got the job in 1995 and a group of senior analysts and salesmen left in high dudgeon. In November 1996, Letley reshuffled his management team. O'Donnell and Krishna Patel, the head of derivatives, were appointed deputy chief executives and Price was put in charge of research and sales for Europe. Soon afterwards O'Donnell left the City, leaving Patel in charge. However, management succession was never smooth at Capel and Price was unhappy with this appointment and left at the end of 1997 after strong words with Asher. These frequent changes damaged continuity, discouraged long-term planning and gave plenty for the staff to gossip about.

With no strong drive for integration from the top and a mismatch in the market positions of broking and corporate finance, it took a long time for HSBC to link the two. A former head of research at Capel told me: 'Integration with Samuel Montagu? There was nothing for us to integrate with. Their strengths were venture capital and project finance, they had very little in pure big company corporate advisory or capital markets work.'[1] Using the Acquisitions Monthly UK deal league table as a proxy for standing within the industry, HSBC's corporate finance ranking slipped from a respectable position of third in 1992 into a sequence of seventh, eighth, nineteenth, fourteenth, fourteenth, thirteenth and ninth for 1999. In European advisory business, HSBC was ranked eighteenth in January 2000. Although HSBC and James Capel on the corporate broking side could boast a large number of clients amongst smaller companies (which brought it third place in the 2000 league table for the number of advisers published by Crawfords) it did not have a major presence amongst big blue chips.

In January 1996 some efforts were made to drive the two together:

Capel's analysts have historically worked almost entirely in isolation from Samuel Montagu and have focused on selling their research to institutional clients. This has become an increasingly unprofitable market, generating lacklustre returns for HSBC. Now analysts are to be encouraged to become more involved in assisting HSBC's corporate financiers. 'We're aiming to improve the use of research to generate more primary equity product', said Keith Harris, chief executive designate of HSBC's new investment banking division. In order to motivate analysts to come up with corporate finance ideas, HSBC is working on a formal remuneration structure.[2]

Many of the integrated merchant banks and brokers had introduced such schemes in the early days of Big Bang as a means of fostering a new culture. But by the second half of the 1990s, cooperation between research and corporate finance was second nature at most investment banks and at many places research was a shared resource between corporate finance and institutional sales. The explanation for HSBC being so late into this is that, within a year or two of Big Bang, senior enthusiasm for investment banking had gone and it became an exercise in damage limitation.

Whether HSBC is seen as a success or a survivor depends on one's perspective. For the HSBC main board, the later 1990s achieved the goal set for Asher when he started out in 1990: he kept the broker and the investment bank from being a serious embarrassment to the parent. There were periodic personnel scuffles and reshuffles at James Capel that caused a flurry in broking circles and the odd bad year for profits, but by and large it kept out of the limelight. The broader investment banking business never got going. If anyone in the City thought about it, some minor discredit would attach to HSBC for allowing the investment bank to slumber on, but no one hardly ever did think about Samuel Montagu.

For the staff, particularly those at James Capel, however, these were not happy years. Analysts, salesmen and traders all complain about the lack of drive, direction and vision and a large number of high-profile defections bear out the fact that it was not a particularly happy place to work. All the Capel staff I interviewed gave me the same story: 'the bank clearly were not interested'; 'there was no strategy, it was a total disaster, we struggled on but it was run by administrators not brokers'; 'I never felt we would get the resources. We paid bottom quartile which is OK if you are a partnership or have staff participation or if you are going forwards but you can't do that with backward momentum'; 'Bernard managed it as though it was a game of chess, his soul was not in the business. Our results and external reputation were starting to recover but it was a very unpleasant environment.' One of his senior managers told me: 'I wanted to quit within a week of starting. The job was undoable. Senior hires had to be approved and were often rejected, so were salary increases. Guarantees of over £150,000 had to be signed off by the group chief executive at a time when average people in London needed double that to even think about joining. There was no delegated power, no trust, we were always being second guessed and not given responsibility.'[3]

For shareholders there was a middling investment bank and as a whole the results were satisfactory. Thanks in part to some hefty disposals from the venture capital portfolio, HSBC Investment Bank made a good return on equity most years in the 1990s but shareholders are entitled to ask whether there was a missed opportunity.

The leading broking franchise of the 1980s was expensively acquired and left to wither. Bernard Asher did a superb job at bringing it under control and showing that the pampered egos of the broking community could be managed for profit as well as prizes. He was one of the few independent minded thinkers in the City in the 1990s and had the courage of his convictions. Many of us thought of doing it Asher's way but became frightened at bad publicity, falling morale and loss of client reputation. Asher knew that he could rely on the long-term support of his board, had no fears for his own position and was prepared to tough it out. If he had managed to instil more confidence into his own appointees, to have recruited a handful of high-profile client pleasers and launched an integration drive, HSBC's shareholders might have got full value for the money and management time spent on James Capel. Instead, their gratitude that losses and reputational issues in investment banking have not damaged the share price is tempered with regret that a top-brand name became tarnished and was not developed into a rounded investment bank.

THE AMERICANS: 'OVERPAID AND OVER HERE'

At the end of 1994 the American investment banks were retreating from London in disarray; by the year 2000 they were in control. How did they turn it round so quickly? They were fortuitous that several of their British competitors blew up or gave up through incompetence or a lack of will. In 1995, while the big US investment banks were still recovering from the bond market problems of 1994, Barings, Warburg, Kleinwort and Smith obligingly rolled over. The US firms had the ambition and skills to take full advantage of this. They were just experiencing a surge in profitability at home which gave them the confidence and the money to be expansive abroad. The great Wall Street bull market enabled the large US investment banks to make returns on equity of 26 per cent in 1996, 23 per cent in 1997 and a still respectable 16 per cent in 1998.

While the British were in disarray, Goldman and Morgan Stanley stepped up their organic growth plans and continued to hire some of the best analysts, salesmen and traders. They went about this more cleverly than some of the European start-ups, such as Deutsche Morgan Grenfell, who were rebuilding again in equities, but too aggressively and with insufficient regard to cultural integration. By contrast, the Americans interviewed slowly and carefully, tended not to take large groups from any one firm and to supplement senior recruits with large numbers of graduates and MBA students.

Three firms, Credit Suisse First Boston, Merrill Lynch and Salomon Smith Barney, went the acquisition route with BZW, Smith and Schroders respectively. Merrill went for rapid and total integration, including the removal of the Smith name and the introduction of American management work practices into London and to begin with it did not look as though this would be successful. The rapid integration was not popular with some of the Smith veterans who took time to come to terms with the loss of Smith's identity and found the American approach to risk management and compliance cumbersome and bureaucratic. The firm wobbled in 1996, recovered in 1997 and was set back again in 1998 when the summer's mini-crash brought heavy cost control from head office including redundancies, restrictions on travel and reduced entertainment budgets. However, Merrill ended the 1990s with a powerful position in corporate finance and secondary broking.

Smith's chairman, Michael Marks, became co-head of equities at Merrill and, in 1997, London-based chief operating officer for Europe, the Middle East and Africa. He is a forthright defender of the rapid assimilation approach:

I am very unimpressed when I ring up friends in the old London broking houses and they answer the phone 'Phillips & Drew' or some other name that has long since gone. We had a strong view that we should not try to run a business within a business and we said 'if we are going to do it we are going to do it'. Reunion parties are banned; we are a meritocracy or we are nothing. We packed up on a Friday night and opened again as a new firm on the Monday morning. Merrill were scrupulously fair about picking the best person for the job where there was overlap. 1998 was a setback but I am sure we took the right decisions even if we might have communicated them better. We had got fat and we needed to take action.[4]

Not everything went well all of the time for the Americans in London. While Morgan Stanley, Goldman and Merrill were steadily improving their position, Salomon continued to behave like an American investment bank of the eighties, retreating and advancing in turn. Salomon was traditionally a bond house with a reputation for proprietary trading rather than client service, so there was little reason to believe that it would be a serious equities player. However, developments in the US in the early 1990s showed that the firm was interested in broadening its business away from bonds. A US equities business was developed under the leadership of Rod Barens and Bruce Hackett and by 1995 was generally ranked in the top three by investing clients in America. This served to encourage Salomon to build up a global equities network and it turned to London.

David Turnbull, who had built up a successful Japanese equities business for Salomon, was given the task of converting Salomon's London equities operations from proprietary trading into a client-oriented sales, research and trading unit. He faced enormous budgetary and cultural problems and the City is full of ex-Salomon people who want to speak out about this period:

Turnbull did an OK job but he faced a credibility gap because he was not a European specialist and because of our reputation on the street for hiring and firing. Bert Richards was head of research, great at the big picture, marvellous recruiter but not so interested in the daily bump and grind of research. He took it up from a handful of analysts in 1995 to fifty or sixty by the time of the Travelers takeover. It was a good mix of stars like Richard Dale in media and good talent from the consultancies and the US business schools.[5]

By 1997 recognition with the institutions was improving but pressures were mounting from New York. London was given a budget of $12 million in 1997–8 to hire a dozen salespeople to help bring in revenues now that the research product was well established and winning plaudits from the clients. This final piece of investment was essential to get leverage from the work of the previous years but the budget was sliced regularly over the summer until, in the end, $2 million was available to hire four salespeople. A senior analyst told me: 'This happened all the time, we could see it. We would get momentum and then New York would panic and all development would be put on hold. This, together with a lack of progress in corporate finance in Europe, really held us back.'[6]

A Salomon middle manager told me:

The trouble came from New York. They viewed the business as a bond not an equity, always looking for an annual return with no concept about longer term growth. Peter Middleton ran the London operations and he was also strong on cost control and short-term results. It was the same on the trading floor. Turnbull used to get terrible pressure from the proprietary traders about hiring people who could not bring in an instant return. It was a problem for him in 1995 and 1996 when we had all the cost of the hires but clients were watching us rather than paying us and they got very impatient with him. You could see the strain on his face for about eighteen months.[7]

The key to Salomon's cost-conscious approach at this time was its credit rating which it needed to protect. It reported quarterly earnings and the central management was under enormous pressure not to deplete reserves so that, every time there was a poor quarter in trading, expenditure had to be cut back elsewhere to protect the bottom line. As an independent entity it would have taken the firm a long time to build a solid earnings platform and then to shed its image of inconsistency.

The turning-point came in 1997 when it was bought by the Travelers Group, bringing with it the US broking firm of Smith Barney. The introduction of a stronger balance sheet, a broader equity culture and experienced equities management helped the firm to a global investment banking business. This was reinforced when Citigroup bought Travelers and real muscle was put behind investment banking. In 1998 and 1999 strong progress was made in London. A good equities platform was built and Salomon Smith Barney came seventh in the Reuters Survey of fund managers published in January 2000.[8] Corporate finance lagged but was only just outside the top ten in the league tables for 1999. However, Citigroup was eager to see Salomon Smith Barney match its top three position in equities and investment banking in the US with a similar position in Europe and its purchase of Schroders was intended to accelerate that process.

Citigroup's re-entry into London in the late 1990s appears to be more carefully thought out than its efforts in the 1980s and to be pursued with greater commitment and conviction. A crucial difference is that the current European initiative is in support of a strong presence in investment banking in the US whereas in the 1980s, Citicorp had hoped to make its initial entry into investment banking through a European product. There are very few precedents for investment banks succeeding abroad without a good position in their domestic market and the firm would have needed to break the mould for its 1980s strategy to have worked. Ten years later with Salomon and Smith Barney bought and integrated, the European proposition looked much more realistic.

A consequence of the success of the US firms in London was that the American investment banking model became accepted as the norm. They focused on pan-European research rather than the traditional separation of the UK and Continental Europe favoured by the British firms. As monetary union in Europe became a reality and US ownership of European equities increased, this model became increasingly relevant. The Americans made great play of teams of analysts around the world all following the same sector and sharing information and views and, although this looked better on paper than in practice, it was something that the European firms could not replicate with ease.

Institutional and corporate clients responded positively. The Reuters Survey of the broking firms following the top European companies demonstrated the grip of the American firms. The fund managers voted Morgan Stanley first, Goldman Sachs second and Merrill Lynch third. The corporates voted Goldman Sachs first, J. P. Morgan second and Merrill Lynch third. The leading positions were a clean sweep for the Americans amongst both constituencies.[9]

The principal characteristics of the American model were the subjugation of broking to corporate finance and capital markets and the elevation of transaction banking above relationship banking. The subsidiary role of broking can be seen from the Goldman Sachs prospectus issued in May 1999, when the firm went public. The firm described itself as 'a leading global investment banking and securities firm' with three principal business lines:[10]

- Investment Banking;
- Trading and Principal Investments; and
- Asset Management and Securities Services.

Broking is tucked away after investment banking, amongst trading and principal investments. Throughout the document the primacy of the needs of corporate clients is apparent. In common with the other leading American firms, global investment research is a separate department, not part of equities. This at least makes it clear to the staff where their loyalties lie but the institutional clients may believe that they are getting an independent service when they are really coming second to corporate finance.

The Americans' preference for transaction banking can be shown by their position in four league tables. The *Crawford's Directory* league tables measure relationships with British corporates, the *Acquisitions Monthly* tables measure deals done. The high value that the American firms have put on transactions rather than relationships is reflected in their positions: not in the top ten for corporate broking or advisory relationships, dominating the leading positions in deals done. The leading three Americans feature higher in the tables for the value of deals than they do for the table for number of deals, illustrating the golden rule of transaction banking: the bigger the deal, the harder they try.

CAZENOVE: A CLASS OF ITS OWN

Cazenove's future, always a popular topic in the City, was debated especially keenly after the firm announced in November 2000 that it planned to incorporate and go public.[11] Many interpreted this as a sign that its predominantly domestic and relationship-based business model was under pressure from the alternative offering of globalism, scale and transaction investment banking, but the pressure for change came through staff not clients.

Cazenove was being squeezed by the pay offered to investment bankers by the large American firms. Senior employees and even some partners compared their pay and prospects at Cazenove with the huge sums routinely on offer at the American investment banks and wondered whether they would be better off moving. With no exposure to Wall St's super returns and no equity to offer, the partnership was unable to match US style packages and during the summer of 2000, the managing partners reviewed the firm's position.

A number of alternatives were considered, including sale of the firm, but it was decided that the client offering was strong enough to sustain independence provided that a solution could be found to the pay question. The decision reached was to incorporate, to sell 10 per cent of the shares to outside investors, to make 20 per cent available to staff and to float the company in 2002, possibly raising extra capital at this time. In this way it is intended to create a currency in the form of shares and share options with which to reward and lock in existing staff and to attract new employees. It is hoped that this will restore competitiveness in the labour market although it is recognized that in certain phases of the investment banking cycle, the broadly based global giants will often be able to pay better.

Incorporation and flotation answer some but not all of the questions facing Cazenove and also raise some new issues. With the bond of partnership dissolved, will the firm become vulnerable to senior level defections? Previously partners had so much capital tied in the firm that they were unhirable and the current partners are all locked in to the new structure. But in future Cazenove will be like other firms where at even the most senior level, job changes are increasingly common and this may in time erode one of Cazenove's competitive advantages. There are also cultural challenges arising from the new structure, notably how to retain the partnership attributes of self sufficiency and mutual support whilst also serving outside shareholders. Cazenove has always enjoyed a certain mystique, an aura which has attracted clients and exasperated competitors. Can this advantage be retained despite the increased transparency and public scrutiny that a stock market listing brings? Can the product offering be maintained at the levels that clients require or will the fact that senior managers have to spend more time running the new public entity lead to management stretch and a decline in client service?

The key structural challenges which existed before incorporation still remain, not least in its core business of corporate broking. The

Table 13. Transaction versus Relationship Banking 1999[12]

Firm	Rank by value of deals	Rank by number of deals	Broking rank	Advisory rank
Morgan Stanley	1	11	Below 15	Below 15
Goldman Sachs	3	15	Below 15	Below 15
Merrill Lynch	5	8	10	Below 15
CSFB	6	6	4	12

UK is the only developed market where companies appoint a separate adviser for general corporate finance matters and a different firm to give stock market advice and it is only recently that the big American firms have alighted on corporate broking as a way of building broader relationships. As the firm with the most FT-SE corporate broking relationships – fifty – Cazenove has the most to lose from increased competition in this area. A further threat to Cazenove would come from any reduction in London's role as a central market since the firm is especially valued by corporate clients for its intimate knowledge about tactics and procedures in the London Stock Exchange.

Globalism is perhaps the biggest challenge. Cazenove's strengths are primarily domestic, with British institutions and British corporates. It does have knowledge of overseas markets and foreign investors but it lacks the same special relationship it enjoys with its clients in the UK. Increasingly, British equities will be owned by non-British investors and it will be harder for Cazenove to act with the same authority as intermediary between its corporate clients when their shareholders are based in Los Angeles and Frankfurt than when London and Edinburgh were the limit of the shareholders' register.

A similar issue arises in corporate advisory work, where more and more companies see themselves as pan-European and global. The broadly based investment banks portray themselves as being better informed about global capital flows and developments in the industries which interest their clients than specialist firms such as Cazenove. In this respect, Cazenove will face a credibility gap about its global capabilities especially amongst clients headquartered outside the UK.

These challenges are considerable but it is not by chance that Cazenove has flourished for so long. An ability to read its own industry and to adapt accordingly has seen it through great change in the past and the company has already responded to some of the current issues by initiatives such as incorporation, a major commitment to the new economy and an expansion of the financial advisory business into the ground vacated by the merchant banks. The ability to raise new capital from outside shareholders will give even more potential to grow the business.

A senior member of the firm told me: 'We no longer see ourselves merely as corporate brokers but as an investment bank'[13] and this vision is backed up by joint adviser and broker appointments to a number of major companies and some important advisory mandates. With the sale of Flemings and Schroders to American owners, Cazenove no doubt sees a gap in the market for an independent integrated corporate adviser and broker. The business challenge is to be big enough to be important whilst at the same time avoiding the middle ground, a graveyard for investment banks. To do this it needs to remain innovative, differentiated and focused, characteristics it has always displayed in the past. The key issue will be how it responds to the global challenge. Can it remain competitive without being big on Wall St? Can it be big on Wall St whilst remaining independent? The merchant banks all failed to answer these questions. In order to flourish, Cazenove must learn from their mistakes as well as exploit the vacuum they have left. How it answers the US question will probably determine its future.

SURVIVORS: CONCLUSION

At the beginning of this chapter the question was posed: how did they do it? The simple answer is that those who survived did so by aligning their resources with their ambition. That is true of the industry leaders, of middle-ranking firms like HSBC and of differentiated firms like Cazenove.

The American bulge bracket brought immense financial and managerial resources to London from 1995 onwards and they rightly decided that they should reproduce their positions as industry leaders in New York in London. They could not have succeeded in building their positions in London without the advantage of a very profitable home market. The surge of profits at the US investment banks in the late 1990s was unprecedented, generating surplus cash for re-investment overseas and creating the confidence to go for it. They were able to afford a cost base in London that exceeded revenues by cross-subsidizing from profits earned in the US. The pressure point, as ever, was compensation costs. Money was no object as the Americans went on a hiring spree, particularly for research analysts. By 2000, the pay differential between London and New York for top analysts had virtually disappeared; five years before it had been 2:1 in favour of New York.

The surviving British firms also got the match between ambition and capabilities right. HSBC identified that it had the financial but not the managerial resources to build a leading integrated investment bank, lacking as it did critical skills in corporate finance. Once that decision was made, it survived by not trying too hard, avoided serious embarrassment in broking but never achieved the potential its staff desired and which the bank's shareholders might have expected given the strength of James Capel's broking franchise in 1986.

The smaller merchant banks also survived by not trying too hard. After the sale of its equity capital markets partner Smith, Rothschilds reached a similar distribution agreement with the Dutch bank ABN Amro but had no intention of getting any deeper into equities: 'We could build a securities arm but it would take a long time and cost a lot of money. This way we get the benefits for free.'[14] Sir Evelyn Rothschild had no doubts about the consequences of over-ambition in securities: 'We are not dogmatic but we do not want to be bought out by a clearing bank.'[15] Another mid-sized merchant bank, Lazards, was even more wary. It concentrated on advisory business and has been able to remain viable and profitable with Lazard Capital Markets, a small team to provide equity underwriting, distribution and research across Europe, its only concession to securities.

Cazenove is the ultimate example of how to live within one's means and has prospered and delivered consistently to staff and clients throughout. The adoption of the American model of investment bank-ing amongst British and European clients offers further challenges but while Cazenove remains innovative and has a collective will to survive, the firm can carve out a new and viable position for itself.

The survivors from Big Bang did not have the field all to themselves at the start of the twenty-first century. Amongst the Americans, Lehman Brothers built again in London in the late 1990s, and Bank of America were also set on an organic growth strategy in London. Citigroup, with the acquisition of Schroders to reinforce Salomon Smith Barney in Europe, and Chase, following the purchases of Fleming and J. P. Morgan in 2000 were also formidable threats.

Many of the firms that fell by the wayside in the 1990s found their way to Continental European owners and re-emerged in a different guise. Deutsche Bank bought Bankers' Trust, acquiring with it the bulk of NatWest's former equities business and has used this to mount a serious challenge to the bulge bracket. The equities and corporate finance arm of BZW was sold to Credit Suisse First Boston which further boosted its business by buying DLJ. Following the merger of UBS and Swiss Bank, Warburg now operates with the United Bank of Switzerland as its parent. ABN Amro still retains the old Hoare Govett broking business and Kleinwort Benson has remained with Dresdner Bank since the takeover of 1995. Dresdner added the US investment Banking boutique Wasserstein Perella to its portfolio in 2000 which broadened its global capability. Commerzbank has started up an equities business in London and is in the lower reaches of the top twenty along with another European, Société Générale Securities. Which of the Europeans, if any, will mount a serious challenge to the Americans? What lessons can be drawn from the last twenty years to help us predict the future?

PART SIX

THE CITY UNPLUGGED

27

What Happened?

The gentleman capitalist is about as rare these days as the gentleman farmer. The gifted amateur has given way to the dynamic investment banker. The day starts at 7 a.m. not 9 a.m., 70 per cent of analysts work over sixty hours per week and designer water has replaced the boozy lunch. Dress down, not dress up, is the order of the day. The product range has been broadened so that derivatives, programme trading and international securities now form as big a part of the City's routine as straightforward British equities.

Firms that formerly employed a few hundred now employ thousands, spread across the world, and are often themselves part of even bigger enterprises. The business has become more complicated and correspondingly harder to manage. The accidents that have befallen a number of investment banks have brought home to shareholders and staff alike the need for controls and infrastructure. Management, once despised as a burden on the cost base, is now recognized as an essential discipline. Information technology, formerly just a mechanism for doing the job better, is now also seen as an alternative to stock exchanges and a threat to the very existence of the broking industry.

CHANGE AND CONTINUITY

Personal relationships are different. The partnerships and family companies that dominated the City in the 1980s built up strong bonds with their employees. All things being equal, partners and staff were loyal for life, but frequent changes in ownership and the imposition of regular redundancies on the one side and the lure of the head-hunters' gold on the other have eroded these bonds. Loyalty has been replaced by commitment – while the relationship lasts. Hard work is rewarded by high pay but everyone is a volunteer in investment banking.

Bonds used to exist between firms as well as within firms but these have not survived. Screen-based dealing has replaced personal contact and it is dog eat dog in the global market place. Formerly the unwritten code was as powerful, perhaps even more powerful, than the Stock Exchange rulebook. It was very hard to cheat on someone you saw every day. Now people play strictly by the written rules with anonymous counterparties in cyberspace and it is the letter rather than the spirit of the law that matters.

There has been so much change that you have to look very hard for continuity in the City. The grip of the English upper middle classes is reduced but still exists. An analysis of *City Lives* suggests that 75 per cent of the Big Bang generation had been to public school. To make an equally approximate modern-day comparison, I asked all the people I interviewed for this book about their own educational backgrounds. Although the proportion is down, still a third of the current generation of senior investment bankers and brokers had been to an English public school. It is no surprise that the English country house look lives on. The meeting rooms at many of the banks located in Canary Wharf are only a few years old but you could easily be in a stately home in the West Country, not twenty floors high in Docklands. I constructed an inventory of one such meeting room the last time that I was in one: two framed prints of English hunting scenes, one gilt-framed mirror, one brass standard lamp, one brass table lamp resting on a carved occasional table, one antique side table, brass door handles and plate, Regency striped curtains with drape ties, antique dining table and traditional chairs.

The trappings of old English life are accompanied by some of the old attitudes. It is still a male-dominated society. The January 2000 Reuters Survey shows that only 15 per cent of brokers' analysts are female; the proportion is only slightly higher in sales and is even lower in sales trading. Some females who have done well retain a suspicion that they are paid less than their male counterparts. The City is still no place for minorities: gay people keep a low profile, and ethnic minorities are under-represented. The only photograph of non-white faces I have come across in researching this book was of a West Indian steel band playing at a Cazenove partners' garden party. Look around the average City dealing room and it still bears a striking similarity to the profile of the crowd at Twickenham. The City is meritocratic but not yet egalitarian.

HOW TO THROW AWAY MARKET LEADERSHIP

Radical change, however, has occurred in the structure and ownership of the firms that operate in the City. The previously separate activities of jobbing and agency broking were joined into single capacity broking in 1986. Merchant banks bought brokers and became so intertwined with them that the resulting institutions developed along US lines into investment banks. Once the merchant banks got involved in broking, the business became so complicated, so demanding of management, that the institutions came tumbling down. It was this decision that caused the problems. By opting for an integrated corporate advisory and securities strategy the British banks got into deep water. That strategy took them into head-on competition with the global giants and required more scale, management resources and shareholder support than was available. As a result, ownership has been thrown on its head. Partnerships, quoted companies and family businesses have been sold and resold before ending up in the hands of large global banks.

Taking the top ten merchant banks in London in 1983, only two – Lazards and Rothschilds – were still independent at the beginning of the twenty-first century and then only by avoiding the full-blown corporate advisory-securities strategy. The top ten brokers of 1983 have been through so many changes of name, management and ownership that they are nearly all unrecognizable today. None of the leading investment banks that took over from the UK's merchant banks and brokers is British-owned. There are five pure American firms, two international firms with strong American influences (Lazards and CSFB), and three Continental Europeans.

Outside the top ten there is only a handful of British investment banks with any significant market reputation and none that can be

Table 14. Leading European Investment Banks, 1983–2000

Merchant banks, 1983	Brokers, 1983	Investment banks, 2000
Morgan Grenfell	Hoare Govett	Goldman Sachs
Warburg	James Capel	Morgan Stanley
Hill Samuel	Scrimgeour	Merrill Lynch
Lazards	Phillips & Drew	CSFB
Kleinwort	Cazenove	J. P. Morgan/Chase
Schroders	De Zoete	UBS Warburg
Rothschilds	Rowe & Pitman	Lazards
Samuel Montagu	Wood Mackenzie	Deutsche Bank
Barings	Grieveson Grant	Citigroup SSSB
County NatWest	Greenwell	Dresdner Kleinwort

described as a leading global firm. Cazenove pursues an integrated corporate finance and securities strategy in chosen areas that appeal to them but has neither the ambition nor the resources to mount a global challenge to the leading Americans. Rothschilds has a good advisory position but lacks a broking arm and does not aspire to full service, preferring a distribution agreement with ABN Amro. HSBC needs an acquisition to be regarded as a credible global investment bank.

Given that in 1983 all of the top ten merchant banks in the UK were home-owned; that Continental Europe was so far behind that it scarcely had an equities culture let alone an interest in investment banking; and that the Americans regarded London as a last posting for retiring partners, this turnaround is remarkable. It is currently unfashionable to talk about national interests, commentators preferring to view large corporations as 'stateless', but the fact remains that none of Europe's leading investment banks is British. Taking three criteria to define corporate nationality – parental headquarters, majority shareholders and home stock market – each of the supposedly stateless institutions that now occupy the leading positions can be readily identified as belonging to a particular country, be it the US, Switzerland or Germany. Is it not startling that a market dominated by British banks fifteen years ago should have been vacated in favour of American and Continental European banks? I believe that the speed and totality of the submission of the City's leading firms is one of the most abject surrenders in business history. The next chapter will assess whether this matters but first we need to understand how this extraordinary state of affairs arose.

LACK OF DIRECTION

Nicholas Goodison for the Stock Exchange and Cecil Parkinson for the Department of Trade and Industry did not get much wrong back in 1983. They set out an outline agreement and allowed a reasonable preparation time before implementation. It would have been better if the process had been phased more gradually, and Goodison did argue for a longer transition period, but the City had reasonable warning of what was to occur and adequate time to prepare its response.

After the 1983 agreement, the devotion of the Government and the Bank of England to the doctrine of free market competition was an important factor in the failure of the British investment banks and brokers. This policy exposed the British firms to attack from Americans who had more experience of running integrated broking, trading and capital markets operations. With a fifty year advantage the Americans had made and learned from their mistakes and were already established as powerful companies. It was optimism bordering on negligence for the UK authorities to expose immature domestic financial institutions to such competition, an act of omission guaranteed to cause the British banks to fail.

This mistake was compounded by the establishment of a very light regulatory regime at a time when the brokers should have been compelled to raise their standards of control. Higher standards of qualification for practitioners, more specialized examinations for managers, more rigorous requirements for reporting risk positions and more regular and thorough inspections would have instilled the belief that management mattered at a much earlier stage than did occur. Instead, until the early 1990s, the old broking attitudes prevailed and management was dismissed as 'more red tape and bureaucracy'. It took years of losses and scandals for the importance of management to be appreciated but by then the pass had been sold and the UK's investment banks were already in trouble.

The absence of a single, strong regulator allowed gaps to appear between the SFA, responsible for regulating the broking firms and the Bank of England, the lead regulator for all British banks. Once expansion overseas had occurred, a third set of regulators were involved which should have warned the lead regulator to be especially vigilant. Self-regulation, lack of clarity in responsibilities and under-resourced inspection teams allowed the brokers to get away with sloppy management in a way that was impossible in the US where the SEC has greater reach. Does the new FSA have the resources to enforce its clarity of powers? Weaknesses in the control infrastructure, the prime focus for strong regulators, were directly responsible for the trading mishaps that led to the collapse of Barings and the sale of NatWest Markets.

Originally the Bank of England had appeared to support the need for an indigenous investment banking industry, Robin Leigh-Pemberton stating when Governor: 'Recognition of the benefits that foreign participation can bring does not imply indifference to where control of major participants in our markets lies and we would not contemplate with equanimity a Stock Exchange in which British member firms played a clearly subordinate role.'[1] This view was not heard in the 1990s when Eddie George became Governor. Convinced of the benefits of free markets and that it was location that mattered, not ownership, the Government and the Bank of England stood aside while the investment banks were sold. Either it was regarded as not being important to have a British-owned investment bank or the matter was felt to be beyond Government control and for the shareholders to decide. Bunkum on both counts. There are many occasions when the Government and the Bank intervene discreetly behind the scenes when national interest is at stake, and the slow death of a strategic industry should have been just such a case. It may or not prove to matter whether there are British-owned investment banks but it would be nice to have an option. The Bank certainly had the influence to have achieved such a result. It had regularly dabbled in the micro-management of firms, for example letting its displeasure be known when too much poaching was going on from one firm to another or guiding firms together in the run up to Big Bang. It is inconsistent to have interfered at this level in the 1980s but to have stood aside while the entire industry failed in the 1990s.

THE BIG BANG GENERATION FAILED

The senior partners of the brokers and jobbers who were responsible for guiding firms through the reforms of 1986 must also share in the blame. They were not able to adapt to the increased scale and complexity of the firms that were being put together. As a result several years were wasted so that, by the time the full force of global competition was turned on London, the British firms were still struggling to establish their roots.

It was in part a class thing as a generation trained to believe in hierarchy and order was suddenly exposed to rapid change in every part of their business. The self-confidence inbred by their educational background in the public schools and reinforced by the arrogance that our profession encourages and even requires meant that they did not take advice or ask for help early enough. They had worked in small businesses, usually on an agency, risk-free basis and were primarily domestic. They were suddenly asked to cope with several new dimensions of risk management and globalization and had neither the managerial skills to cope nor the humility to ask for help.

Motivation also came into it. The Big Bang generation became millionaires at the same time as they were freed from the responsibility of looking after the partnerships. They found themselves able to invest using other people's money, their personal position was secure and they became less prudent. The practice became widespread of investing in new businesses while the existing ones were still in loss, which would never have occurred under the old partnership system. It was more exciting to open a new business than to fix an ailing one and this resulted in overblown strategies and the creation of long chains with some very weak links.

The new owners of the brokers contributed to the poor start made by the new investment banks. They did not exert control over the new businesses until too late, falling for the brokers' self-confidence, and even then failed to grasp the nettle firmly. They did not invest sufficiently in infrastructure. Expediency was much more common than long-term planning and cool analysis of the risks and rewards.

Throughout the late 1980s and early 1990s, the British firms trying to build investment banks paid very little attention to cultural issues. Team-building and structured compensation packages to foster long-term commitment were ignored and too often the new organizations 'were bound together only by a common love of money and lacking any distinctive esprit de corps'.[2]

Neither the brokers nor the parent companies were honest with each other. Martin Taylor's account of life at BZW matches with my own experience at NatWest and Schroders and will be recognized by anyone involved in management in the City at this time: 'They [management] craved reassurance all the time. There was so much you could not say to them. BZW was dressing up the numbers in the way that they always had done and the board was just hoodwinked. It's the dishonesty of BZW that rankles. They were not prepared to make the trade offs.'[3]

OWNERSHIP MATTERS

On the day that Barclays announced that it was selling the corporate finance and equities arms of BZW, G. W. Mallinckrodt rang me up. He asked me for my views on the move and I asked him for his: ' "It's the difference between ownership and management," he said. "There is no one at Barclays able to take a long-term view. The chief executive probably thinks he's only got a year or two to sort it out. The institutional shareholders are working on an even shorter time horizon. Building an investment bank is a thirty year process and Barclays are about a third of the way through it but no one is around for that long." '

As the sale of Schroders' investment bank was to show, the owners are not the only relevant stakeholders, but the institutional pressure on Barclays and NatWest to exit from investment banking highlights the issue of short termism among pension funds and other financial institutions.[4] Investment banking was unpopular with the institutional shareholders in Barclays and NatWest because it was expensive, volatile and offered poor returns and they wanted out. They had never bought into the strategy and were not inclined to support initiatives that would require thirty years to pay off. They preferred the strategy of Lloyds which had avoided investment banking and was held to be an example of a well-run British financial services company.

Derek Wanless, who as NatWest's chief executive was on the receiving end of much of their criticism, does not blame the fund managers: 'I've got more sympathy with the fund managers than you might think. Their sole brief is to perform so that's what they try to do. Pension fund trustees are where the problem starts; they set the rules for the fund managers. It is wrong to blame the fund managers for the failures of capitalism.'[5] The fund managers at the institutions work in an industry that is every bit as competitive as corporate finance and equities. Performance league tables are issued quarterly for each fund and are pored over by consultants who report to the boards of trustees. Fund management houses that regularly under-perform are sacked. It is no wonder therefore that shareholders pressurize the companies for short-term results. But when strategic issues are at stake, institutional ownership is inappropriate and that is why it is important for the Government to protect the public good. That, after all, is why we have Government.

Families, partners and employees appear to have been more appropriate owners of investment banks. The Schroder, Kleinwort and Fleming families have been more stable and always committed to the business. Their investment banks were sold, but the pressure to do so came from the management not the shareholders who acquiesced in but did not precipitate the sales. Partnerships worked best and Cazenove and Goldman will no doubt try to retain the partnership ethos post incorporation. As Morgan Stanley and Smith have shown, significant staff ownership, encourages a community of interest amongst the staff and shareholders.

There was very little lateral thinking on this issue, no alternative ownership pattern to 'salary plus bonus employees' being seriously attempted. The tragedy of Schroders is that the potential for a new model of ownership with substantial staff participation was not taken up.

AMERICAN POWER

The weakness of the UK firms might not have mattered but the US firms finally got their act together. Even as late as 1994 the Americans were misfiring in London, their constant retreats and advances giving them a poor reputation with staff. However they were consistent with corporate clients, guessed rightly that they could be more cavalier with the institutions, and finally timed their move well.

There appears to be a rule in investment banking that foreign firms can only dominate a market that is smaller than their own, which is fortunate for the Americans since their Stock Market is the biggest in the world. A larger domestic market than the one being tackled gives experience of scale, of complexity and a good stream of profits to reinvest. Unfortunately for the UK banks, the Americans targeted Europe for expansion with London as the base: 'There is a view within the bank that goes right to the top that Europe is the next growth opportunity.'[6] The super returns earned by the US investment banks after 1994 enabled them to loss-lead in London. They could afford to bid up for staff and to over-resource teams safe in the knowledge that their domestic business was highly profitable.

This can be illustrated by Goldman Sachs' five-year record during the middle and late 1990s. Nineteen ninety-four was a depressed base year but the recovery in revenues in 1995 and the surge in 1996 and 1997 created awesome returns. The most impressive figure, however, is the consistency of the ratio between remuneration and revenue. Despite the explosion in compensation rates in the investment banking

Table 15. Goldman Sachs' Revenues and
Compensation, 1994–8, $ million[7]

Year ending November	1994	1995	1996	1997	1998
Pre-tax profits	508	1368	2606	3014	2921
Compensation / Net revenues	51%	45%	40%	42%	45%

industry over these years – the annual compensation of a good senior analyst trebled between 1994 and 2000 from $800,000 to $2,600,000 – Goldman paid out to staff a steady 40–45 per cent of net revenues after 1994.

Goldman and the other leading US investment banks were in a virtuous circle. The more business they won, the more they could pay their staff, the more they could attract the best people and the more business they won. The UK investment banks, on the other hand, were in a vicious circle. The more they had to pay to keep staff, the more money they lost and the worse morale got and the more they had to pay to keep people happy.

They were not able to grow revenues anything like so fast as the firms with a strong position on Wall Street but had to keep up with bulge bracket rates of pay if they were to keep their staff. This can be illustrated by the relationship of net revenues and compensation at Schroders in the late 1990s. It was the inverse of the picture at Goldman, with compensation taking a bigger proportion of revenues, keeping profits flat.

The Americans' ability and willingness to pay aggressively for top quality staff caused serious problems for all of London's investment banks. In addition to the financial implications, staff wars ground down the management. The resignation of a valued member of staff was emotionally draining for their managers, damaging to the morale of those who remained and a distraction from other pressing business issues. Competitors rubbed salt in the wounds. I was shown an internal memorandum from a firm that had just made a senior recruit from Schroders: 'We also did something equally stunning last week in

Table 16. Schroders' Revenues and
Compensation, 1995–9, $ million[8]

Year ending December	1994	1995	1996	1997	1998
Pre-tax profits	195	197	239	245	232
Compensation / Net revenues	42%	45%	48%	50%	52%

Europe. We hired xyz from Schroders to capitalise on the strides we've made among the blue chip UK and European companies ... Last week I was sitting with abc ... he thought it was a very interesting statement that someone of such high personal integrity and professional achievement, who was so successful in the UK merchant bank, would join us.'

Whenever a senior recruit was made, news spread through the grapevine, sowing the seeds of self-doubt at the losing firm and instilling confidence at the winner. Staff would think, 'If he or she has left us for them, what does that say about my judgement in staying here?' or 'If he or she is joining, I must be right to stay here.' Managers knew this, that's why they fought so hard to hire and retain. Many of them told me that they became wearied by the constant struggle to turn round potential leavers. Faced with a steady stream of staff with big offers to join the Americans, it is not surprising that many of these senior managers concluded that it was easier to give up.

GLOBALISM AND SCALE

During the 1990s many of the world's industries experienced mergers amongst leading participants on an altogether new scale. In sectors as diverse as oil, telecommunications and pharmaceuticals, today's giant became tomorrow's pygmy. Investment bankers played a key role in putting these mergers together so it is no surprise that their own industry, financial services, also experienced consolidation. Combinations of businesses on the scale of Citigroup/Travelers/Salomon Smith Barney, Morgan Stanley/Dean Witter, Bank of America/NationsBank/Montgomery Securities redefined the notion of critical mass and posed real challenges for other firms that sought a position at the top of the financial services industry.

The megabanks had a number of advantages. They could use one part of their product range to open a relationship for another, for example loans to fund acquisitions could be used to open a door for the corporate finance department. Profits were so large that huge teams were assembled irrespective of cost, enabling a very good service to be delivered to clients.

Capital was readily available for clients and, with sales teams in every part of the world, global distribution of securities could be offered.

Clients liked this model and expected all investment banks to offer something comparable. This produced a squeeze on medium-sized investment banks in the US as well as the UK and many concluded that they would be better off as part of a financial services conglomerate. Bankers Trust purchased Alex Brown and was then itself swallowed up by Deutsche Bank. Another mid-ranking generalist firm, Oppenheimer, was sold to Canada's Imperial Bank of Commerce. The Californian investment banks also found it hard to go it alone and in 1997 NationsBank paid $1.3 billion for Montgomery Securities, a San Francisco-based bank specializing in high technology companies. Robertson Stephens, another San Francisco firm, was sold for $540 million to Bank of America and then on to BankBoston. In 1999, Hambrecht & Quist, the doyen of West Coast investment banks, sold itself to Chase Manhattan for $1.35 billion.

As the critical mass required to become a leading global investment bank rose and as the bulge bracket turned their attention to hot spots like California and London, the medium-sized banks struggled. The 1980s' vision of a Warburg or a Morgan Grenfell becoming world-class competitors became unattainable for the medium-sized banks. Either they had to sell themselves or redefine their market position. By the end of the 1990s it was clear that only the largest of British institutions, the clearing banks, had the scale to compete on a full global basis in investment banking.

ONE MISTAKE AND OUT

The power of the Americans, the step change in scale and complexity required and the pressure on margins from rising compensation gave the British investment banks a tightrope to walk. For the medium-sized banks the global vision became unattainable under independent ownership. Either the vision needed adjusting, as Kleinwort attempted after 1990, or, if a global role was still sought after, the business needed to be sold, the route followed by Warburg and Smith. With a limited capital base, the mid-sized UK investment banks had no margin for error. The competitiveness of the industry given globalization, scale and high profitability on Wall Street meant that implementation had to be perfect. The managements of the medium-sized UK investment banks had to define and deliver their strategies faultlessly, which was a real challenge. As Schroders proved, it was a case of one slip and you are dead in the competitive market that prevailed.

Of the larger banks in the group we have followed, only the UK clearers after the merger of SBC and UBS had the scale and the resources to compete globally in investment banking. However, having wasted the years immediately after Big Bang in a muddle of mismanaging, they were not in as strong a position as they might have been when the Americans turned on the heat after 1994. This meant their results were poor, shareholder pressure mounted and directors found it difficult to maintain enthusiasm. It was significant that, during the crucial years in the mid 1990s, the chief executives of Barclays and NatWest, Martin Taylor and Derek Wanless, were much less supportive of investment banking than were their boards.

At a crucial period, the two British banks which combined the resources to develop in investment banking with a reasonable market position lacked high level enthusiasm. They elected not to buy the mid-sized US investment banks that were changing hands in 1996–7, at prices that either firm could easily have afforded and that could have provided a satisfactory US bridgehead. Instead, they left the industry. HSBC maintained a low profile throughout the period, has a weak position but at least has all its options still open.

The UK's investment banks were brought down by a combination of external forces and self-inflicted wounds. The trends to globalism and scale and the power of the Americans set a formidable challenge to the City. Its failure to respond effectively was due to negligence born out of a cultural system that inhibited good management and to the existence of a vacuum where the authorities should have been. Whether or not this matters is a debate that needs to be had.

28

Does It Really Matter?

This book started with a conversation that I had with a future Governor of the Bank of England over a decade ago and the Wimbledon tennis tournament analogy: played in London, dominated by foreigners but still a great provider of jobs and cash for the UK. The analogy is beguiling but imprecise. Wimbledon is British owned, the performers are foreign; the City is foreign owned, the performers are British. Ownership brings control and it is the City's lack of control over its own destiny that creates concern. If you are looking for a sporting analogy in London SW 19, a better one is Wimbledon Football Club which was once a focal point for a section of the local community. A few years ago, the owners moved Wimbledon FC several miles across London to share another club's stadium and then tried to move out of London altogether to Dublin and then Milton Keynes. The football club's only remaining connection with the suburb of Wimbledon is the name, all economic and emotional ties are gone. Football, not tennis, is the right Wimbledon analogy for the City.

In May 2000, two days after Wimbledon Football Club was relegated from the Premier League, I visited Eddie George, the man with whom I discussed the Wimbledon theory back in 1987. By this time he had been Governor of the Bank of England for nearly seven years.

IN AN ENGLISH COUNTRY GARDEN

I have already commented on investment banking's taste for the English country house. Whether on Park Avenue or in Canary Wharf, the prevailing décor is fake old England. The Governor's office at the Bank of England is the real thing. Antique tables, leather sofas and chairs, Persian rugs, a mahogany cabinet for the computer and, on the day I called, open French doors leading to an impeccable English lawn: a secret country garden between Threadneedle Street and Lothbury.

Appearances, however, can be deceptive. Sir Edward George, Governor since 1993, is no gentlemanly capitalist. In fact, his conviction that the efficiency of markets should be encouraged, not resisted, has been pursued with an intellectual rigour that has left the old City gasping. Under his regime, in contrast to the Bank's earlier belief that the survival of domestic firms was important, a policy of non-intervention in the affairs of individual banks has been ruthlessly followed. As Barings found on the weekend of 25–26 February 1995, there would be no help from the Bank of England for firms in trouble. And as countless others discovered as they wrestled with and finally sold their investment banks, it was a matter of indifference to the Bank of England whether individual businesses survived or failed.

Underlying this are a number of core beliefs. Market forces create economic efficiency and should not, indeed cannot, be resisted. Central planning is impossible: the authorities would not be able to judge how many firms should be encouraged to compete in a given market or which ones should be favoured. Companies no longer have a national identity because of globalization amongst clients and shareholders. Free market competition will have such a positive effect on the size of the European financial services industry that any loss in London's relative position – which is inevitable given its high starting point – will be more than balanced by an increase in the size of the total cake. We are invited to just accept that market forces will work and to shed emotional, patriotic beliefs in the need for British banks.

Superficially these arguments are compelling. Foreign exchange and eurobond trading continues to gravitate to London and the City retains a high share of international equity trading. It is hard to meet the Governor's challenge: 'Show me a single statistic where the City is in decline.'[1] But the debate is about the future, not the present. It was only in the second half of the nineties that the British gave up investment banking and it is too soon for statistical consequences to appear. There are good reasons to believe that ownership matters and that the consequences will appear in due course.

HOME IS WHERE THE HEAD IS

The old merchant banks – for example Warburg, Schroders, Rothschild – were all set up and owned by European families. In the early days they were not popular, the culture of a foreign institution like Warburg being deeply inimical to the City. However, the owning families became Anglicized, they lived in Britain and the banks had their headquarters in London. There is no parallel with modern banks with their headquarters in New York or Continental Europe and ownership scattered across the world's financial centres.

There is a view that these modern companies do not have 'nationality'. National identity, this argument runs, will disappear as the ownership of companies' equity spreads across the global investor base and as their business becomes more international: 'The nationality of the global financial conglomerate becomes less relevant as deregulation, competition and technology erase geographic borders and large organizations and teams from varying cultural backgrounds work together regardless of location.'[2]

The Governor of the Bank of England holds this view and recounts that: 'I go to meetings where it is impossible to tell from the people seated round the table the nationality of the companies that they are representing.'[3] This is not how it looks from the shop floor. Goldman and Morgan Stanley have been the most successful of the American investment banks at bringing British people through to senior management positions in London. If there was anywhere that the staff would be unaware that their employer had a nationality, it would surely be there. I asked a number of Goldman and Morgan Stanley people in London if they knew the nationality of their firm. All stated 'American' and a few looked at me as though the answer was so obvious that my sanity was in doubt. A similar picture emerged at the German and Swiss institutions.

Even the virtual organizations of the future will have headquarters. The location of head office will be determined by historical factors: the composition of the board, relations with regulators, proximity to clients, concentration of staff. Head office will take the important decisions on business policy and set the firm's culture in matters of style, work ethic and values. British investment bankers that work for American or Continental firms consistently state that it is very easy to detect national identity whenever head office gets involved. None of the top ten investment banks in Europe have parent companies with headquarters in London and that is unlikely to change. The key decisions about London will be taken in Frankfurt, Zurich or New York. In that sense, companies do have a national identity.

The issue of ownership is a matter of economic concern, not one of patriotism. Eddie George asked me to 'just accept that London will do well out of free market competition. It is not the World Cup final where there is a winner and a loser. This is not a zero sum game, it is a positive sum game. The whole industry will expand at a great rate. The City cannot expect to own all of that.'[4] If the scenario unfolds as the Governor describes, the City would indeed do well but the question is, would it do as well as if it had owned, not just housed, the investment banks?

Ownership brings influence, that's why branch offices always feel different to head offices. As Sir Evelyn Rothschild has noted, 'London cannot claim to be a true financial centre if it loses the spectrum of institutions.'[5] Without ownership, much depends on the other countries also setting aside national interest. They might but they might not. We do not believe in war but we maintain an army just in case. We believe that economic nationalism is dead, but should we not maintain British financial institutions in case we are wrong?

RESPONSIBLE COMPETITION NOT PROTECTIONISM

As the Governor puts it, 'The idea that we would have done better by keeping them out is wrong' and I agree. No one would wish to see the City resort to the closed shop ways of the old Stock Exchange or the kind of protectionism in favour of domestic firms that damaged Tokyo's global competitiveness for so long. But protectionism is not the only alternative to laissez faire. Occasional intervention in the manner that central banks have done over the years would have ensured the survival of at least one British investment bank without damaging in any way the City's reputation for openness.

There were a number of occasions when the Bank could have inter-vened. It is widely believed that for many years it promoted the cause of Warburg as the British company most likely to have succeeded as a global investment bank. When Warburg was in trouble, a word from the Bank to those Warburg executives who preferred to work for the Swiss than NatWest would have been very influential. When Barclays was under pressure from their UK shareholders to exit investment banking, the Bank of England might have got a sympathetic hearing if it had encouraged management to persist: 'The Barclays board was full of notions that it was their national duty to be the UK's investment banking champion.'[6]

Intervention at a few crucial moments is not protectionism and is not anti-competitive, it is just good Government. It is difficult to believe that a policy encouraging responsible competition would have had any negative impact on the City's reputation and it might have ensured the survival of one or two British-owned investment banks.

WHAT HAPPENS NEXT?

The model for the world's financial services industry that was envis-aged at the time of Big Bang is much altered. Fifteen years ago it was thought that there would be three legs to the global trading stool: London, Tokyo and New York. Since then, the Japanese economy and Stock Market has collapsed, New York has flourished, London has sold out and Continental Europe has developed an equities culture. As equity investment gathers pace on the Continent, Swiss, German, French and other nationalities will grow to rival the funds under management in London and these centres will develop a critical mass of their own. A hub-and-spoke model around New York will replace the three-legged stool.

This will be reinforced by trends in technology, which jeopardize the position of every financial services centre except New York. Dis-intermediation and e-commerce have made the vision of a central market place obsolete. Increasingly stocks will be crossed elec-tronically, hardly going through a recognized stock exchange and the financial centres will become places where investment bankers and their clients work rather than homes for markets. The *Financial Times* has caustically predicted that: 'On this form Europe's stock exchanges will soon find themselves consigned to obscurity by nimbler, cheaper, electronic trading networks.'[7] The drift to integration amongst the world's stock exchanges points to a lesser role for single centre markets. As the largest of the existing European Stock Exchanges, London will be putting most into the pan-European melting pot and pinning the most hopes on it turning out to be the positive sum game promised by the authorities.[8]

The next bear market will be a real test for London. Whether a full blown affair as in the early 1970s, a short sharp shock as in 1987 or a rap on the knuckles as in 1998 investment banks will respond by cutting back on numbers of staff. London can expect harsh treatment. It contains a big infrastructure left over from the days when the City's investment banks were independent and its people are more highly paid than in any financial capital except New York. When pressure on revenues returns, the US investment banks will use modern technology to cut right back on overseas overhead especially London. What will emerge is a hub-and-spoke model run out of New York with a number of subsidiary centres on the rim. London will be just another city at the end of a spoke. It will be no worse off than Frankfurt, Paris or Zurich but as the current world number two after New York, its relative status will be much diminished.

FATE OF THE SURVIVORS

One of the original reasons that the British clearing and merchant banks bought brokers was that they believed cross-selling opportunities would exist between the corporate and the investment banks. In the UK such a development was slow to happen: 'Many clients did not want us on the corporate finance side. They saw us as a bank, just a bank and they would tell us that's how we see you, please don't try to sell us corporate finance.'[9]

Recently, however, there have been signs that the time of cross-selling has at last arrived. In part this is because, as companies themselves have scaled up, they expect their financial advisers to do the same: big companies want to deal with big banks. The commercial banks have been able to respond to this as a result of the erosion of the most stringent provisions of the Glass–Steagall Act, enabling deposit-taking banks to own investment banks in the US. This prompted a number of the US commercial banks to acquire investment banks and made it easier for European commercial banks to enter investment banking in the US. As the combinations have been made, the leading banks have become much more skilled at cross-selling. Citigroup in particular has found good synergy between corporate lending and investment banking: 'Clients were hungry for the creation of a single platform for loans and bonds and it has led to a slew of equity and M&A mandates. While pure investment banks have struggled to develop their lending capabilities the new Citigroup could provide this service at a stroke.'[10]

The acceptability of one-stop shopping in corporate financial services will probably cause the American and European commercial banks to develop further the integrated corporate and investment banking models. For example, Chase Manhattan has bought Fleming and JP Morgan and hopes that these will form transformational acquisitions in the investment banking industry.[11]

The leading Continental banks have also developed investment banking arms. Deutsche Bank paid $10 billion for Bankers Trust in June 1999. Bankers Trust had bought Alex Brown and NatWest's European equities business to broaden itself away from its traditional base in derivatives and trading. When set alongside the old Morgan Grenfell corporate finance business and Deutsche's own strengths in Germany, this is a powerful combination. Credit Suisse has developed its investment banking arm, CSFB, in Europe by acquiring BZW's equities business and globally by adding DLJ.

ABN Amro has a developing European equities reputation built around Hoare Govett and Alfred Berg, the top Scandinavian equities house but as yet lacks a presence on Wall Street. Dresdner's acquisition of the US firm Wasserstein Perella follows inconclusive discussion with prospective European partners. UBS has a strong position in Europe through the old Warburg and Phillips & Drew businesses and a good niche in North America through Dillon Read. ING, however, the Dutch acquirer of Barings in 1995, is scaling down its investment banking ambitions, indicating how difficult it is for all but the leaders to prosper.

The British clearing banks are in a different position. Barclays and NatWest sold out of investment banking. Barclays and NatWest's new owner, the Royal Bank of Scotland, may find themselves at an increasing disadvantage as the global and top European competition offers its corporate clients the full range of financial products. They may find themselves – like the medium-sized investment banks of the 1990s – being squeezed out of relationships with corporate clients because they do not have the full suite of products. They would then be forced to make a choice: restrict themselves to the personal sector, go back into investment banking or get taken over.

The dark horse is HSBC. Since 1990 it has kept well clear of a heavy investment banking involvement. It has kept the former Capel and Montagu businesses alive and has developed a broader range of debt based products. It bears no psychological scars from large scale losses, scandals or retreats from investment banking. If the trend to one stop shopping continues, HSBC is well placed to buy a large investment bank to round out its portfolio and is probably the UK's last hope in the sector.

The movement to scale will be accompanied by a revival of specialized investment banks and brokers. The large investment banks tend to neglect the small and medium sized end of the market and niche operations have already sprung up to do business in this area. In London, Close Brothers, under the chairmanship of Sir David Scholey, Warburg's last leader, has already done an excellent job in building such a position. Banks of this kind are more likely to flourish if they remain focused and remember not to get too big to be small. They may also win some surprisingly large clients for, although at present corporates are choosing the largest investment banks, skill may come to be regarded as more important than scale by a few clients. Just as in asset management the very large firms have found it hard to retain entrepreneurial skill amidst the bureaucracy of a large organization, so too will the big investment banks. This will create some opportunities for the smaller players.

Between the giants and the specialists, the medium-sized investment banks must resist the big squeeze. For firms such as Cazenove,

Lazard and Rothschild, differentiation is essential. With clients, this means offering a service that does not appear to be merely a pale imitation of that which the bulge bracket can supply with greater resources. With staff, they must counter the big bonus battalions from Wall Street with the prospect of meaningful equity participation. A mid-table ranking is perfectly viable provided that it is achieved by excellence in the areas where a bank has chosen to compete and not by a mediocre performance across the board. Excellence, selectivity and equity participation are the keys to survival for medium-sized firms.

The arrival of a sustained bear market will have profound consequences for all investment banks, bringing capital markets activity and mergers and acquisitions down to much lower volumes. This will expose the firms that have been throwing businesses together with insufficient regard for costs or culture. In some cases, the consolidation of recent years will be reversed as the less well-considered mergers of the nineties are undone. From this fragmentation, a number of specialized independent firms will re-emerge. There will be a hasty retrenchment and London will bear the full brunt of this.

It will be the bear market that marks the next stage in the migration to a New York-based hub-and-spoke model, with London occupying a much reduced place on the rim. Would London have been better placed if it still had a strong independent investment banking presence? I believe that if Barclays, HSBC or NatWest had developed (or develop in future) strong and successful investment banking arms the City would be able to occupy a position midway between the hub of New York and the rim of the other financial services capitals of the world. Big commercial and corporate banks with headquarters in London would ensure that London's natural advantages would, in turn, better ensure the City sustains its position. A group of mid-sized independent investment banks focusing on small and medium-sized corporates with occasional successes at the higher end would have represented a useful hedge in case clients decided that, after all, they prefer skill to scale.

The City used to have a heart and a soul that stemmed from the central market and ownership of the firms. Now the central market is under threat and ownership has gone. The City is a branch office of

New York with no control over its own destiny. Its position relative to the other European capitals can only get worse. The only issue for debate is the extent of the decline.

29

Herding Cats

It is a fair question to ask whether managing a broker or an investment bank is any harder than running any other organization. Aren't investment bankers just a bunch of overpaid cry babies, making a fuss about nothing?

THE PAY QUESTION

I have always felt guilty at the amounts investment bankers get paid. The public is probably unaware how far down the broking industry the big rewards go, how simple it is for mediocrity to survive for long periods, and how big the numbers really are. The tables below show the packages paid by Deutsche Morgan Grenfell to attract top names when it was rebuilding in 1995–6 and compensation levels in broking in the City during 2000. They reflect the booming conditions for investment banks that prevailed in the late 1990s. Table 17 is a composite of market rates and does not catch the outliers, the few individuals who earn much more than the bands indicate or, indeed, those who work in niches earning less than these levels. However, the figures are typical of the 50, 000 registered representatives of the broking firms that now work in the City and they represent an enormous pool of spending power that fuels the economy of south east England.

The money paid to brokers is a social and moral disgrace. With the most basic skills, a broker can earn four times as much as a teacher, twice as much as a GP, and about the same as the finance director of a medium-sized quoted plc. Even if the broker lacks flair but is pushy

Table 17. How Much Do Brokers Earn?*

Altitude	Skills needed	Sales	Trading	Research
Foothills	Technical only	£50,000– 100,000	£100,000	£150,000
Mid-station	Technical+drive	£300,000	£200,000	£300,000
Peak	Technical+drive +instinct	£500,000	£500,000– 1,500,000	£1–2,000,000

*Total annual compensation.

Table 18. Directors' Emoluments, Morgan Grenfell & Co., 1995–6[1]

Emoluments band, '000	1995	1996
£500–1000	15	30
£1000–1500	6	16
£1500–2000	3	8
£2000–4500	2	15

and determined enough, he or she can earn the same as a leading heart surgeon and more than some chief executives of FT-SE 100 companies. All of this seems outrageous given that the talent required to earn such sums is not particularly rare and the industry is not very profitable in the City. For those with flair, determination and the right technical skills, there is the potential to earn as much as a top sportsman and a middling rock star. This is more defensible: the rarity value of such talent is not dissimilar. But it is the huge sums of money earned by journeymen that chokes the industry's profitability and makes it so hard to defend.

To help understand how the middle rankers not just the stars manage to earn a fortune, imagine that you have to get to the top of a mountain and that you need some tools to get you there. The tools are technical skills, competitive spirit and instinct. The technical skills will get you a third of the way up the mountain to the top of the foothills. To get further, you need extra tools in the form of competitive spirit. The combination of technical skills and competitive spirit will get you out of the foothills onto the mid-station. You can stay at the mid-station quite a long time but you will need the full bag of tools (technical, competitive and instinctive) to get to the peak.

Most people who get a job in broking have or can learn the technical skills, and if not they soon fall by the wayside. As they acquire the ratios, the knowledge and the vocabulary they join the crowd on the lowest part of the mountain. After about two years, if they are competitive, some rise into the next group. They are valued by their employer as 'a real prospect' and begin to attract the interest of competitors. Having survived the first and moved into the second stage they have demonstrated that they have two thirds of the skill set and represent a fair bet for someone looking for candidates to get to the top. But the mountain gets steeper as you go up. The right climbing gear and a will to win are necessary to succeed but not sufficient. A touch of genius is now required, and only a few of those at the mid-station have such a talent.

If they do not demonstrate instinct, they stay at mid-station, salesmen living off relationships not ideas, analysts who can report but not predict and traders who can support but not lead. For the few star brokers who move on to the peak, huge riches become available. They can be the difference between winning or losing a big IPO (6 per cent fees even on a billion pound offering) or between their firm placing a big block of stock or being left with a rapidly depreciating asset.

The high rewards earned by the leading brokers trickle down to the rest of the industry. Because the rewards for success are so high, and so clearly identified with an individual star, anyone showing promise will get backed. This drives up the compensation of the crowd in the mid-station until it becomes clear whether or not they can go on to the peak. Those who can, do, those who can't subside gently, working for second- and then third-grade firms before finally leaving the industry. A similar process occurs in the foothills.

This is a classic supply and demand situation where people are the item in short supply. New entrants bidding for staff or existing players seeking to improve their position have driven up wages. The industry operates on such a short time cycle that it prefers to recruit rather than to train. It takes at least three years to bring a beginner up to speed and investment bankers always want quicker results than that. The

American firms have well-developed recruiting programmes at the business schools to replenish the pool of talent but for development areas such as London demand has exceeded supply in recent years. There have only been one or two years in New York and London in the last fifteen when employment levels in investment banking declined, and then only briefly.

The supply and demand situation in broking has been exacerbated by the disproportionate amount of business that goes to the top five firms. This creates constant pressure to finish in the top five and means that the group of aspiring under-achievers always remains large. The top three brokers on any client's list get a high proportion of the available business, around 20 per cent each; the next two get around 10 per cent each and the remaining twenty or thirty brokers are scrambling around for 20 per cent between them. Corporate clients watch the lists published in the financial press very closely and tend to choose their advisers from the leading bunch. There can only ever be five in the top five; the rest are striving to get there, perpetually bidding up the price of talent and reinforcing the position and power of the established players.

IS IT REALLY SO HARD TO MANAGE?

Many of the skills and structures required to manage a global risk-taking investment bank are also required in running other organizations. However, in addition to needing common managerial attributes such as strategic vision, communication skills and financial discipline, the managers of investment banks have to cope with staff who have unique power over them.

In most cases the top producers in an investment bank have a bigger brand name than that of the firm itself. Managing the bottom half of the talent pool has its problems, but it is the top half who present the real challenge. These individuals are on one-sided contracts, they can give a short notice period and move to a competitor, taking most of the business's goodwill with them.

The long-term solution is to build a brand which is bigger than the individuals within it but very few investment banks or brokers have been able to do so. In British broking during my time there has been only one brand that was consistently bigger than the individual – Cazenove – and only one that came close – James Capel – in the early 1980s. By the end of the 1990s, two American firms had managed to build brands in London that were bigger than the individual – Goldman and Morgan Stanley – and Merrill is getting close. Managers everywhere else have to walk the tightrope, balancing the firm's need for shape and style with the need to keep the star performers happy.

The task is complicated by the characteristics likely to be displayed by the stars. Whilst the industry contains its share of warm and wonderful human beings, the safest assumption to make when managing investment bankers is that their demands will be unreasonable, illogical and selfish. They expect the firm to be run with clear, strongly enforced rules applying to everyone but themselves. They consider penalties to be essential for matters such as filling out deal tickets incorrectly, being late at morning meetings, not following the agreed research format – provided that these penalties do not apply to them. More times than I can count I have heard analysts and salesmen denounce management for failing to apply rules they themselves ignore at will. Brokers are very good at dishing it out but not so good at receiving. It is the nature of their job to have a view on everything and it spills over into the way they conduct their professional life. Sometimes this boils over into erratic personal behaviour and this brings its own management challenge.

ECCENTRICS

Back at Fielding Newson Smith in 1978, on my first day I was given a desk facing a blank wall, a book about accounting and told to read it. The subject matter was new to me, I felt strange wearing a suit and there was bedlam all around. Most of the noise was coming from an office next to me and I could hear a man ranting and raving and occasionally thumping the desk. After about an hour I got up and peeped in through the window, half expecting to see some poor individual in a straitjacket desperately trying to escape.

What I saw was a man in his thirties wearing a raincoat, black leather gloves and clutching a telephone on a very long lead. He was pacing the room telling his clients which shares to buy and sell and getting furious with them if they dared to disagree. 'Look, every trader in Rangoon High Street is selling them, why don't you', I heard him yell. This, I later learned, was Angus Phaure, the leading analyst of building shares in the City, and one of the hottest properties around. His written style was eccentric, he felt the cold (the raincoat), he did not like to get newsprint on his fingers (the gloves), he was a strong believer in rules but not for himself and at his peak he had a wonderful ability to spot under-valued building shares.

Ten years later I had the task of managing Angus when I was head of research and he was still a top analyst. He was unmanageable in the conventional sense. He had his own way of writing and laying out the research that conflicted with our attempts at branding. He was as likely to start his research with a story about his dog as about the shares in question; he wrote when he liked about what he liked and the clients loved it. Good management of Angus was just a matter of creating an environment around him where he felt good so that the creative juices flowed and maintaining a control framework that kept him the right side of the compliance department.

ADDICTS

Managing those with an addiction is a sad and testing challenge for any manager in any line of work, the City included. Modern firms take a strong line on drunkenness and drug taking but there are still vestiges of the old City on display, often from the most talented people. One of the firms I worked for had a charismatic sales trader, a big revenue earner for us with a huge client following. He worked hard and played hard but often allowed the two to interfere. I was presenting an investment case to an old friend of his, a serious actuarial type but who had spent a few wild nights with our man in the past, a fact which he clearly wished to forget. Our man was having none of it and, halfway through the presentation, burst in clutching a bag of doughnuts. He squeezed our client's knee, blew a loud elephant trumpeting sound, shouted 'wey hey' and insisted that everyone eat a doughnut. He was having such fun that he stayed for the whole presentation, interrupting occasionally with more trumpeting, wey heying, squeezes and doughnuts as I tried to take the actuary through the equity risk premium.

Why did he get away with it? Ninety-nine days out of a hundred he was fine; he had a genius for spotting share price bargains and a personality that the clients loved. We could have fired him and removed bad behaviour but with it would have gone a great broking instinct and a lot of the firm's magic stardust that helped it stand out. As another friend of mine remarked, 'Talent is hard to manage.'

ODDBALLS

Another of my colleagues combined a great facility with clients with bizarre personal behaviour. One summer the air conditioning in the New York office broke repeatedly and the landlord was slow to fix it. Our man phoned the landlord, announced that in fifteen minutes he was going down to the lobby and would strip unless the heating engineer appeared. He did; the engineer didn't. We were just about prepared to tolerate that but finally our salesman went too far. He was permanently over-excited – that's what drove him on – but it emerged that he was relieving the stress in an unacceptable way. He made regular trips to London and always stayed at the same hotel. After the first visit the hotel noticed that his mini-bar was empty but that he had not filled out the voucher; a similar thing occurred on the next visit. Each time he was questioned by the hotel management but denied all knowledge. On the third occasion the hotel sprung a trap and questioned him as he checked out. Outrage: never had a thing from the mini-bar, regular visitor here, how dare you. They searched his bag and found the lot: peanuts, beer, wine, soft drinks, glasses, even the bottle opener. The salesman earned over half a million dollars a year, had no financial reason to steal but needed his release valve.

These are extreme cases but, because broking attracts characters, such events are surprisingly common. Insecurity is one of the reasons why the top brokers are so good at the job. They are never complacent, they do not pause for self-congratulation, they never assume that they have it mastered. Consequently they tend to stay on top of the shares they are interested in. Once an investment decision has been made it needs constant watching: when to close out the profit, when to cut the losses, what to do next. It is a living world that moves fast and requires quick thinking and the moment you relax you are dead. Neurotics flourish under those circumstances but they are hell to manage.

HERDING CATS

We have four cats at home and, by and large, they all do their own thing. If you let them loose in the garden they go their separate ways and when they go looking for mice they do it on their own, not as a pack. Twice a day we can get them to come together. At feeding time they rush through the door to their bowls, looking every bit like a pack but in reality no more than a collection of individuals all doing the same thing at the same time to satisfy their personal needs. At bedtime in winter they huddle up together in one basket to keep each other warm. This is unlike the dash for the food: it's animals interacting, drawing from each other's warmth and (probably incidentally) giving something back to the group.

So it is with brokers. If you can persuade them on an action where they are all running in the same direction towards a common goal, for a while the firm can look like a united team. The fact that the individuals are all totally focused on personal goals does not really matter; to the outside world it looks like a team. But like the cats and their food, once the goal is achieved, they all go their separate ways again. To produce real team behaviour, like the cats at night the brokers must have a shared interest that can only be achieved if they work together to get it. Good management means persuading individuals in the firm that they can benefit from working together.

FIVE WAYS TO HERD CATS

The close of the twentieth century and the beginning of the present one has been a period in which investment banking in the City has seemed relatively easy: open up shop, hire lots of people, cross-subsidize for a few years and watch the Euros roll in. This environment is seductive and treacherous. It is very easy to forget the lessons of the past and to assume that basic business discipline does not apply to investment e-banking. The traditional signs of bull market excesses are there in the City right now and they will end up in the traditional way: retrenchment, distress to over-expanded firms and debt-laden individuals and promises to do better next time. So, for the next time here are five of the guiding principles which the successful firms of the twentieth century have followed and which might just come in useful again.

Align ambition with resources.

Successful investment banks require a perfect alignment between ambition and resources. Provided that the target market position is clearly defined and supported and is within its financial and managerial means, the bank will work. This is substantiated by the City's successes as well as the failures of the period.

Cazenove did not have the balance sheets of the mega-banks and knew that it lacked the management infrastructure to sustain multi-product, global businesses. It defined a market position that was appropriate to its resources and delivered more or less to plan. Its success illustrates that, if the vision is understood by staff, management and shareholders and is supported by clients, the position is sustainable even if it does not fit the template of the bulge bracket firms. Two of the failures in the UK, Barings and Warburg, illustrate how a mismatch between ambition and management and financial resources can bring a bank down. Barings wanted a derivatives business but lacked the skills to control it; Warburg wanted to be a bulge bracket firm but lacked the financial muscle or management to deliver.

Ensure support of all stakeholders.

No bank can succeed without clients but unless the internal stake-holders all support the enterprise there will be no bank and no clients. The key internal stakeholders in an investment bank are management, staff and shareholders and it is not enough to have two out of the three on side.

The physical and emotional demands on the senior managers

running an investment bank are enormous. Jet lag, long hours, hundreds of e-mails and the need to combine the soft skills of people management with hard-headed risk assessment take their toll and can only be borne by those who are totally committed. The moment that the management doubts in the proposition, the whole business can unravel and at that time management should stand aside either for new management or a new owner to bring in a fresh strategy. Many of the banks that gave up their independence voluntarily did so when the senior management flinched.

Any investment banking strategy is likely to be difficult, volatile and unpopular with shareholders unless it is properly understood by them. They need to comprehend the risks as well as the rewards and to have a realistic appreciation of the pitfalls along the way. This is especially important where there are institutional shareholders who face constant short-term pressure in their own businesses and who can be very demanding on the managements of the companies they own. BZW and NatWest were brought down by this and Warburg's failure to carry MAM with it was a key factor in its collapse. Management needs to work very hard at drawing the shareholders into the strategy.

Carrying the staff is equally important. Investment bankers thrive on momentum and they need to believe that the firm they work for is going places. Bernard Asher's vision for HSBC Investment Bank was realistic and in line with the firm's resources, but did not appeal to the staff. They were more ambitious than the parent bank, they wanted to play a leading role in the investment banking world and were unhappy with the limited vision that they were shown. The support of the staff requires work on culture, team work and compensation.

Build a common culture.

Culture is a word that is tossed around investment banks like confetti at a wedding. It is every management's dream to have a culture that binds in the staff. Siegmund Warburg had one, Lord Cairns lost it; Martin Owen wanted one but could never get it; Cazenove and Goldman still have one; Smith had one and deliberately changed it. Culture consists of shared values (ethics, how staff treat each other, how client business is done) and a common vision. It is hard to define and harder still to build, but there are four essential steps: state the vision and values to all stakeholders; set a good example; build the right team; use compensation to reinforce the message.

The best example of stating the vision and values to all stakeholders comes from Goldman Sachs. The first thing the reader finds when opening the firm's prospectus for its initial public offering in 1999 is 'Our Business Principles'. They are all there from number one, 'Our clients' interests always come first', through to number fourteen, 'Integrity and honesty are at the heart of our business'. They are carefully phrased and intelligently formulated and no sane person would disagree with them. They set the benchmark for the firm's values and, when accompanied by a cogent business plan, form an important point of reference for future generations of staff and management. Other firms have the same values but they are tacit rather than explicit, and it is the act of stating them that is the differentiating factor.

A mission statement helps but is not enough unless the senior management walks the talk. From the top to the bottom, all day every day, management needs to practise what it preaches and reinforce the message by regular signals to the staff. These signals are watched for carefully by brokers: who is promoted and who is overlooked?; what sort of person is recruited?; how does management treat the staff?; how do management interact with each other?

Teamwork, teamwork, teamwork.

Teams have to be put together top down and bottom up, blending imported established talent with home-grown people. Morgan Grenfell in the 1980s and Deutsche Morgan Grenfell in the mid 1990s tried to build from the top down, hiring too many stars and neglecting to assemble complementary skills, personalities and experience. Organizations can only tolerate so much recruitment and the blend of old and new is important. It is simply impossible to form a team out of hundreds of new joiners all starting within a few months and it is much better to accept a slower rate of build-up in market position and revenues in order to give staff time to assimilate each other and their new environment. At Schroders in 1995, I was fortunate to find the products of the group's graduate intake and earlier attempts to build securities already in place. These men and women were well-versed in Schroders' values and formed the core of the new firm that was put in place, passing on to the newcomers the firm's folklore and best practices. There is no doubt that Goldman's intensive trawling of the best of British graduates and MBAs has enabled it to grow its own bottom up culture in London alongside its existing model in New York. The only way to build a firm with roots is to do it slowly, blending existing staff with incomers and a range of skills, characteristics and experience.

Bonds can be forged in a variety of ways: by bloody-minded determination to succeed against the odds as displayed by the Smith New Court underdog; by collective pride in being part of a winning team as shown by James Capel in the 1980s; or by paternalistic mutual support as occurred at the pre-Big Bang partnerships. However it is done, bonding the brokers into a team plan is an important task for managers in the industry.

Compensate well and wisely.

The right form and amount of compensation helps to establish the culture and forge the right bonds. Linking remuneration to the performance of the whole firm not just the individual is a big factor in this. One of the failures of the Big Bang generation and their successors was that cash was allowed to remain king for too long. The new investment banks did not succeed in giving the staff significant ownership of the business and compensation was nearly always in the form of cash. Only recently have deferred compensation and a linkage to the firm's overall performance become widespread. Equity participation is even more powerful as a driver of team behaviour.

ROUND UP THE USUAL SUSPECTS

Cazenove and the best American firms display all of these five key success factors: alignment; stakeholder buy-in; strong culture; teamwork; and equity or near-equity participation. Some other firms are currently succeeding in the benign business conditions of the bull market, believing that they are building a brand with stakeholder loyalty whilst paying only lip service to the principles of good management. These firms will be caught out when market conditions get really choppy. Falling revenues will expose inflated cost bases and losses will appear. Shareholders, staff and management will get discouraged, firms will unravel, and we will all promise to do better in future.

Here's to the next time.

Notes

1

1. *Financial Times*, 13 December 1983
2. ibid., 7 March 1984
3. ibid., 12 September 1983
4. *Evening Standard*, 4 February 1986

2

1. The boom in equity pension funds is generally credited to George Ross Goobey, of the Imperial Tobacco Pension Fund, in the 1950s. He realized that the combination of capital and income growth offered by equities fitted well with the liabilities of pension funds.

2.   Leading Pension Fund Managers, 1982, £ million

Managers	Funds under management
Merchant banks	
S. G. Warburg	2200
Robert Fleming	1800
Schroder Wagg	1800
Morgan Grenfell	1785
Hill Samuel	1667
Insurance companies	
Prudential	2200
Legal & General	2000

Littlewood, John, *The Stock Market, Financial Times*/Pitman Publishing, London, 1998, p. 308

3. Unit trusts are open-ended mutual funds and the share price reflects the net asset value of the securities held in the portfolio. They are not listed on the Stock Exchange. Investment trusts are also mutual funds but, unlike unit trusts, they are limited companies with shares in them being traded on the Stock Exchange. Investment trusts are close ended in that new capital can only be raised on a pre-emption basis from existing shareholders

4. Littlewood, op.cit., p. 457; Hayes, Samuel, and Hubbard, Philip, *Investment Banking*, Harvard Business School Press, Boston, 1990, pp. 210–16

5. John Moore, the Finance Secretary at the Treasury, to the House of Commons, *Financial Times*, 4 April 1984

6. Various sources including City Research Associates, 1983; Extel survey 1984; *Crawford's Directory*, 1984

7. *Financial Times*, 3 July 1984

8. Endlich, Lisa, *Goldman Sachs: The Culture of Success*, Knopf, New York, 1999, p. 85

9. *Financial Times*, 3 July 1984

10. ibid.

11. Flotations may be through an 'offer for sale' in which the underwriters buy a block of shares from the vendor and offer them to investors at a slightly higher price or through a book-building process on a best endeavours basis

12. The method of issuing new equity contrasts with the US system where the lead underwriter and the lead distributor are synonymous. Fees are 4–6 per cent but the equity is priced at a less steep discount

3

1. Courtney, Cathy, and Thompson, Paul, *City Lives: The Changing Voices of British Finance*, Methuen, London, 1996, p. 65

2. ibid., p. 123

3. Gapper, John, and Denton, Nicholas, *All That Glitters: The Fall of Barings*, Penguin Books, London, 1997, p. 110

4. Jack Spall, in Courtney and Thompson, op. cit., pp. 96–7

5. With the exception of research analysts who spent 8 per cent of their time – just four days a year – with corporate finance

6. John Holmes, interview 1999

7. Endlich, Lisa, *Goldman Sachs: The Culture of Success*, Knopf, New York, 1999, p. 237

4

1. Blakey, George G., *The Post-War History of the London Stock Market*, Management Books 2000 Ltd, Chalford, 1997, p. 247
2. Hutton, Will, *The State We're In*, Vintage, London, 1996, pp. 21–2; P. J. Cain and A. G. Hopkins, *British Imperialism, 1914–1990*, Longman, London, 1993, pp. 292–6
3. Courtney, Cathy, and Thompson, Paul, *City Lives: The Changing Voices of British Finance*, Methuen, London, 1996, pp. 164–5
4. ibid., p. 175
5. Mike Geering, interview 1999
6. George Nissen, in Courtney and Thompson, op. cit., p. 195
7. Courtney and Thompson, op. cit., p. 195

5

1. *Financial Times*, 18 October 1983
2. ibid., 26 September 1986
3. ibid., 30 January 1985
4. Quoted in Hayes and Hubbard, *Investment Banking*, Harvard Business School Press, Boston, 1990, p. 206
5. Lawson, Nigel, *The View from No. 11: Memoirs of a Tory Radical*, Bantam Books, London, 1993, p. 399
6. Courtney, Cathy, and Thompson, Paul, *City Lives: The Changing Voices of British Finance*, Methuen, London, 1996, pp. 164–5
7. *Financial Times*, 8 January 1986
8. Courtney and Thompson, op. cit., p. 161
9. *Financial Times*, 17 July 1984

6

1. The Royal Bank of Scotland bought the Liverpool broker, Tilney, in 1986 to go with Charterhouse but remained on the fringes of investment banking and is not covered in this study
2. Lorenz, Andrew, *BZW: The First Ten Years*, BZW, London, 1996, p. 12
3. ibid., pp. 11–12
4. *Financial Times*, 12 July 1985. NatWest's chief executive, Tom Frost, was

persuaded by County's chairman Charles Villiers that the bank could not run the risk of being left behind if its competitors successfully created integrated investment banks

5. ibid., 3 July 1986, Corporate Finance supplement, p. 2
6. Lorenz, op. cit., pp. 12–13
7. Peter Quinnen, *Financial Times*, 22 October 1986
8. Lorenz, op. cit., p. 19
9. Barclays senior executive, in Lorenz, op. cit., p. 19
10. Simon de Zoete, in Lorenz, op. cit., p. 14
11. *Financial Times*, 27 October 1986
12. ibid., 10 September 1984

7

1. Jim Barton, head of Prudential Bache's international division in New York, *Financial Times*, 23 December 1983
2. Interview 1999
3. *Financial Times*, 22 February 1985
4. Brian Peppiatt, senior partner, Akroyd, *Financial Times*, 20 December 1983
5. *Financial Times*, 22 February 1984
6. *Financial Weekly*, 22 June 1986
7. *Financial Times*, 21 May 1984
8. Christopher Reeves, *Financial Times*, 16 May 1986
9. *Financial Weekly*, 22 June 1986
10. ibid., 22 June 1986
11. Kleinwort director, interview 1999
12. Wake, Jehanne, *Kleinwort Benson: The History of Two Families in Banking*, Oxford University Press, Oxford, 1997, p. 423
13. *Financial Times*, 4 October 1984
14. Hill Samuel, *Investment Banking – A New Era*, p. 2, brochure produced by Hill Samuel
15. *Financial Times*, 4 June 1984
16. ibid.
17. ibid., 1 May 1985
18. ibid., 4 June 1984
19. ibid., 26 June 1985
20. ibid., 10 June 1986
21. ibid., 26 June 1986

22. Courtney, Cathy, and Thompson, Paul, *City Lives: The Changing Voices of British Finance*, Methuen, London, 1996, pp. 250–51

23. Jacob Rothschild, *Financial Times*, 4 November 1983

24. Securities Industry Association, in Hayes, Samuel, and Hubbard, Philip, *Investment Banking*, Harvard Business School Press, Boston, 1990, p. 391

25. *Financial Times*, 9 October 1984

26. *Financial Weekly*, 22 June 1986

27. Wake, op. cit., p. 425

28. *Financial Times*, 10 November 1984

29. ibid., 1 June 1985

8

1. Endlich, Lisa, *Goldman Sachs: The Culture of Success*, Knopf, New York, 1999, p. 85

2. Eurobonds were traded globally from London after the US Government, fearful of large dollar outflows to European borrowers, pushed the market out of New York. In June 1963 Warburg's $15 million placing of 5.5 per cent bearer bonds for Autostrade helped to establish the City as the world's Eurobond capital. US investment banks set up Eurobond teams in Europe in the late 1960s and 1970s. By the early 1980s six of the top twelve Eurobond houses were American but this was a specialized business. Hayes, Samuel, and Hubbard, Philip, *Investment Banking*, Harvard Business School Press, Boston, 1990, p. 50

3. Interview, August 1999

4. Glass–Steagall's underwriting restrictions on US banks reached as far as London and as a result Security Pacific had some practical problems to solve if it was to make full use of its new broking arm. It got round Glass–Steagall by forming a syndicate of leading buy side institutions (Legal & General, Norwich Union, the Prudential, Royal Insurance and Standard Life) to underwrite large issues. In return for joining the syndicate, the members were entitled to a share of the underwriting commission, with Hoare Govett retaining the management fee. Hoare Govett then formed a number of separately capitalized subsidiaries, none of which was to underwrite more than $2 million, therefore avoiding breaching the Glass–Steagall limit (*Financial Times*, 29 September 1983, 9 April 1984, 24 and 25 July 1984 and 25 October 1986)

5. *Financial Times*, 8 November 1983

6. ibid., 4 September 1984, 1 November 1984 and 16 April 1985

7. ibid., 29 September 1983

8. Extel survey, 1984

9. *Financial Times*, 23 December 1983
10. ibid., 27 October 1986. Prudential Bache was a US retail broker that had successfully grafted on an institutional business. It was amongst the earliest Wall Street builders in London and enjoyed some early success. In 1983 it pre-empted the reforms by establishing a new firm as a joint venture with two individual members of the Stock Exchange, Ashley Dunn and Christopher de Boer, who had headed up James Capel's corporate finance department
11. Endlich, op. cit., p. 86

9

1. J. Dundas Hamilton, senior partner, in Courtney, Cathy, and Thompson, Paul, *City Lives: The Changing Voices of British Finance*, Methuen, London, 1996, p. 65
2. Gerald Dennis, finance director, Wedd, in Lorenz, Andrew, *BZW: The First Ten Years*, BZW, London, 1996
3. Sir John Craven, in Courtney and Thompson, op. cit., pp. 109–10
4. Lorenz, op. cit., pp. 19–20
5. *Financial Times*, 6 November 1984
6. John Chiene, interview 1999
7. Interview 1999
8. Hobson, Dominic, *The Pride of Lucifer*, Mandarin, London, 1991, p. 213
9. Ken Taylor, Scott Goff partner, interview 1999
10. *Financial Times*, 21 December 1984
11. ibid., 28 November 1985
12. Cazenove partner, interview 1999
13. ibid.
14. Kynaston, David, *Cazenove & Co.: A History*, B.T. Batsford, London, 1991, p. 301
15. Cazenove partner, interview 1999
16. ibid.
17. *Financial Times*, 11 September 1986
18. Kynaston, op. cit., pp. 313–14
19. *Financial Times*, 11 September 1986
20. Davinia Walker, in Courtney and Thompson, op. cit., p. 132
21. George Nissan, ibid., p. 82

10

1. *Financial Times*, 27 October 1986
2. Interview, 2000
3. Ken Taylor, interview 1999
4. Smith New Court annual reports 1985–8
5. *Financial Times*, 19 November 1984
6. Howard Coates, interview 1999
7. Nick Whitney, interview 1999
8. *Financial Times*, 27 October 1986
9. ibid.
10. Wake, Jehanne, *Kleinwort Benson: The History of Two Families in Banking*, Oxford University Press, Oxford, 1997, p. 422
11. Beecham went to Wood Mackenzie as corporate broker and Racal to Scrimgeour Kemp Gee in large part because these firms had ranked analysts following the stocks (*Financial Times*, 11 January 1984)
12. *Financial Times*, 27 October 1986
13. ibid., 21 February and 5 August 1985
14. ibid., 5 April 1986

11

1. *Financial Times*, 13 January 1984
2. ibid., 24 July 1984
3. ibid., 13 March 1984
4. ibid., 1 September 1984
5. Gapper, John, and Denton, Nicholas, *All That Glitters: The Fall of Barings*, Penguin Books, London, 1997, p. 107
6. *Financial Times*, 13 March 1984
7. Stamp Duty was halved to 1 per cent in the 1984 Budget. The 1986 Budget then stimulated a further surge by halving the rate again (except on ADRs) to 0.5 per cent. The rate on ADRs was cut from 5 per cent to 1.5 per cent in response to complaints by the Stock Exchange that London was an uncompetitive international centre

8. Smith New Court Bull and Bear Positions,
1983–7, £ million

	1983	1984	1985	1986	1987
Bull	49.4	85.1	92.7	246.5	466.5
Bear	38.7	53.3	39.3	155.2	393.8

Smith New Court plc Annual report and accounts,
1983–7

9. Courtney, Cathy, and Thompson, Paul, *City Lives: The Changing Voices of British Finance*, Methuen, London, 1996, p. 125
10. *Financial Times*, 'City Revolution', 27 October 1986
11. Gapper and Denton, op. cit, p. 105
12. *Financial Times*, 11 April 1985
13. Lorenz, Andrew, *BZW: The First Ten Years*, BZW, London, 1996, p. 31
14. ibid., p. 35
15. Wake, Jehanne, *Kleinwort Benson: The History of Two Families in Banking*, Oxford University Press, Oxford, 1997, p. 426
16. Gapper and Denton, op. cit., p. 107
17. *Financial Times*, 12 March 1984
18. ibid., 24 January 1986
19. ibid., 7 August 1986
20. ibid., 26 April 1984 and 7 October 1985
21. ibid., 'City Revolution', 27 October 1986
22. Charles McVeigh, in Courtney and Thompson, op. cit., p. 117
23. Lewis, Michael, *Liar's Poker, Two Cities, True Greed*, Hodder and Stoughton, London, 1989, pp. 182–3

12

1. Enfield, Harry, *Harry Enfield and his Humorous Chums*, Penguin Books, London, 1997, pp. 24–6
2. Philip Leeder, interview 2000
3. ibid.
4. Richard Wyatt, interview 1999
5. David Atkinson, interview 1999
6. Littlewood, John, *The Stock Market*, Financial Times/Pitman Publishing, London, 1998, p. 358

7. Tony Cole, interview 1999

8. Littlewood, op. cit., p. 355

9. Rolls-Royce, British Airways, British Airports Authority and British Petroleum

10. Tony Cole, interview 1999

11. Blakey, George, *The Post-War History of the London Stock Market*, Management Books, Gloucester, 1997, p. 308

12. Tony Cole, interview 1999

13. Ms A in Courtney, Cathy, and Thompson, Paul, *City Lives: The Changing Voices of British Finance*, Methuen, London, 1996, p. 141

14. ibid.

15. Tony Cole, interview 1999

16. *London Stock Exchange Quarterly*, 1988–90

13

1. Rudolf Mueller, interview 1999

2. Keith Brown, interview 1999

3. Donald Macpherson, interview 1999

4. Lorenz, Andrew, *BZW: The First Ten Years*, BZW, London, 1996, p. 44

5. James Capel executive, interview 1999

6. *Daily Telegraph*, 7 December 1988

7. Donald Macpherson, interview 1999

8. Keith Brown, interview 1999

9. ibid.

10. Tony Cole, interview 1999

11. Donald Macpherson, interview 1999

12. Keith Brown, interview 1999

13. Interview 1999

14. Keith Brown, interview 1999

15. *Financial Times*, 16 January 1988

16. Lorenz, op. cit., p. 47

17. ibid., p. 52

18. Rudolf Mueller, interview 1999

19. Howard Coates, interview 1999

20. John Chiene, interview 1999

21. Lorenz, op. cit., pp. 33–4

22. Interview 1999

23. Interview 1999

24. Rudolf Mueller, interview 1999
25. Tony Cole, interview 1999
26. Former James Capel partner, interview 1999
27. *The Times*, 10 June 1989

14

1. S. G. Warburg 1989 accounts, p. 9
2. Company accounts, calendar year, Warburg March year end shown as previous calendar year
3. S. G. Warburg 1988 accounts, p. 12
4. ibid., p. 17
5. Warburg director, interview 1999
6. Nick Whitney, interview 1999
7. S. G. Warburg, 1988 accounts, p. 14
8. S. G. Warburg 1989 accounts
9. Nick Whitney, interview 1999
10. ibid.
11. S. G. Warburg 1990 accounts, p. 19
12. S. G. Warburg 1989 accounts, p. 11
13. David Clementi, interview 1999
14. *Daily Telegraph*, 4 January 1988
15. David Clementi, interview 1999
16. Interview 1999
17. John Chiene, interview 1999
18. Hobson, Dominic, *The Pride of Lucifer*, Mandarin, London, 1991, p. 246
19. John Holmes, interview 1999
20. Hobson, op. cit., p. 295; and *Financial Times*, 11 November 1986
21. John Holmes, interview 1999
22. *Daily Telegraph*, 7 December 1988
23. Courtney, Cathy, and Thompson, Paul, *City Lives: The Changing Voices of British Finance*, Methuen, London, 1996, pp. 111–13
24. The decision to pull out of equities left Morgan Grenfell vulnerable to approaches. There were discussions with BZW and Banque Indosuez before Deutsche Bank stepped in with a bid of £950 million
25. Courtney and Thompson, op. cit., p. 111
26. *Daily Telegraph*, 7 December 1988
27. *Economist*, 10 December 1988

28. Gapper, John, and Denton, Nicholas, *All That Glitters: The Fall of Barings*, Penguin Books, London, 1997, p.134

15

1. Smith New Court director, interview 1999
2. Michael Marks, interview 1999
3. Smith New Court 1988 accounts, p. 6
4. Michael Marks, interview 1999
5. ibid.
6. ibid.
7. Smith New Court 1987 accounts, p. 8
8. Ken Taylor, interview 1999
9. Smith New Court 1988 accounts, pp. 22–3
10. Michael Marks, interview 1999
11. Smith New Court 1989 accounts, p. 2
12. Obligations for market makers to deal with each other at SEAQ prices and sizes were dropped and a twenty-four-hour trade reporting delay on publishing prices on bargains over £100,000 was introduced
13. Smith New Court 1988 accounts, pp. 22–3
14. *Financial Times*, 11 December 1987
15. Smith New Court 1988 accounts, p. 15
16. Michael Marks, interview 1999
17. The company raised a tranche of £15 million loan stock during 1986–7 and £63 million largely through convertible issues in 1987–8
18. Smith New Court accounts 1987, p. 3
19. ibid., p. 30
20. Smith New Court, 1988 accounts, p. 2
21. ibid., pp. 22–3
22. Cazenove press release, 29 January 1987
23. Cazenove partner, interview 1999
24. Cazenove partner, interview 1999
25. After the closure of Morgan Grenfell, Cazenove recruited the team of investment trust market makers, but team hiring was unusual for Cazenove. Kynaston, David, *Cazenove & Co.: A History*, B. T. Batsford, London, 1991, pp.319–33

16

1. Michie, Ranald, *The London Stock Exchange, A History*, Oxford University Press, Oxford, 2000, p. 580
2. Securities Industry Association data
3. Endlich, Lisa, *Goldman Sachs: The Culture of Success*, Knopf, New York, 1999, p.85
4. Keith Brown, interview 1999
5. John Holmes, interview 1999
6. Jim O'Donnell, interview June 1999
7. ibid.
8. *Financial Times*, 14 October 1987
9. *Observer*, 30 March 1986
10. Interview 1999
11. ibid.
12. *Financial Times*, 5 January 1989
13. Hoare Govett employee, interview 1999
14. Interview 1999
15. Citicorp Scrimgeour Vickers employee, interview 1999
16. ibid.
17. *Financial Weekly*, 26 October 1986
18. *Economist*, 3 December 1988
19. Endlich, op. cit., p. 86

17

1. *Stock Exchange Quarterly*, spring 1994, p. 17
2. *The Times*, 27 February 1991
3. Interview 2000
4. Lorenz, Andrew, *BZW: The First Ten Years*, BZW, London, 1996, p. 80
5. BZW director, interview 1999
6. UBS Executive, interview 1999
7. Hector Sants, interview 1999
8. James Capel director, interview 1999
9. Interview 1999
10. James Capel senior executive, interview 1999
11. Bernard Asher, interview 1999
12. ibid.

13. HSBC executive, interview 1999
14. Bernard Asher, interview 1999
15. ibid.
16. James Capel executive, interview 1999
17. Bernard Asher, interview 1999
18. ibid.
19. ibid.
20. ibid.
21. *Guardian*, 22 November 1994
22. *Financial Times*, 21 November 1994

18

1. S. G. Warburg 1994 interim results statement
2. Gapper, John, and Denton, Nicholas, *All That Glitters: The Fall of Barings*, Penguin Books, London, pp. 150 and 177
3. S. G. Warburg and Kleinwort annual reports. Group pre-tax profits minus asset management. Warburg years ended in March and have been shown as previous calendar year
4. S. G. Warburg 1991 accounts
5. S. G. Warburg 1992 accounts, pp. 15–16
6. S. G. Warburg 1994 accounts, p. 8
7. *Financial Times*, 16 February 1993
8. S. G. Warburg 1994 accounts, p. 7
9. S. G. Warburg 1993 accounts, p. 6. In May 1993 it was agreed to buy KC-CO, a Chicago-based derivatives firm
10. S. G. Warburg 1994 accounts, p. 6
11. S. G. Warburg 1994 accounts, p. 28
12. *Sunday Times*, 9 May 1993
13. Kleinwort 1990 accounts, p. 3
14. Interview 1999
15. *Mail on Sunday*, 20 January 1991
16. David Clementi, interview 1999
17. Kleinwort 1993 accounts, p. 6
18. *Financial Times*, 1 February 1995
19. Kleinwort 1994 accounts, chairman's statement
20. Robert Fleming executive, interview 1999
21. *The Times*, 9 September 1991; and *Mail on Sunday*, 8 September 1991
22. Bill Harrison, interview 1999

23. *Evening Standard*, 23 October 1995
24. *Management Today*, 31 August 1987

19

1. *Sunday Times*, 27 June 1993
2. Ken Taylor, interview 1999
3. Smith New Court 1993 accounts, p. 2
4. Kynaston, David, *Cazenove & Co.: A History*, B. T. Batsford, London, 1991, p. 331
5. Smith New Court employee, interview 1999
6. Smith New Court 1993 accounts, p. 6
7. *Sunday Times*, 27 June 1993
8. *Financial Times*, 2 May 1991
9. Smith New Court 1995 accounts, p. 3
10. Cazenove partners, interviews 1999 and 2000

20

1. *Financial Times*, 12 December 1990
2. ibid., 15 October 1990
3. Interview 1999
4. Salomon managing director, interview 1999
5. *Sunday Express*, 11 March 1990
6. *Sunday Telegraph*, 29 September 1991
7. *Financial Times*, 8 November 1991
8. ibid., 12 June 1991
9. Blakey, George, *Post-War History of the London Stock Market*, Management Books, Gloucester, 1997, p. 354
10. *Observer*, 24 March 1991
11. *Independent*, 21 October 1992

21

1. Fay, Stephen, *The Collapse of Barings: Panic, Ignorance and Greed*, Arrow Books, London, 1996. Gapper, John, and Denton, Nicholas, *All That Glitters: The Fall of Barings*, Penguin Books, London; Report of the Board of Banking

Supervision into the Circumstances of the Collapse of Barings, London, 1995
2. Board of Banking Supervision, p. 9
3. ibid., p. 10
4. ibid., p. 11
5. ibid., p. 12
6. Gapper and Denton, op. cit., p. 4
7. Board of Banking Supervision, p. 21
8. ibid., p. 21
9. ibid., p. 22
10. ibid., p. 23
11. ibid., p. 254
12. ibid., p. 254
13. ibid., p. 28
14. ibid., p. 252
15. ibid., p. 253
16. ibid., p. 244
17. ibid., p. 244
18. ibid., p. 244
19. ibid., p. 244
20. ibid., p. 245
21. ibid., p. 248
22. ibid., p. 248
23. ibid., p. 13

22

1. This account taken from the article by Gapper, John, 'The Takeover of S. G. Warburg – A Year That Killed the Global Dream', *Financial Times*, 22 May 1995; Stormonth Darling, Peter, *City Cinderella: The Life and Times of Mercury Asset Management*, Weidenfeld & Nicolson, London, 1999, pp. 226–51
2. *Financial Times*, 22 May 1995
3. S. G. Warburg 1995 accounts, p. 4
4. *Financial Times*, 22 May 1995
5. ibid., 22 May 1995
6. S. G. Warburg 1995 accounts, p. 4
7. *Financial Times*, 10 January 1995
8. ibid., 11 January 1995
9. ibid., 22 May 1995

10. ibid.
11. *Financial Times*, 14 February 1995
12. John Holmes, interview 1999
13. *Financial Times*, 22 May 1995
14. S. G. Warburg 1994 accounts, p. 24
15. ibid. 1995 accounts, p. 23
16. ibid.
17. Courtney, Cathy, and Thompson, Paul, *City Lives: The Changing Voices of British Finance*, Methuen, London, 1996, p. 213
18. ibid., p. 220
19. A senior Warburg source told me: 'Scholey was never chief executive and decisions were thrashed out in the Chairman's Committee by the half dozen business heads. The discussion process saved us lots of mistakes. Cairns was chief executive and the division heads reported to him individually, and the overall scale of what was being done was lost. The old Chairman's Committee would have stopped this.' Interview 1999
20. Michael Verey, in Courtney and Thompson, op. cit., p. 222
21. Stormonth Darling, op. cit., p. 250
22. *Financial Times*, 14 February 1995

23

1. *Financial Times*, 30 January 1995
2. Financial press, week commencing 27 February 1999
3. Simon Robertson, deputy chairman, *The Times*, 1 February 1995
4. *The Times*, 1 February 1995
5. ibid., 1 February 1995
6. *Daily Telegraph*, 17 February 1995
7. Wake, Jehanne, *Kleinwort Benson: The History of Two Families in Banking*, Oxford University Press, Oxford, 1997, pp. 438–41
8. Dresdner Bank press release, 26 June 1995
9. *Financial Times*, 16 June 1995
10. 'The groups' performance so far in 1995 has been substantially below the board's expectations', Kleinwort press release, 26 June 1995
11. Financial press, 16 June 1995
12. ibid.
13. Michael Marks, interview 1999
14. Smith New Court Director, interview 1999
15. Michael Marks, interview 1999

16. Ken Taylor, interview 1999
17. Smith New Court director, interview 1999
18. ibid.
19. ibid.
20. ibid.
21. *Mail on Sunday*, 5 May 1996
22. Ken Taylor, interview 1999

24

1. BZW executive in Lorenz, Andrew, *BZW: The First Ten Years*, BZW, London, 1996, p. 166
2. Martin Taylor, interview 1999
3. ibid.
4. ibid.
5. Buxton, Middleton and Taylor
6. Martin Taylor, interview 1999
7. Bill Harrison, interview 1999
8. Martin Taylor, interview 1999
9. Bill Harrison, interview 1999
10. Barclays Director, interview 2000
11. Martin Taylor, interview 1999
12. *Financial Times*, 4 October 1997
13. ibid., 23 April 1997
14. Martin Taylor, interview 1999
15. *Sunday Telegraph*, 5 October 1997
16. *Daily Telegraph*, 4 October 1997
17. Sir Peter Middleton, interview 1999
18. Interview 1999
19. Martin Taylor, interview 1999
20. Interview 2000
21. Martin Taylor, interview 1999
22. *Financial Times*, 4 October 1997
23. Derek Wanless, interview 2000
24. NatWest director, interview 2000
25. NatWest director, interview 2000
26. NatWest director, interview 2000
27. Derek Wanless, interview 2000
28. Derek Wanless, interview 2000

29. Former UBS executive, interview 1999
30. Former Phillips & Drew UBS equities analyst, interview 1999
31. NatWest director, interview 2000
32. Lorenz, op. cit., p. 166
33. Stormonth Darling, Peter, *City Cinderella: The Life and Times of Mercury Asset Management*, Weidenfeld & Nicolson, London, 1999, p. 243

25

1. Internal memorandum, Philip Augar 1995
2. The retention of pre-emption rights reduced the risk of bond market-style bought deals becoming the norm which would almost certainly have been done by the bigger investment banks on an integrated basis

26

1. Interview 1999
2. *Evening Standard*, 29 January 1996
3. Interview 1999
4. Michael Marks, interview 1999
5. Salomon analyst, 1999 interview
6. ibid.
7. Salomon executive, interview 1999
8. The Reuters Survey 2000, Tempest Consultants
9. ibid.
10. Goldman Sachs prospectus, p. 3
11. 'After Flemings, can Cazenove be far behind?', *Independent*, 24 March 2000; *Financial Times*, 28 November 2000
12. *Acquisitions Monthly* and *Crawford's Directory*, 1999
13. Cazenove partner, interview 2000
14. Tony Alt, N. M. Rothschild, in *Financial Times*, 11 May 1996
15. *Financial Times*, 11 May 1996

27

1. Banks, Erik, *The Rise and Fall of the Merchant Banks*, Kogan Page, London, 1999, p. 406

2. Hobson, Dominic, *The Pride of Lucifer*, Mandarin, London, 1991, pp. 262–3
3. Martin Taylor, interview 1999
4. Hutton, Will, *The Stakeholding Society*, Polity Press, Cambridge, 1999, pp. 53–7; and *The State We're In*, Vintage, London, 1996, pp. 304–5
5. Derek Wanless, interview 2000
6. Lehman Brothers spokesman, *Sunday Times*, 24 October 1999
7. Goldman Sachs prospectus May 1999, p. 10
8. Schroders accounts 1994–8

28

1. Sir Eddie George, interview 2000
2. Banks, Erik, *The Rise and Fall of the Merchant Banks*, Kogan Page, London, 1999, pp. 528–9
3. Sir Eddie George, interview 2000
4. ibid.
5. *Financial Times*, 13 May 1996
6. Interview, Barclays Director, 1999
7. *Financial Times*, 21 September 1999
8. Don Cruickshank, chairman of the London Stock Exchange, appears to share this view with Eddie George, *Financial Times*, 22 April 2000
9. Martin Taylor, interview 2000
10. *Euromoney*, January 2000, p. 30
11. *Financial News*, 24 January 2000; and *Euromoney*, November 1999; *Financial Times*, 13 September 2000

29

1. Morgan Grenfell & Co. accounts 1996, pp. 15–16

Glossary

Based on Bannock, Graham, and Manser, William, *Penguin International Dictionary of Finance* (Penguin Books, London, 1999)

Agency broker A stockbroking firm working for a client as an agent for commission.

American depository receipt (ADR) A certificate giving title to a number of shares in a non-US-based company deposited in a bank outside the USA. These certificates are traded on US stock exchanges.

Back office The department in a firm of stockbrokers that deals with settlement procedures, such as the forwarding of share certificates to clients and the maintenance of accounts.

Bank of England The central bank of the UK responsible for the execution of national financial and monetary policy, under the overall direction of the Government. In mid 1997 the UK Government announced that the Bank's responsibility for supervision of the banking system would pass to the Financial Services Authority (Financial Services Act). At the same time the Bank was made solely responsible for determining UK interest rates, a function until then exercised by the Treasury.

Bear position A short position in securities.

Best execution The best price available in the relevant size at the time of dealing in the securities in question.

Big Bang The term used to encapsulate the changes culminating on 27 October 1986 with the abandonment of the commission agreement between members of the London Stock Exchange and of strict segregation of jobbers and brokers.

Bonds Interest-bearing securities.

Bought deal Large line of stock in a single company bought as principal by an investment bank or broker with the aim of reselling at a profit.

Bulge bracket The handful of leading US investment banks.

Bull position A long position in securities.

Capital employed The capital in use in a business. There is no universally agreed definition of the term.

Chinese wall A communications barrier between members or departments of a financial institution intended to prevent the transfer of price-sensitive information.

Commercial banks Privately owned banks otherwise referred to as clearing banks (UK), national banks and state banks (US), joint-stock banks and, in Western Europe, credit banks, to distinguish them from investment banks.

Compliance department, officer All official stock exchanges and many large financial institutions have people responsible for ensuring that laws and regulations governing share dealing and investment are complied with.

Conflict of interest A situation where a financial institution is acting for the parties on both sides of a transaction, or where the institution itself has a financial interest in the outcome of the transaction; i.e. a merchant bank both placing shares on the Stock Exchange on behalf of a client company and recommending the purchase of those shares to an investor client whose portfolio it manages; or a securities house offering to an investor shares with which it is itself over-supplied and that it is under pressure to sell.

Convertible bond A bond that can be converted at a fixed price into the shares of a company, usually within a given time period.

Corporate broker A company's official appointed stockbroker responsible for that company's dealings with the London Stock Exchange and its shareholders.

Corporate finance Strictly speaking, the provision of money for commercial use but more generally used to describe advice given to companies about strategic matters as well as financing requirements.

Derivative A generic term for futures, options and swaps, i.e. instruments derived from conventional direct dealings in securities, currencies and commodities.

Disintermediation Flows of funds between borrowers and lenders avoiding the direct use of financial intermediaries.

Dual capacity The situation where a market maker can buy or sell shares to and from members of the public or other members of the Stock Exchange without the need for a broker. The market maker acts as both jobber and broker.

Equity capital markets A department in an investment bank responsible for organizing equity placings on behalf of companies.

Eurobond A bond issued in a currency other than that of the country or market in which it is issued.

Fixed interest Generally refers to securities such as bonds on which the holder receives a predetermined and unchanging rate of interest on the nominal value (par value); as opposed to the non-guaranteed, variable return on equities.

Flotation The issue of shares in a company on a stock exchange or unlisted securities market for the first time. The method may be an introduction, an intermediate offer, a placing or an offer for sale. When a private company becomes a public company and has its shares listed in this way, the process is known as going public.

Gilts, gilt-edged securities Fixed-interest UK Government securities traded on the London Stock Exchange. They are called gilt-edged because it is certain that interest will be paid and that they will be redeemed (where appropriate) on the due date.

Glass–Steagall Act 1933 legislation prohibiting commercial banks from acting as investment banks or owning a firm dealing in securities. The Act has been challenged by banks offering money market mutual funds and other investment services.

Initial public offering (IPO) The offering of the shares in the equity of a company to the public for the first time. New issue.

Insider dealing The buying and selling of shares while in possession of price-sensitive information obtained unlawfully, i.e through employment in the company whose shares are being dealt with. Insider dealing is illegal in the UK, the USA and France, among other countries.

Investment analyst Someone who studies companies and financial securities and makes recommendations to buy and sell shares and other securities. Analysts work not only in investment banks and stockbroking firms (the sell side), but also in the financial institutions such as pension funds (the buy side), which own the majority of stocks and shares.

Investment bank A financial intermediary that advises corporates, governments and investors on financial transactions including the issue and trading of securities. Cf *Merchant banks*.

Jobber A dealer in securities who will buy and sell specific securities at all times, a market maker. Prior to the Big Bang, jobbers were members of the London Stock Exchange who were permitted to deal only with brokers and not with the general public.

Lex column Influential daily column on the back page of the main section of the *Financial Times*.

Market maker A broker–dealer who is prepared to buy and sell specified securities at all times and thus makes a market in them. Prior to the Big Bang, this function was carried out by jobbers, who were not allowed to deal with the public. Since the Big Bang all members of the Stock Exchange may deal with the public as broker–dealers.

Merchant banks Institutions that carry out a variety of financial services, including the acceptance of bills of exchange, the issue and placing of loans and securities, portfolio and unit trust management, foreign exchange dealing and some banking services. Merchant banks advise companies on mergers and other financial matters. The term 'merchant banks' is now giving way to investment banks as their activities are absorbed into large global concerns.

Offer for sale Shares may be offered to the public at a fixed price in an advertised offer for sale (US=public offering). Those who purchase the shares are said to have subscribed, i.e. it is an offer for subscription. Issues over a certain size (£50 million) have to be offered to the public in their entirety, under the rules of the London Stock Exchange, instead of by a placing or an intermediaries offer.

Personal equity plan (PEP) A scheme introduced in the Finance Act 1986 to provide tax relief on the proceeds of personal investments in equities listed on the stock exchange.

Portfolio trading Cf *Programme trading*.

Pre-emptive rights The right of shareholders of a company to have first refusal to purchase any new shares issued by the company. These rights have legal backing in the UK.

Primary Of the stock market, that part of the market concerned with new issues: Cf *Secondary*.

Privatisation The sale of government-owned equity in a nationalized industry or other commercial enterprises to private investors.

Programme trading Purchases or sales of a large basket of securities, usually through a single broker and sometimes computer generated.

Quoted company A company (incorporation) whose shares are listed on an official stock exchange.

Rights issue An offer for new shares to existing shareholders. A company will offer the rights in a certain proportion to existing holdings, depending upon the amount of new equity capital it wishes to raise. Thus in a one-for-one rights issue, shareholders will be offered a number of new shares equal to the number they already hold. To ensure that the issue is taken up, the new shares are offered at well below the market price of the existing share, i.e. at a discount, which will usually result in some fall in the price of existing shares.

Secondary Stock market activity in which securities are resold and repurchased. Cf *Primary*.

Settlement Payment of an obligation, i.e. payment in cash for securities.

Single capacity A term used to describe a situation where a market maker on a stock exchange deals only with other professionals and not with the investors.

Stock exchange A market in which securities are bought and sold. There are stock exchanges in most capital cities, as well as in the larger provincial cities in many countries. The New York Stock Exchange, London Stock Exchange and Tokyo Stock Exchange are the largest in terms of market capitalization.

Stockbroker A member of a stock exchange who buys and sells securities as an agent for clients in return for a commission.

Underwrite 1 To guarantee to buy or find buyers for all or part of the issue of a security. Normally done in return for a fee by a bank or group (syndicate) of banks to ensure sale of any part of an issue not bought by the public to which it is directed. 2 To accept on behalf of an insuring firm or syndicate an insurance risk.

Starters and Finishers, 1983–2000

Twenty-two companies are covered in this book, including all of the principal market participants of the period and a representative sample of other players. These twenty-two companies are listed below together with the most significant corporate events in their London broking activities. A firm's name without an entry below it means that it is continuing to pursue an organic growth strategy.

THE COMMERCIAL BANKS

- Barclays
  Bought de Zoete & Bevan and Wedd Durlacher, 1984–6
  Equities and corporate finance sold to CSFB, 1997

- NatWest
  Bought Bisgood Bishop and Fielding Newson Smith, 1984–6
  Bought Wood Mackenzie, 1987
  Bulk of equities business sold to Bankers Trust, 1997

- HSBC
  Bought James Capel, 1983–6
  Bought Midland Bank, 1992

- Midland
  Bought Greenwell, 1985–6
  Closed equities, 1988
  Sold to HSBC, 1992

- UBS
  Bought Phillips & Drew, 1986
  UBS merged with SBC, 1998

- Citigroup
  Bought Scrimgeour Kemp Gee and Vickers da Costa, 1983–6
  Closed equities 1990
  Bought Travelers, including Salomon Smith Barney, 1998
  Bought Schroders' investment bank, 2000

- Security Pacific
  Bought Hoare Govett and Charles Pulley & Co., 1983–6
  Sold equities to ABN Amro, 1992

THE MERCHANT BANKS AND INDEPENDENT BROKERS

- Warburg
  Bought Rowe & Pitman, Akroyd & Smithers, Mullens & Co., 1984–6
  Group sold to SBC, 1995
  SBC merged with UBS, 1998

- Kleinwort
  Bought Grieveson Grant, Charlesworth & Co., 1984–6
  Group sold to Dresdner Bank, 1995

- Hill Samuel
  Bought Wood Mackenzie, 1984–6
  Group sold to TSB, 1987
  Wood Mackenzie sold to NatWest, 1987

- Morgan Grenfell
  Bought Pember & Boyle, Pinchin Denny, 1984–6
  Closed Morgan Grenfell Securities, 1988
  Group sold to Deutsche Bank, 1989

- Barings
  Group sold to ING, 1995

- Schroders
  Investment bank sold to Citigroup, 2000

- Flemings
  Sold to Chase Manhattan, 2000

- Cazenove

- Smith New Court
  Bought Scott Goff, 1986
  Group sold to Merrill Lynch, 1995

- Lazards

- Rothschild

THE US INVESTMENT BANKS

- Merrill Lynch
  Bought Smith New Court, 1995

- Goldman Sachs

- Morgan Stanley

- Salomon
  Sold to Travelers Group, 1997
  Travelers Group sold to Citigroup, 1998

Index